A GUIDE TO HIKING THE LIBERAL ARTS

The Washington College Kiplin Hall Program

Richard Gillin

A GUIDE TO HIKING THE LIBERAL ARTS

The Washington College Kiplin Hall Program

Richard Gillin

COMMON GROUND RESEARCH NETWORKS 2020

First published in 2020
as part of the New Directions in the Humanities
http://doi.org/10.18848/978-1-86335-228-4/CGP (Full Book)

Common Ground Research Networks
2001 South First Street, Suite 202
University of Illinois Research Park
Champaign, IL
61820

Library of Congress Cataloging-in-Publication Data

Names: Gillin, Richard, author.
Title: A guide to hiking the liberal arts : the Washington College Kiplin
   Hall Program / Richard Gillin.
Description: Champaign : Common Ground Research Networks, [2020] | Includes
   bibliographical references. | Summary: "Hiking the Liberal Arts tells
   the story of an annual program in North Yorkshire, England, and West
   Cork, Ireland whose purpose is to connect students ever more deeply to
   the literature written in or about various landscapes, by having them
   experience the landscapes directly on foot to intensify their reading of
   literature"-- Provided by publisher.
Identifiers: LCCN 2020038782 (print) | LCCN 2020038783 (ebook) | ISBN
   9780949313416 (hardback) | ISBN 9780949313904 (paperback) | ISBN
   9781863352284 (adobe pdf)
Subjects: LCSH: English Literature--Study and teaching (Higher)--Activity
   programs--Great Britain. | Washington College Kiplin Hall Program. |
   American students--Great Britain. | Foreign study--Great Britain. |
   Environmental education--Great Britain. | Hiking--Great Britain.
Classification: LCC PR53.W37 G55 2020 (print) | LCC PR53.W37 (ebook) |
   DDC 820.900071/141--dc23
LC record available at https://lccn.loc.gov/2020038782
LC ebook record available at https://lccn.loc.gov/2020038783

Cover Photo Credit: Kelley Holocker

Table of Contents

Acknowledgements

Neither *A Guide to Hiking the Liberal Arts* nor the Washington College Kiplin Hall Program occurred without help. In addition to Barbara's full scale support to write the book in the first place, Bob Mooney's guidance in developing my ideas into writing was quietly appropriate at each stage of development, and provided the reassurance to move on. Jeff Christ's painstakingly critical reading of the manuscript, and his editorial advice made the editing and rewriting process serve for a leaner and more clearly focused final draft. Jean Baker brought good sense and enthusiasm in her advice to complete the book; her belief in the project gave me purpose.

Ralph Wolfe, Professor Emeritus, from Bowling Green University introduced Barbara and myself to Romantic Poetry when we were his graduate students and to the Lake District. On our first visit to Rydal in 1970, Barbara and I were enchanted by the natural environment; the experiences in that visit were elemental in shaping the program.

Jay Griswold, Emeritus Chairman of the Board of Visitors and Governors and Emeritus Interim President of Washington College was steadfast in his belief in the program from its inception. For twenty years he was a vital financial supporter, but even more than that he went out of his way to engage students by visiting us at Kiplin Hall, sitting among students at noisy dinners, and speaking with students about their interests. His trust in us was unwavering. President of Washington College, John Toll and Provost Joachim Sholtz were also enthusiastic supporters of the program. They saw the Kiplin Hall Program as a new and valuable addition to the college curriculum.

Lew and Marie Gillin gave me faith in myself, among a myriad of things, and an abiding capacity for love. Since Barbara's death, in particular, Erin and Jake and Courtney and Frank were relentless in pushing me to complete this book, and I am forever grateful.

Of course the Program would not have been a Program without students. Sharing the challenges and difficulties in hiking, often in daunting weather together for three weeks at a time, made for the formation of significant bonds among us. Barbara and I came to know students in a more nuanced way as they talked about their experiences with literature and landscapes while on the move. The stories about various incidents, I believe, will live on in good ways for all of us. The program brought great joy to Barbara and me, and I feel extraordinarily fortunate that Washington College believed in us.

Preface

Figure 1: Vale of Grasmere

Source: Kelley Holocker

A basic element in the Kiplin Hall Program is getting students to encounter the physical world with their senses uncluttered by the distractions endemic in our time. I often see students on campus and at the gym or running around campus and in town with earbuds in place, the music cutting their senses off from a myriad of impressions otherwise surrounding them. In conversations there is the continual checking of text messages, interrupting verbal communication, as thumbs flash in response to some perceived urgency. Multi-tasking is a fool's errand from my point of view. A clear focus on the immediacy of where we are and what our relationship to the physical features surrounding us, I believe, centers us. Capturing the rhythm of human interaction, and the rhythms of nature in various landscapes is a way to begin the development of a lifelong contemplation of our place in the world.

To that end the Kiplin Hall Program requires students to hike into the mountains and moors of Northern England, the mountains and valleys of West Cork and Kerry in Ireland for the purpose of connecting the literature written in or about the landscapes we encounter. The physical demands of climbing mountains, traversing moors, or walking along sea cliffs are daunting at times, especially when cold rain blows sideways on days with no hope of dry periods. Selections from Wordsworth, Coleridge, Emily Bronte,

Matthew Arnold, Caedmon among others in England, and Leanne O'Sullivan, Seamus Heaney, and Patrick Kavanagh in Ireland form the basis of readings the students must work through. For many students it is their first encounter with the assigned writers, and many have only a superficial knowledge of literature. Making meaning from our experience of the physical and emotional world we live in by removing the invasive filtering of our electronic devices is a primary step in the program. The next step is for students to develop a rich, subjective understanding of their own, unique experiences. Beginning an ascent of a mountain on a windy, wet, and cold day requires resolution and physical determination. It fosters self-perception and a recognition of personal identity forged in the tug of will and thoughts of the physical strain of completing the mountain climb. In writing about their experience students gain the power and perspective to understand their individuality and enrich what their life means. Possessing their world in their own words is a creative act to capture what is authentic, and a form of resistance to the drive toward conformity.

Questions of "How" and "why" in relation to these goals must be answered. I outline the "how" in my description of the Kiplin Hall Program below, and the "why" stems from my love of literature and belief that in analyzing challenging poems from earlier historical periods the satisfaction in understanding what has been thought, and equally important, what has been felt by talented poets in the past gives students access to their maturing perception of their relationship to the world we live in.

Screens, computer screens, television screens, telephone screens, movie screens, and to borrow from the English, wind screens, seem to be the way we face the world. We look on screens and through them; we confront the world with the screen as a filter, removing us a degree from the actual; virtual reality by habit becomes real in a host of ways. Screens aim our attention and dictate what we see. Watching a baseball game on a television screen keeps us riveted to the director's choices, in person at the ball-park we can look all around and see what is conspiring at first or third base, or how far back the infield is. Like the option of choices to see a baseball game the way we want to, the freedom to see the world from our unique perspective enfranchised the value of what we can offer society; both we, and society, benefit. Thoughtful consideration of our unique experiences as human beings is the stepping-stone to shaping our will to make judgments in society. The skills of learning are bedrock to the life-long commitment to learning. Too often in our time this aspect of college education is smothered in concerns about getting a job. Having a good job is clearly not incompatible with good thinking; fostering the way to develop the way we construct our relationship to understanding comes first.

Many aims go with the Kiplin Hall Program: I want students to experience an initial exposure to foreign cultures in England, Scotland, and Ireland, I want them to read literature connected with the various landscapes we visit, I want them to write honestly about what they experience, I want them to find ways of getting along with others in intense situations, developing ways of respecting differences among them, and I want them to discover how their way of confronting difficult challenges in hiking, often in trying circumstances, makes them aware of how they have greater powers of will, intellectual depth, and physical strength than they expected. But most of all I want them to unplug from the distractions of our electronic society and find in themselves a resonance between what has been written about the landscapes we visit and their own, unique reactions to what we encounter. Making a sensual, physical connection is an important stride toward internalizing personal meaning, which, I believe, is a way to bring focus to the power of learning. I aim for them to discover poetry in their movements, their developing insights in literature, and their hopes in life.

In the last several years, voices have been raised about the value of higher education, and in particular Liberal Arts education. In a report by Harvard University, "The Teaching of the Arts and Humanities at Harvard College: Mapping the Future" we are warned that, "Knowledge of the Humanities is no practical response to most pressing practical challenges we face." My experience over the last four decades runs counter to the Harvard warning. Students who studied 18th and 19th Century English writers with me during those years have found success in their professional lives, not because I taught them useful technical knowledge and provided them with training, but because they learned how to write effectively, knowing how to "read" a period poem, and how to understand the cultural context in which the poem was written. They comprehended the need to communicate their ideas about poems they studied in clear, concise, and appropriate language. While the students today are under significant financial pressure to be able to stay at a liberal arts college, and are potentially distracted by the myriad of technological devices, each with its own lure, they are still captured by the power of literature and the meaning it has for their lives. Gaining mastery over how the study of literature, for example, opens a realm of understanding others, providing the basis for taking leadership roles and avenues of cooperation is fundamental for our age. The elements of this sort of knowledge are tied to individual works and not easily, if at all, deducible to a metric. Understanding comes from immersion in the subject. My bedrock belief is that the shaping of intellect and fostering the power of the imagination are the most useful things we can do in our age.

For the last forty-six years, I have been teaching at Washington College a liberal arts college that is old and hangs onto its core values in spite of threats from MOOCS (Massive Open Online Courses) and assorted advanced technological methods of teaching undergraduates. I do not wish to suggest that we have submerged ourselves in a sort of academic cocoon resisting the use of technology, far from it, technology is widely used but its focus, along with traditional methods of instruction, is on individuals. Classes are small and access to professors is expected and encouraged. It was in the context of continual innovation that my wife, Barbara, and I were encouraged to begin a summer program in England at Kiplin Hall in North Yorkshire, later expanded to include time in West Cork, Ireland, that has had a powerful effect on our lives and the lives of student participants. The program continued for twenty years, and as the criticism of liberal arts colleges and deep skepticism about their importance has become commonplace, I realized that the Washington College Kiplin Hall Program embodies the essence of what is primary in a liberal arts education. I do not want to suggest that our program as it is should be duplicated or imitated exactly, but I do want to make the point that the experiences in the program enhance and give focus to essential matters escaping assessment reports and the tendency to quantify what an education means, a tendency much in vogue today. The proponents of the quantification of learning can put a number on pages read, assignments completed, the number of pages turned in at the end of the term, and so forth. But when it comes to meaning, things become open-ended. Many years often elapse in before an individual comes to understand the value of something learned. The role of the imagination and the way it is stoked makes numbering arbitrary. Charles Dickens, a particularly gifted social observer, in his novel Hard Times, takes to task the rise in using statistics in his time to portray ironically the dreadfulness of the Gradgrind method of education. Thomas Gradgrind "was a man of facts and calculations. With a rule and a pair of scales, and the multiplication table always in his pocket, Sir, ready to weigh and measure any parcel of human nature and tell you exactly what it comes to." Dickens' withering satire speaks directly to us; it would behoove educational bean-counters to read Dickens closely.

Curricular issues in the liberal arts are under constant discussion, perhaps in the hope of formulating the perfect balance of courses from diverse fields of study. Opinions supporting the "Western Tradition" clash with multiculturalists, assorted theoretical approaches to knowledge, canonical and non-canonical material, to name a few. The opinions are well intentioned, often complicated, and strongly held. From my point of view, I believe that specific courses in particular disciplines, whether they are canonical or non-canonical, western or other, are less important than establishing deeply felt connections to learning and instilling ways to foster interest in diverse subjects. Fascination with knowing something for personal satisfaction, heretical as it sounds in our age of accountability to useful ends, is elemental in the liberal arts. Making something learned into a cherished part of our identity is an elemental step in developing our authenticity as human beings. Creating the ways to making that step is of prime importance to me as a teacher, and in what follows I hope to show one way, not the only way, to the starting point. In referring to particular students I have often changed their names to protect their privacy, or with their permission I have used their real names.

In addition to illustrating the value of the Washington College Kiplin Hall Program, I offer a guide in this manuscript to the places where the program has taken place to help anyone who is interested in developing a program of their own or creating a literary holiday. The landscapes of northern England and southern Ireland offer a wide variety of possibilities for hiking and making literary associations, I submit our choices to you for your consideration.

Teaching English Literature

Signs of fall are rising as I stand at the edge of the campus. Cars are filling the parking lots, people are walking with a purpose between buildings, and there is a feeling of anticipation in the air. For forty-six years I have taught graduate and undergraduate students at Washington College, a small, old, liberal arts college on Maryland's Eastern Shore. Today students are reanimating the college after the humid press of high summer as they move into their dormitories, hauling a significant amount of baggage with them. Like a very heavy-footed ballet their movements and gestures follow the choreography laid down decades earlier by former students. The campus was very old when I arrived in 1973 and physical connections to the deep past, and my past within, are linked to the oldest red brick buildings before me in the relentlessly glaring sun, but the most palpable link to the past is in the labored movements of the students and their excited voices. Sweating under the sun, the bulky loads of stuff, ascending staircases in their enthusiasm to meet up with friends and meet new people is hardly diminished as they high five each other and in loud voices greet newcomers across the parking lot. I am drawn in by their youthful energy and their emotionally charged expectations for the new academic year as they shout greetings to each and all. Seeing them hauling their possessions across grass frizzled by the summer heat, and quiet puffs of dust rising and coating their sandaled feet, I am reminded of caravans in faraway places that set out to new destinations in never ending movement. The impression lingered in my mind until I drifted into the realization that movement, change, and the challenge of the new is integral to what I do as a Professor of English. The beginning of my journey in a metaphoric caravan will begin again in a short period of time I knew, bringing with it a new cycle of the academic year, and the satisfying prospect of working with the energy the students bring with them.

On my way to my office, I have the urge to look into the classroom where I have been teaching for many years, and where I will teach again this year. The room has been refinished over the summer; the thick smell of new wax on the floor mingles with the heavy air, as yet un-air-conditioned creating an almost tactile sensation of thickness. Standing in front of the empty seats, I visualize the wraithlike overlay of faces from years and decades past and reminds me of wonderful moments here. The sure look of recognition when a student discovers the meaning of a complex literary text always brings a frisson of delight to me, and for a moment the student and I share the intersection between insight and wonder. The power of that kind of moment transcends easy description.

In my first year of teaching I can distinctly remember the surprised shock of awareness on a young woman's face lock into a moment as if it were engraved in marble as she understood what I was saying. It was a freshman class and we were discussing Yeats' poem, "The Lake Isle of Innisfree" where he proclaims that "I will arise and go now and go to Innisfree." In my aim to consider the visual and auditory images in the poem I asked the class why Yeats was so precise in his depiction of the various natural elements in the poem, "a small cabin build there, of clay and wattles," "Nine bean rows," "a hive for the honey bee" living alone "in the bee loud glade" where"

1

the cricket sings?" I was hoping that they would come to understand how the specific natural perfection of the place early in the poem was set off against the grayness of the pavement with its suggestive power at the end and made the depiction of the isle a personal ideal. To get them started in that direction I told them that Yeats was crossing a busy London street when his imagination took him to the lake isle. How many of you have become lost to reverie amid immediate commotion and found yourself briefly, and delightedly, disconnected? Their smiles confirmed what I expected. My next question was to be how does the ideal landscape work toward meaning in the poem? Several students noted how the visual imagery made the landscape in the poem clear and a believably real place, but they were not working through the implications. Then the young woman in a quiet but resolute voice simply said that the landscape was a place in his imagination that he could move his mind into emotional security and fulfillment from the harsh realities of the work-a-day world. The peace "dropping from the veils of morning' where midnight "is all a glimmer, and noon a purple glow" made the isle seem like a fairytale to her. The air seemed to hesitate in the room, and I felt my breath stop for several heart-beats. I knew that I needed to move the conversation to the next level of perception gently; I needed to ask the right question in the right way. So, I made eye contact with each of the students and inquired about why the speaker was confident that he would have "some peace" there, because "peace comes dropping slow?" "The kind of peace he talks about is intense, rare, and in nature away from the distractions and pressure of urban life" one student added. Other students then talked about the way that sounds of nature in the poem intensified the speaker's yearning to find peace so that he could "hear it in the deep heart's core," a logical incongruity, but imaginatively understandable none-the-less. How can the "water lapping" be heard in the heart's core, I asked. A thoughtful silence ensued, and then a very honest discussion about the way poetry works, where each element in a poem links to another through suggestion and the poem's structure. How peace in the poem and the speaker's desire to go to Lake Isle was really about finding a place within himself where things were centered and away from the "pavements grey" led to an awareness from the students that we can develop our own internal Lake Isle. The departure away from a logical understanding into the realms of imagination made meaning in the poem much more satisfying and richly complex. It's how poetry captivates us.

In that classroom on that autumn morning I knew that I was hooked, nothing in my working life before gave me such a sense of blended excitement and satisfaction. My aim as a teacher to create more moments like the one I had bound me into a sort of personal pledge to myself. But things are different in a host of ways now. So much emphasis now is on acquiring technical competence, seeing the world as a series of more or less interconnected metrics, which it is believed will give us power over all that is measured. Education and learning as a product, a commodity to be marketed, stripped of the human context is a stance filtering into political debates and creating misunderstandings about what learning entails. A college education, from that point of view should lead to a specific end: a good, well-paying job. I have a very different view. What I aim for in my classes are ways to train the power of intuition and cultivate the imagination. As athletes train their bodies to go beyond perceived limits, so too can students develop their sensitivities to the world around them that they can expand their intuitive and imaginative understanding of their place in the world. A good well-paying job is desirable but developing our interior life and comprehending our meaning in the world gives us the foundation of how to live in the world.

Delight in those moments is bedrock to why I have taught and still teach. I feel assured that what students learn in those moments will stay with them, and travel forward in time, shaping their lives in ways I cannot measure. By focusing on particular passages and thinking through what they mean specifically is the way I teach literature. For undergraduates I feel it is essential that they come to know the primary texts intimately. It takes time to work through all texts this way, particularly difficult ones, but I am sure that going through the process, laborious as it is, sets up a way to confront a number of challenges. Like climbing a mountain, a first impression of a mountain from some distance might make an ascent seem impossible, but in nearing the base of the mountain various ways into and onto the mountain appear, and each step reveals the next. Success or achievement comes in a series of contingencies. Discussions about higher education in our time often place the commodification of learning ahead of discovery, where the place of feeling and imagination are absent or dismissed as fluff. That moment and others similar to it happen in classes frequently and serves as the incentive to keep teaching in a classroom environment for me. I firmly believe that substance in learning comes from the effort to wrestle with challenging ideas and ways of expressing them and doing so in a positive environment.

In a few days the seats will be filled with a new group of students in various degrees of eagerness and interest in studying English Literature, and the cycle will begin again. Old now, I think often about when I will have to break the cycle and cease in my position as a professor. While friends and family suggest gently and respectfully that I should use the time I have left to do things I want to do for myself, I have not reconciled my life-long habit of reading widely and thinking about ways I can use what I read in my courses, to a life away from the classroom. For now, I put off thinking about it. With the new students I know I have a chance to bring my years of experience and whatever fragment of wisdom I have and come to know them and their lives.

The decades of being a faculty member have not been blissful. My academic salary proved to be a continual challenge especially in raising two daughters. The things available to their friends were often out of range from our budget. A prolonged period of renting, making do with dodgy automobiles, limiting expenses continually on all fronts, framed our lives. My wife and family had to endure much so that I could teach. Barbara, my wife, especially, never wavered from her belief that teaching was a noble enterprise, and her support of me sustained us all in difficult financial times. Because of the examples I had from the best teachers in my education I believed that sacrifice was a large part of being a faculty member when I first began my career, and that a life focused on intangibles had greater value than the acquisition of material goods. Weathering the difficulties and experiencing the intense gratification stemming from the give-and-take of the classroom has convinced me that I made the right choice. Students return to campus or contact me to tell me how much they appreciate what I have done for them, and I feel humbled and fulfilled. These reflections take me to central questions about the value of college and specifically of a liberal arts education.

3

Beginnings

> *Great hopes were mine*
> *My own voice chear'd me, and, far more, the mind's*
> *Internal echo of the imperfect sound*
> (Wordsworth, *The Prelude,* 63-65)

Figure 2: Scafell Pike Approach

Source: Kelley Holocker

The Kiplin Hall Program at Washington College was launched in 1998, the first year we travelled with students, but it really began for me, and Barbara, decades earlier. In 1970 my wife and I were asked to assist Ralph Wolfe, an English professor at Bowling Green University, in Ohio in his study abroad program in England. Ralph was my dissertation chairman, and a dynamo in the classroom. His warm and engaging personality and relentless devotion to the Romantic Poets gave me much to aspire toward since I was at the beginning of my teaching career. Though modest in stature the magnitude of his effect on me regarding the Romantic Poets belied his physical size, it was his sensitive understanding of the way poetry works that has stayed with me through the years. Barbara, also a graduate student and full-time teacher at the time, took on the task of

4

making travelling arrangements for the group, a task that she has continued to perform for the Kiplin Hall Program. It was a fine preparation.

In 1970, the first Rydal Mount Summer School in honor of William Wordsworth's bicentenary took place in the Lake District in Wordsworth's home, Rydal Mount. During the weeks of the program Barbara and I were introduced to the landscapes surrounding Rydal, Ambleside, Langdale, and Helvellyn by fellow graduate students enrolled in the summer program. Perhaps we should have been reading our assignments more intensely, but the special charm of the unspoiled landscapes pulled us outdoors. In between lectures we impulsively abandoned our student selves to climb the surrounding fells and valleys. Our classmates illustrated how to hike on the cheap. Without special clothing or equipment, we launched into the youthful glee of following our sensibilities into the landscape. There was an element of childishness in giving ourselves to the moment, but with that there was the joy of feeling the exuberance in such freedom. With Wordsworth and all the importance, he gives to childhood in our collective, somewhat guilty minds, since we had abandoned the Common Room where academic discussions were taking place, we felt a sort of vindication.

During our time outdoors we were arrested, literally stopped and taken, by the unique particulars in the landscape. The air was cool and bracing, the sun made the green in the landscape glitter with a freshness that seemed primeval. Only our heavy breathing disturbed the environment, but then the deep breaths were a way to internalize the ambient vitality of the air. The distant Lake Windermere shrouded in mist that swirled in what appeared to be ethereal strands of light and dark seemed to be taken from a fairy tale vision. The cool, bracing air underscored the rarified moment-to-moment apprehension of a landscape I had only known through Wordsworth's poetry. Seduced by the sensuousness of the landscape that carried a promise of some as yet unknown meaning, and inebriated by enthusiasm, off we went. With energy to spare we rambled through the mountains absorbing the nuances of each vista with a breathless anticipation. The strain on my legs and my burning lungs was compensated in the elation of rising above the next rock formation. Discomfort seemed irrelevant. As demanding as each challenge was, there was deep pleasure in pushing myself beyond what I thought were my limits. The impression of this moment in the natural world, and as rendered in the poetry of Wordsworth travelled to my bones. In the Prelude Wordsworth traces his own development as a poet by illustrating his deep and abiding love of the natural world, and how that particular sensitivity led to the contemplation of his mind at work in association with nature. My self-discovery made palpable what Wordsworth wrote about in describing his sense of fulfillment that came in connection with his walks up and around these same mountains almost two hundred years earlier:

> To drink wild water, and to pluck green
> herbs, And gather fruits fresh from their
> native bough. Nay more if I may trust
> myself, this hour
> Hath brought a gift that consecrates my joy;
> For I, methought, while the sweet breath of
> heaven Was blowing on my body, felt
> within
> A corresponding mild creative breeze
> (Wordsworth, *The Prelude*, 1805)

The meaning of that fulfillment, that we can understand moral and ethical dimensions of our lives from our interaction with the natural world, and discover the substance of our self, made a forceful impression on me. The "creative breeze" was the blending of my physical exertion into the way I absorbed the summer beauty and what it meant to me. This realization came through my muscle burn and rapidly beating heart: it was intuitive, physical, and later rational. Seated at the top of Heron Pike surveying the three-hundred-and-sixty-degree view of the world before me I felt deeply centered in the scene, literally, and emotionally elated in myself. I knew that I had discovered something timeless and enriching in the experience of climbing to this point, and I knew with certainty that it was not in the achievement of summiting the mountain that meant the most to me, it was the process of getting there. At that time, new as I was to so many things, I understood intuitively that the meaning of the best poetry had to do with finding those links to the world where we live, and the emotions that instigate and shape personal understanding. In poetry it was not about the reading of words on a page, but an experience of where those words transported me. Metaphorically that place was captured by the experience of climbing. My subjective feelings led to contemplating myself as the center of a constellation of physical and emotional influences in the context of remarkable beauty. Wordsworth's "creative breeze" linked me to the essence of his meaning, a meaning made all that more powerful and enriching by my climbing experience.

It was England, and the Lake District with all of its literary associations came vividly alive. Filled with lines from Wordsworth's poetry, especially *The Prelude*:

> The Admiration and love, the life
> In common things; the endless store of
> things Rare, or at least so seeming, every
> day
> Found all about me in one neighborhood
> (117 – 120)

The special bonding that developed between our newfound comrades, sharing lunches, struggling up almost vertical climbs, and having special interests in poetry, and especially Wordsworth's, stretched into our sensibilities accompanied by feelings of delight. We felt not only what Wordsworth wrote, but we felt what poetry is: that unique fusion of feeling, thinking, and imagining. In short, we were young and open to the world. Since we were graduate students with high hopes that we would find academic positions, I remember speculating on the desirability of bringing students to this place to experience what we had found. Weeks later in a wistful conversation with Barbara about our joint experiences, as we prepared to leave England, I knew that an awakening of poetry's power, felt in conjunction with physically taking in the landscapes of the Lake District, had unsettled me because I was unsure about how to translate those experiences into an ordinary classroom. On the way home to the United States Barbara and I talked in somewhat dreamy tones about bringing future students to this place that we had learned to love, but elementally doubtful that we would ever have the opportunity to do that.

Things Come Together

*And so, his senses gradually wrapt
In a half sleep, he dreams of better
worlds, And dreaming hears thee still,
O singing lark, That singest like an
angel in the clouds!*
            (Coleridge, *Fears in Solitude*, 25-29)

Figure 3: Sunburst

Source: Kelley Holocker

Then it happened. Seventeen years after our summer in the Lake District the president of Washington College, John Toll, asked me to come to his office so he could ask my opinion about an opportunity that had just come to light. I had found a home at Washington College for twenty-four years at that point, all the while cherishing the idea of taking students to the landscapes haunted by Wordsworth and Coleridge. President Toll told me that the University of Maryland had established a Study Centre at Kiplin Hall, the ancestral home of the Calvert family who founded Maryland, and they had space available for Washington College if we wished to develop a program. Immediately I said that I had an idea which I felt would work well for Washington College. Along with

8

John Toll was the then Chairman of the Board of Visitors and Governors Mr. Jay Griswold who spoke enthusiastically about the historic importance of Kiplin Hall for the state of Maryland, and especially Washington College as the tenth oldest college in the United States.

In his quiet and unassuming way Jay communicated a depth of sincerity and passion for developing a program that would have Washington College connect with Kiplin Hall that made turning him down impossible, a negative thought that never entered my mind. In time these two men, and especially Jay, would have a shaping influence on the success of a newly born program, just in its infancy as we talked. Jay continued to spur interest in Kiplin Hall through the years, and he would make annual visits to us while we were there, his main purpose being to talk with students. He would stand in the dinner line like everyone else, and for the students it was the first time they had contact with a Chairman of the Board. The legacy of his good work is incalculable. Dr. Toll and Jay's clear support for taking on something more or less unconventional was unprecedented in my experience, and I was onboard immediately. I told President Toll and Mr. Griswold that I would have a plan and course description in writing in short order.

The prospect of realizing a long-delayed dream spurred a wide range of feelings, emotions, and hopes in me, and they were amplified when I shared the good news with Barbara. Taking on the responsibility for a new program in a foreign country was a challenge, and the logistics of seeing to the needs of a dozen college students, not to mention making sure there were meals on the table at the appropriate time, and transporting the group to specific sites was sobering. Barbara, steady in her belief that none of the issues was intimidating, said she was ready to begin.

Evolution

If I may trust myself, this hour
Hath brought a gift that concentrates my joy
(Wordsworth, *The Prelude,* 39-40)

Figure 4: White Moss Common

Source: Barbara Gillin

The nature of the American college experience for students and faculty has evolved and changed since 1982. In my early days in the 1970s English faculty members were expected to have significant depth in one literary period as well as a generalist's knowledge of the English canon. The pursuit of generalist knowledge was always before me like a threat and a reward. Reading the works of major literary figures made me keenly aware of how to read the works of authors I particularly valued. The unsuspected links among writers and cultural realities that they had to confront helped me to develop a richer perspective on literature's relationship with life's challenges. The opportunity to develop a program in England pushed me into thinking about the value and purpose of a college education, and the importance of English as a discipline. The situation called to mind passages from the Prelude as Wordsworth contemplated the course of his life:

And, in the shelter'd grove where I was couch'd
A perfect stillness. On the ground I lay
Passing through many thoughts, yet mainly such
As to myself pertain'd.

(The Prelude, 69 – 72)

Finding stillness and having time and a place to focus on discovering the meaning of ourselves in our 24/7 became a goal for my sense of the program. As ideas about the prospective program became clearer in my mind, I established as a prevailing principle that my purpose was to move students through their reading of poems and link the literature we would study with specific sites that we had to reach on foot and with varying degrees of difficulty. Combining physical exertion and poetry, I believed, would allow students unique ways of understanding what they felt and thought. The emotional context I wanted was joy.

The physical challenges of hiking and climbing would be difficult, but the satisfaction of completing each day's experiences in a supportive group, I believed, would lead to joy in personal satisfaction. Learning takes place best in a positive environment. Understanding poetry requires concentration, open mindedness, precision, cultural and historical awareness and imagination. Physical exertion demands discipline, will power, confidence, and physical fortitude. The elements of each part of my goal I conceived as being complementary. I wanted them to go where poetry goes, taking them to new perceptions and new ways of understanding their experience, and how they read poetry. By studying and experiencing poetry along with the demands of hiking in various landscapes, searching for connections between the natural world and the poems they would read, I believed would reach the particular level of understanding the knowledge derived from poetry and their physical effort, fusing their unique experiences. Ambition about my high hopes for the program led me in time to consider the larger issue of the liberal arts. By describing the Kiplin Hall Program, what we have done and do now, I hope to illustrate the essence of what the liberal arts embody.

Organizing the Design

> *Yet I was often greedy in the chace,*
> *And roam'd from hill to hill, from rock to rock,*
> *Still craving combinations of new forms*
> *(The Prelude, 190-193)*

At the outset we understood that the Study Center at Kiplin Hall consisted of three bedrooms, two bathrooms, a kitchen, and a sitting room. Twelve students could be housed in the bunk-bedded bedrooms, and we would stay in a flat on the property. The aim of the program was to have students hike in the landscapes of the Lake District, the Yorkshire dales and moors, as well as the cliffs along the North Sea. The students were assigned readings and asked to connect the readings with their own experiences in the landscapes written in or about by various writers.

As we developed plans for what would be called the Washington College Kiplin Hall Summer program we were faced with financial issues immediately. Everything in England seemed to be much more costly than in the USA. Groceries, fuel, van rentals, and parking put immediate pressure on our budget. To cut costs we decided to shop for and cook our own meals, thereby saving the cost of hiring a cook. To get around the North of England ordinary public transportation was too complicated, time consuming, and limiting, hiring private drivers was too expensive, so we decided to hire vans giving us the freedom and flexibility to drive students to various sites of literary and historical importance. In the past we had driven in England, though not in vans. We would discover very quickly that there is a significant difference between driving a small compact car and American style van that seemed to devour road width. But that came later. The program as I outlined it in my mind had at its center the physical experience of particular landscapes in the North, and the relationship between specific landscapes and the literature that was written about or in that landscape. To accomplish my goal for the program I determined that walking and hiking in as many landscapes as we could cover would create the elemental links between that literature we would read and the environment we would be in. Wordsworth was a clear example for inclusion, as well as Coleridge, Shelley, the Brontes, Bram Stoker, Caedmon, Ted Hughes, Arnold, Ruskin, and Sir Walter Scott. The list grew long fairly quickly. To give a sharp focus to the program since it was only for three weeks we needed to sort out the logistics and calculate the distances we would need to travel, the time involved, the amount and cost of fuel, and the relevance of particular landscapes to literature.

The clear potential for realizing what we had dreamed of propelled us in rapid order to sort out a clear and reasonable plan. Students were to be invited with the aim of having between eight and twelve students join the program. In about a month we had developed a working outline of our itinerary and a budget, which the Dean and the President approved. At that point we needed to get the word out to students. Fortunately, email had arrived on campus and after one email sent to the students describing the essential characteristics of the program, we had twelve very interested students signed on. We met with the students and suggested what they needed to bring and not bring, and above all to pare down what they intended to bring since space in the vans was going to be very limited. They seemed to understand, for the most part.

An unforeseen adventure began as we departed from Chestertown to the Baltimore Washington Airport. Being somewhat nervous about the tasks that lay ahead and the need to meet and gather students at the airport, we set out earlier than we thought we had to. The Bay Bridge connects the Eastern Shore of Maryland to the rest of the state. As we approached the bridge feeling confident now that we would be very early on our arrival at BWI we were somewhat appalled that the traffic just before the bridge was at a standstill. At first, we tried to convince ourselves that the traffic would move in short order since we had never encountered this kind of absolute standstill traffic on the bridge. Fifteen minutes went by, then thirty, then forty-five, then an hour. The dryness in my throat helped to suppress the cyclone that was fast developing in the pit of my stomach. I had all the tickets, ours, and the students, in my pocket. On a good day the airport would be a forty minute drive from where we were stopped. People emerged from their vehicles hoping to find out what the holdup was. This was taking place in the era before near universal cell phone use. Fortunately, a man who stopped to talk with us said that he had a cell phone and called the police to find out why the bridge traffic was not moving. They told him that there had been a serious car crash, but it had been cleared and forward motion was imminent. Barbara asked if she could use the phone to make a call to the airport. This stranger was glad to help out. She called and alerted the airline officials about our situation, and they said that they could hold the plane for a brief time.

Encouraged, and now in motion, we roared to the airport in heart pounding record time. Close to panic we found that trying to sprint with luggage was counterproductive and torturous. In the vision we had of our time at the airport before takeoff we imagined meeting the students with their parents and reassuring the parents that their children would be well taken care of, and safe to the best of our abilities. As it turned out we arrived at the departure gate sweating profusely, out of breath, haggard, and looking fairly dodgy with the tickets and my passport spilling out of my jacket packet. Our luggage was with us. But those were the days when screening and security measures were minimal, so the crew simply took our luggage into the plane, and we met with the students, some for the first time. Their looks of apprehension were not hard to miss. In that moment the full weight of my responsibility for the students, the program, and the college's reputation made my spirits sink. My gleeful confidence about the program I had imagined during the planning stages, and the sweaty, gritty reality of the first few hours, gave me a new centering. I felt unnerved, my breathing shallow making me lightheaded, and somewhat fearful that making a dream into a working program required disciplined nerves and copious amounts of faith. This was an object lesson in experiential learning, one I had not anticipated. The pressure in the situation skirted with what I perceived to be the boundary of my abilities. Under the threat of disaster, it was the scrambling of will and good fortune that brought about success, and a personal confirmation that formidable situations also contain solutions. We have to search actively if we are to achieve a favorable resolution.

The apparent hopelessness of the situation, the urge to give in to my worst fears, and then the rapid turnaround, bringing about an unanticipated way though the problem paralleled what I have experienced often enough in my life, and something I knew needed to be communicated to students from me as a teacher of English Literature. In writing about "spots of time," Wordsworth comments on the power of memory in keeping our spirits up:

> Our minds
> Are nourished and invisibly repair'd
> A virtue by which pleasure is enhanced
> That penetrates, enables us to mount
> When high, more high, and lifts us up when fallen.
> *(The Prelude,* 11.264-268)

A careful and steady focus in sorting my way through outsized difficulties, combined with a resolute belief that solutions can be discovered, emerged in me as I matured in my studies of writers who against formidable challenges gave the world works of great beauty profound insight. Providing students with the will to extend the belief in themselves was associated with my intentions for the Kiplin Hall Program. Little did I understand at the outset how quickly that would be tested.

I have never been able to sleep on airplanes, and during this trip there was no hope given the very close call of logistical disaster at our departure. If we had not made it to the plane either the students would be on their way to London or we would all be at the airport waiting for the next evening's flight. Neither scenario was desirable. But we were on our way, sleeplessly for me. But we were all together and heading East. Next morning in London the full measure of what the students brought with them, in spite of clear directions to travel light, staggered us as we stood amid a good sized midden of suitcases, backpacks, and duffle bags. We hired two vans for the journey north and I had asked for roof racks just in case we needed them. After completing all the paperwork that accompanies car hires, we all followed a young Indian gentleman to the vans. Along the way he kept shaking his head from side to side. Before showing me the vans, in an exasperated voice, he said to me, "Sir you cannot fit all these people and their belongings into the vans, impossible!" My heart sank when I looked at the assembled luggage and what looked like Lilliputian vans. Barbara is never one to be put off, so she immediately began organizing each van. Students first, then luggage on top of their laps, and anywhere else bags could fit. Our car representative was close to tears when I asked him about roof racks. "You cannot do that," he said. Not wanting to be the entirely ugly American, I shook my head in agreement as if I understood. I did not, but I did not want to upset the man any more than we had so far. With vans filled to bursting we went in pursuit of the motorway and the North. What lay ahead was the core of the project. In setting an outline for each day the plan as I explained it to the students was to have them encounter various landscapes in the North of England, and to make their own links between what they experienced physically and emotionally with the literature written in or about the landscape we were in. Our first visit to the Lake District was planned to include a visit to Wordsworth's home at Rydal Mount and then a hike up a trail to Nab

14

Scar. The hike was to serve as a sort of shake-out introduction to the physical aspect of the program. Nab Scar rises directly behind Rydal Mount and tops out at about 1200 feet.

The drive from Yorkshire to Cumbria went through some breathtaking scenery characterized by dramatic changes from farmland, to moors, to mountains. Following the hour and a half journey we were all eager to stretch and begin walking. As planned the students sorted their way through Rydal Mount, a little bit quicker than I anticipated. As a Professor of English this was holy ground of sorts for me. What seemed like a cursory drift through the house by the students perplexed me. I had to work through why the students were not enchanted by all things Wordsworth. My perspective, as I would learn on the first trip and again and again on subsequent ones, was not theirs. I knew that I had to earn their interest; the very thing that every teacher faces. The link between what we were going to do in England and its relevance to the meaning of literary study started to take shape in more substantial liniments. No time for that at the moment though since there were twelve people aged eighteen to twenty-two pulsating with eagerness to take on a climb.

Framework

> *To unorganic natures I transferr'd*
> *My own enjoyments, or, the power of truth*
> *Coming in revelation, I converse'd*
> *With things that really are, I, at this*
> *time Saw blessings spread around me*
> *like a sea.*
> (The Prelude, 2. 410 –414)

Each subsequent year of the program specific incidents did not fall into exactly the same pattern as the first, but over the years certain places we visited were revisited. The overlay of year upon year in my memory provides me with the ability to use examples culled from different years and illustrate what I see as connections between the physical demands of hiking, reading poetry, and the aim of a educated liberal arts student. What follows is a distillation of events and years. The terrain covered is not the most daunting in the world, but it is challenging. The literary and historical associations connected to each day's hike, in combination with the physical exertion required to traverse the landscapes, provide the centering for unique, individual insights, derived from experience.

Nab Scar

> *With a heart*
> *Joyous, nor scared at its own liberty,*
> *I look about; and should the chosen*
> *guide Be nothing better than a*
> *wandering cloud, I cannot miss my*
> *way. I breathe again!*
>
> *(The Prelude*, 1.15-19)

Figure 4: Nab Scar

Source: Barbara Gillin

Beginnings are transformations. Perceptions in mind at setting out inevitably transmute into something very different at the end. The ideas and plans I had in mind set out a general direction and order for the day, and the single day as part of a larger whole in the context of a coherent program. As human beings we seem to function with a greater sense of emotional security and purpose when there is a plan. Like a compass we find and feel true north, from there we can deduce where to go. Associated with beginnings is change, and inevitably transformation. Shifting to something new requires emotional fortitude, the will to encounter what change brings, relies on an open mindedness and an increase in vulnerability. The

17

transformative dimension inherent in beginnings emerges quickly, and often not gracefully. The goals we establish gather our conceptions of who we are and what our relationships are to the world around us and give them focus into our sense of self as it emerges. Beginnings are exciting given the anticipation of what might be, and the special joy of physically moving. For me the moments leading up to the first hike embodied thoughts and feelings that were contradictory: how would the students react to what we were embarking on physically, will we be safe, and would the links to the literature I wanted them to experience be truly enhanced by hiking? The contradictions and reservations made me especially restless and pushed me into movement forward. These thoughts and feelings did not leave me alone as we started to engage with the trail; they were quickly pushed to the side of my consciousness because the crush of immediate necessities in moving the group upwards was my responsibility and required full attention to their well-being and safety.

But those thoughts and feelings would haunt my awareness of what I was engaged in throughout the program in 1998 and all the years to follow. At the time I could clearly recognize something deeply affecting in the initial phase of the program's beginning. There was something about choosing to do what we were about to take on that struck me as significant in itself. We were all agreeing to do something together, knowing that it would be physically tumultuous and emotionally demanding. The ability to choose, I sensed, was connected to the restlessness I felt in starting. That restlessness and the ability to make a choice and to follow through in attempting to fulfill the goal we had in common gave me an initial insight into a portion of the human condition. In choosing, we have some control over the formation of ourselves. As the group readied for the climb there was a nervous tension in their voices and movements. Each person was assuring herself or himself that they would measure up to a standard they perceived for themselves. The nervous tension led to some weak laughter, followed by louder laughter as each person summoned up reserves of energy and will power to ascend.

Off we went, immediately uphill at about a fifty-degree angle. After a hundred yards two students panting and sweaty wanted to know when we would have lunch. I was a little miffed since I had made it clear that we would stop on top of Nab Scar for lunch and a class, so I simply added, "Later." Some of the other ten students looked up toward the summit with a mixture of doubt but open-minded about going on, while others looked longingly at the path downwards. My sense that I could read the motions and thoughts of each member of the group just before we began our journey was brought up short as I realized that creature comforts and getting things done was more of a priority for them than my imaginings about the meaning of what we were engaged in. Still I believed that I was not entirely wrong about the meaning of shared trek. So, on we went. The ascent is very sharp, almost deceptively so. A series of switchbacks seemed to make progress toward the summit an intensely slow-motion affair. About halfway up, a woman distinguished by her love of cigarettes, sat down wheezing loudly and theatrically grumbling with sustained vigor. She rambled on in a way that I was to become familiar with over the years of the program; a degree of physical distress and self-doubt leading to complaints. "Why are we doing this?" "You did not tell me that hiking is so hard." Or my favorite, "I never knew that we were going to hike!" "Really," I replied, "Then why are you wearing hiking boots, and hiking clothes?" It was far from a typical response, but for many years it came up in various forms. Instead of just dismissing the comments I began thinking seriously about why the comments would arise in the first place. How do we delude ourselves? Why would it be necessary to make a statement, "Why are we hiking?" when it was entirely clear from the beginning that hiking was a major element in the program? These interruptions in the flow of my plans were in one sense irritating, and yet, I discovered, important in significant ways. I reasoned that what students heard and what I intended could often be at odds with each other. It was not that I had left out important information or did not share it with the group, but that what I thought I had made clear was filtered out in their understanding of what would be happening. The gap between intention and understanding at times seemed to increase, and I was intrigued as to why. A clear answer would evolve in subsequent years.

> *To the brim*
> *My heart was full: I made no vows, but*
> *vows Were then made for me; bond*
> *unknown to me Was given, that I should*
> *be, else sinning greatly, A dedicated*
> *spirit. On I walked*
> *In thankful blessedness, which yet survives.*
> *(The Prelude*, Book 4)

My intuition told me that the program was moving into positive territory. Near the top, without saying anything at first, there was a shared sense of accomplishment. Palpable were feelings of joy and very good will as the strain of the ascent gave way to hoots and fist pumps. Looking out over Lake Windermere, Rydal Water, and Grasmere in bright sunlight and cobalt blue skies, elevated everyone's spirits even higher: we had earned the view. As I thought about the feelings of the group including myself on this our first full hike of the program I could not help but to reflect on my first ascent in this same place years before, and the deep sense of connectedness I felt with the landscape, and I began thinking about what was happening to each of the students, at least as much as I could surmise. The effort to ascend the mountain was considerable and absorbed each individual's physical effort and emotional determination. With lungs burning, ironically, in the cool air, the body pulsating with heat steaming from the core like an out-of-control furnace, and sweat saturating clothes, puddling in boots, will power is what pushes us up to the next recovery spot. What feels like an all-out effort physically is tempered by the recognition of the actual slow movement upwards? The conflict between significant physical effort and a rational understanding that progress is painfully slow can easily dry up the determination to move onwards. At each switchback we stopped so that all members of the group could stay together; there was time to assess each level of ascent and arrive at a dispiriting sense of no end to what lay ahead, and above. Having moved through the switchbacks, a momentary feeling of relief in seeing what looks like the summit just ahead, only to find on arrival that there is still more to climb, tests resolve. False summits seem to be a cruel game played by the mountain's texture. From the intense amount of body heat produced through the early stages of the climb, reaching the third false summit provided a shocking change with a blast of cold wind from the direction of Grasmere. The unexpected surge of wind, and the accompanying cold air changed our focus away from the strain of climbing to keeping covered against the cold and maintaining balance high up on the mountain. I could see each person clench against the wind, as I reacted the same way. At that transition point there was a wonderful view of how high up we were, and a gut-clenching awareness of how close the edge, with a considerable fall away, was to where we stood.

A sort of emotional slump followed. It had been very hard work to get to this point, and yet there was clearly more to go. The very last stage of the ascent, I think, is most challenging because our physical reserves were spent and movement happens directly from the will, and the pull of the group. Without complaint we kept rising successfully to the top. By the time everyone settled for lunch it was not just the food that tastes especially good and different, but the internal sense that each person realized that they had to overcome challenging physical and emotional obstacles to arrive here. Sofia wrote in her journal later in the day, "The second important lesson from day one was that the view from the top was worth it. When we finally reached the overlook and sat to read our poetry and eat our lunches, Wordsworth's words told of the view I was looking at and it was a truly spiritual moment for me. My body was not completely exhausted as I had assumed it would be and my mind was more awake then at any other part of the day." Our senses were excited and calmed at the same time. Ordinary things such as eating a squashed peanut butter and jelly sandwich, and sitting to give our feet a rest, seemed extraordinary. In other words, each individual worked though the variety of transformations emerging from the beginning of the hike, choosing to keep going against near physical exhaustion to the contrary, but reaching the first inkling of their own possibilities. During lunch we read poems by Wordsworth, and the discomforts of the ascent up Nab Scar were slowly supplanted by the feeling of what Wordsworth captured in his description of the very landscape we were in. During the time we sat and talked I believe that the students gathered a new range of associations to the poetry as they scanned the valleys below, rich in color and texture under the bright sunlight. As Wordsworth says in his poem *Influence of Natural Objects*:

Wisdom and spirit of the universe!
Thou Soul, that art the eternity of
thought! And giv'ist to forms, and
images a breath And everlasting
motion! Not in vain,
By day or starlight, thus from my first
dawn Of childhood didst thou
intertwine for me The passions that
build up our human soul

(1 – 8)

Feelings of eternity underscored the vividly clear elements of the landscape below and around us. Breathing deeply from the climb seemed a way of absorbing the colors, textures, and sounds of the wind. In this place at this time Wordsworth's words resonated emotionally and sensitively in each of us as we talked about the poem and the views. The uniqueness and immediacy of the moment I believed would stay with the students in a palpable way when they encountered Wordsworth in the future. I felt confident in my hope that that would be true.

Out of the wind and next to a stone wall there was snuggled comfort in our sweaty clothes alternatingly cooling since we were stationary and warming in the afternoon sun. Coming down was rapid and punctuated by short bursts of running and laughing among the students. I felt assured by this first hike in the first year of the program that I was onto something valuable for the students, and at the same time fulfilling for me as a teacher. While the students went ahead, I had time to think my own thoughts. This process of reflection after and during a hike became a pattern, which continues.

The trail to the top of Nab Scar begins just to the right of Wordsworth's House, Rydal Mount. The paved roadway pitches sharply upward before coming to a gravel path to the right around a farmhouse. The path parallels a stone wall on the left, and the trail is upward toward a series of switchbacks.

The Challenge of Unlimited Possibilities

> *A gracious Spirit o'er this earth*
> *presides, And o'er the heart of man:*
> *invisibly*
> *It comes, directing those to works of love*
> *Who care not, know not, think not what they do*
> *(The Prelude, 5.316 – 319)*

Transformation and the way that it can be guided is what I aim to do as a teacher. The growing connections between what I do in the Kiplin Hall Program and what I do on campus were becoming more evident even though many elements appeared to be at odds. The very idea that studying the liberal arts is a way to learn how to be human, and the way that my experiences in the Kiplin Hall Program and those of the students seem to merge the physicality demanded by the program and way literature resonates in association with physical effort. Novelist Marilyn Robinson in an address at Stanford University, citing Emerson's "The American Scholar" as the inspiration of her talk, noted that by offering a "variety of fields of study and great freedom to choose among them, has served as a mighty paradigm for the kind of self-discovery American have historically valued." Our educational culture "emerged from the glorious sense of the possible and explored and enhanced the possible through the spread of learning." The experiences I was finding in the Kiplin Hall Program resonated with the central concerns I had, and still have, about the way we understand learning, and more significantly about its value.

Thinking independently takes time and effort, but concerted thought opens up a myriad of possibilities in regard to any subject. Human beings represent infinite possibility. Learning from the humanities is a continuous process of renewal. Distilling the aggregate of great works into the current age is a way of clarifying purpose and meaning for individuals. We need to make informed and thoughtful decisions about what life in the United States means, taking the perspectives of great minds can provide a reasonable way forward. The resolve to push the limits of my physical abilities allowed me to know and feel that there were resources I did not know I possessed. This realization was both assuring and a challenge. Knowing that I could do more brought about a strong well-spring of confidence and helped me to see through adversities that seemed insurmountable. The challenging element in this kind of discovery was that my understanding of the conventional appeared very limiting: I knew that I needed to re-envision my perception of order and my understanding of the shaping influences in my life. Insights I was gaining into myself in connection with the physical effort in climbing led more or less directly to a kind of clarity of purpose and a sense of potential fulfillment. Years of reading and study on my part brought a similar kind of satisfaction and value. To find a link between these two seemingly contradictory modes of experience became the focal point of my concern and interest. I felt, rather than knew, that the kind of essential questioning occurring in my reading led to a quiet joy associated with a level of understanding. Thinking led to feeling and molded how I could feel. Nuances of feeling arose as I came to understand various poets and writers with a new sense of vitality.

Thinking and writing about the Kiplin Hall Program for me is the way toward expressing and unifying my experiences as a college professor for over forty years, in conjunction with having developed and led the Kiplin Hall Program for twenty years. By following an amalgam of different aspects of the program I hope to draw attention to the way a liberal arts institution provides space and latitude for different kinds of learning, while at the same time enhancing students' experience of learning. Opening a number of ways that students can use to find a way to develop a sense of themselves, as opposed to the regimentation of utilitarian courses of study, which demand a strong level of conformity is fundamental. Independent thinking leads to living with confidence in hope for the future. Ways through difficulties can be worked through to a fitting resolution. The core of the Kiplin Hall Program is to have students experience the various landscapes of northern England by walking and hiking. To see the landscapes from a car or bus is a very different experience than feeling the texture of the earth on feet and legs. A lovely, sweeping mountain-scape can fill the eyes of people driving by in a motor vehicle with the sense of placid contentment. Seeing that same landscape with the prospect of hiking in it carries with it a number of judgments about relative distances, the elevation of the mountain, the texture of the trail, the time of day, and the weather conditions.

Being prepared includes having adequate clothing for various temperature and weather-related conditions in a pack. Food, water, maps, first aid kit, a proper hat, and sunglasses are among the things essential to encountering a challenging mountain. In other words, the experience of climbing a mountain, as opposed to looking at it, demands engagement and effort of a different sort on the part of the individual. The casual traveler taking in sights from a car or bus window largely uses the sense of sight, and the traveler has a valid take on the landscape, the sort of thing that is the base of fond memories. But other senses such as tactile, hearing, and olfactory are mostly quiescent. The individual who walks into a landscape must use all senses and call on will power to move and keep moving. Past experiences frame a degree of self-knowledge and initiating a climb flows from the self-assurance that the challenge can be completed. The solitude accompanying the choice to go forward can be chilling insofar as reliance on conventional conveniences associated with travel are concerned. Being really alone even within a group makes one sharply aware of individual responsibility. As a hiker what is carried, how it is used, and what the unique personal purpose is in the hike are elemental. As a hiker, I must master my expectations, emotions, and my physical ability. My plan and hope for the student participants in the Kiplin Hall Program was to have them learn how to take the essential preparations for physically engaging with mountains, woods, moors, and cliffs and concomitantly learn how to engage with poetry. Taking on a poem can be done metaphorically with bare hands, but the experience and understanding of a poem can be notably richer by clearing the way emotionally and intellectually. Poetry as a part of a number of subjects aimed at awakening the longing within us to find our way toward our purpose in existence parallels in many ways the kind of hiking involved in the Kiplin Hall Program. Preparations must be made, the proper equipment is essential, and an open receptiveness to take in whatever is encountered is fundamental. As Coleridge notes:

> Such a green mountain 'twer most sweet to
> climb, E'en while the bosom ach'd with
> loneliness—
> How more than sweet, if some dear friend should
> bless The adventurous toil, and up the path sublime
> Now lead, now follow: the glad landscape
> round, Wide and more wide, increasing
> without bound!

(Coleridge, *To A Young Friend*, 14 –19)

Coleridge's point about the value of having a friend join and share the exhilaration in the effort of ascent, and the shared joy of achievement is an aspect of my aims. Disposing of a kind of "drive by" approach to poetry is first. Students, I have learned, often have many sad and destructive experiences with poetry in school. Poetry takes time and puts demands on our knowledge of words, perceptions of structure, history, life in general, and meaning.

The division between useful knowledge in particular, associated with training, and the cultivation of knowledge that entreats us to bring together the sum of our experiences intellectually and experientially and aimed at enhancing our understanding is a starting point in my hope to show how the Kiplin Hall Program evinces these qualities. From my point of view poetry needs to be more than a matter of reading; it must be experienced. Feeling our way to meaning is an integral starting point to experience what a poet expresses. Knowing what we understand a poet to mean is emotionally shaped by the poet's language, analogues, evocations, tone, and cadence among a number of artistic possibilities. To be truly effective learning must capture the attention and focus of students and become an organic part of their being. I also believe that a friendly and enjoyable atmosphere incites a willingness to learn. In Paradise Lost Milton shows us how Adam had to experience solitude before discovering his vital need for companionship. The felt sense of absence of something in his solitude had to be experienced before he could become fully human. What I hope to make clear is that the focus on individuals is time consuming and often complicated, but significantly valuable in their intellectual, and emotional maturation. The core point of the Kiplin Hall Program is the relationship between poetry and the various landscapes of northern England, and southern Ireland. The fortitude required to complete a hike through to its conclusion is analogous to confronting the challenges of reading a complex poem. By tracing the ways students for twenty years have struggled while hiking on sea cliffs and moors, as well as climbing mountains, I want to illustrate how their perceptions of poetry have been deepened and expanded, as illustrated by their comments and actions. To make my point clear I will focus on walks and hikes that have become traditional in the program and illustrate consequential aspects of experience and learning. From the fusion of activities over twenty years I hope to distill insights and revelations that came along the way.

Helmsley and Rievaulx Abbey

Arrived very hungry at Ryvaux...I went down to look at the Ruins—thrushes were singing, Cattle feeding among green grown hillocks about the Ruins. Those hillocks were scattered over with grovelets of wild roses & other shrubs & covered with wild flowers—I could have stayed in this solemn quiet spot till Evening without a thought of moving but William was waiting for me...We walked upon Mr. Duncombe's terrace & looked down upon the abbey. It stands in a larger valley among a Brotherhood of valleys of different lengths & breadths all woody and running up into the hills in all directions. We reached Helmsley just at Dusk.

(Dorothy Wordsworth's Journal)

Figure 5: Rievaulx Abbey

Source: Courtney Fitzgibbon

The landscape today is not much different from Dorothy's impressions. Between the Yorkshire town of Helmsley and Rievaulx Abbey is a portion of a trail known as the Cleveland Way. Helmsley looks to be too precious to be real. The central market square is surrounded by stone buildings, which appear to have always been there. The entire village is constructed on a human scale. The buildings are generally two stories in height, the sidewalks can accommodate a single walker comfortably, especially if he or she is small and slim, and the shops look crisp and inviting. Just to the north of the town's central market is a stream that on most days' flows with a pleasing trickling sound suggesting freshness and vitality. For centuries Helmsley has been notable for its castle, a physical illustration of the town's importance, as well as serving the local area as the focal point of commercial activity. Students have found the town quaint and the subject of numerous photographs.

Once on the trail leading out of town and heading north, the ground rises deceptively through farm fields and animal pasture land. Since livestock are in the fields, gates are provided for walkers. Kissing gates abound, with the associated custom of having to kiss the person next to come through. Students acknowledge the custom but shy away from advancing to the kissing stage. As the trail winds on between woods and fields, conversation flows, with a range from the trivial to the deeply personal. There is something freeing that comes as each person settles into a personal rhythm where footsteps, body movements, and thoughts coordinate connections to the earth itself. Early in the walk everyone is somewhat careful about keeping away from mud and puddles. Well into the walk a splash or mud stripes become the norm. The bonding that emerges in the rhythmic flow of our steps enhances a sense of well-being and muddy clothing seems not to matter.

Winding downhill toward Rievaulx seems to be a walk back in time. The surrounding hills are wooded as I imagine they would have been hundreds of years earlier, and the pasture land with cows languidly present evokes a sense of quiet and peaceful contentment. Scenes from paintings by Constable come to mind. In June, when we visit, the wild flowers are abundantly in bloom adding to a landscape that captures a vision of "Englishness" in a traditional way. The first sighting of the ruins of Rievaulx through a break in the hedge along the road is almost enchanting and reminiscent of Wordsworth's description of the landscape near Tintern Abbey:

> *Once again, I see*
> *These hedge-rows, hardly hedge rows,*
> *little lines Of sportive wood run wild:*
> *these pastoral farms, Green to the very*
> *door; and wreaths of smoke Sent up, in*
> *silence from among the trees!*
> (*Tintern Abbey*)

The ruins at a distance of about a half-mile seem to belong not only to a different age but to a different reality, part ghostly and part substantial. The unroofed arches and the littered remains of former buildings point to stasis and death, the ruination of our effort as humans to create and maintain stability. And yet the stunning workmanship in what remains behind shows the capabilities of individuals to build a monument to beauty and our spiritual longings. Standing on the fractured tiles of the High Altar my imagination races to comprehend the scope and meaning of what was once here in this exact place. For five hundred years life was lived in the abbey, and I think that to those people living in the abbey it seemed that life would continue on as it had been for generations. How often have I done the same thing regarding my sense of order and security? To think that inevitably what appears fixed and permanent shifts to something else is a sobering thought. What is the legacy of our time? What is my place in existence?

> *We are laid asleep*
> *In body, and become a living soul:*
> *While with an eye made quiet by the power*
> *of joy, We see into the life of things.*
>   (*Tintern Abbey*)

These thoughts and related ones are what students talk about as we filter through the ruins and grounds, and they provide a fine mood to talk about Wordsworth's poem commonly known as "Tintern Abbey." A young man looks wistfully at the remains of the central archway, notices me and says that he feels that God is pulling him upwards through the stone-work. As we gather in the bright sunlight in the cloister to talk about the poem the students immediately recognize that poem is not about Tintern Abbey itself, but about the landscape and its meaning to Wordsworth on his second visit to the area. As we talk about the poem, students comment on the way the landscape leading into Rievaulx is parallel to the introductory landscape Wordsworth recounts early in his poem.

By and large in the poem the landscape appears to stay the same, but it is Wordsworth as the speaker who has changed naturally enough because of his maturity. Though the day's experience is the first time the students have come to the landscape where Rievaulx is located they understand the tension between past and present and the substantially different social orders they represent. With the division between how the past was experienced and how it is now we move into the pivotal point in the poem concerning imagination. Wordsworth portrays the way that memory, especially memory firmly connected to visual impressions, sets up the starting point of imaginative insight. The power to bring back the full intensity of what he felt five years earlier with how he feels now connects the past with the present and stimulates the imagination into an essential connection between the speaker reacting to the scene before him, and his particular recollections drawn from the past. The insight growing from the process lets him" see into the life of things" and deepens his self-consciousness. The "life of things" for Wordsworth is a major element throughout his most important poems. By tracing his sensitivity to aspects of the Wye valley and illustrating how those aspects stay with him he discovers the way that the physical world is connected to

28

the workings of his own consciousness. The tension between feeling and his reach to capture the meaning of feelings in words leads him to write in a similar vein in another of his great poems, *Ode: Intimations of Immortality From recollection of Early Childhood*:

> *But for those obstinate*
> *questionings Of sense and*
> *outward things, Fallings from*
> *us, vanishings;*
> *Blank misgivings of a*
> *Creature Moving about in*
> *worlds not realized*
> *High instincts before which our mortal Nature*
> *Did tremble like a guilty Thing surprised:*
>
> (145-155)

His intimations of immortality come as a sort of distillation of his experiences in nature and writing about a sense of something more but not realized particularly as a child. His individual search concludes in his maturity as he understands a fitting of the processes of nature and the parallel movements of self-consciousness. The depiction of the evolution in his growth is tracked through The Prelude as well as Tintern Abbey. As we move through readings and experiences in the Kiplin Hall Program I hope that each student will confront those Blank misgivings that cannot be settled by a formula but must be understood by engagement and keen self-consciousness.

The meditative quality of Tintern Abbey is richly enhanced by the serene landscape of Rievaulx, and students make observant comments about how what they feel today can work in the same way Wordsworth illustrates in the poem. Many students write about their particular sensations and what they feel about their sensual response of Rievaulx, as well as the visual impact the ruins make on them in their journals. Several entries focused on the sensual dimension of the poem and our location in the ruined abbey, but among them there was another that stands out to me. A young man in the group noted "That the rapid destruction of a way of life that had been in existence for many hundreds of years and the wonton desecration of beautiful architecture for largely political aims is a striking parallel to what is going on in the world today." In their effort to gather particulars and to recognize their reactions to them, they take an important step in coming to understand Wordsworth's aims and meaning in" Tintern Abbey." They also have what I hope will be a lasting impression about the way they came to understand the poem. In realizing that the impressions they gather during the day are important and likely to be very memorable, they come to a sensual apprehension of the suggestive dimension of Wordsworth's lines, and set up the basis of their own powers of recollection. Indeed, over the years former participants in the program have delighted in telling me about their cherished recollections of Rievaulx and their memories of discussing Tintern Abbey there. In "Tintern

Abbey," Wordsworth observes the impact his sister Dorothy experiences in the landscape of the Wye Valley in a way parallel to his first visit. He projects a future in which Dorothy will be able to draw upon her unique recollections and find the sort of imaginative insight he has discovered. Even further, Wordsworth points to the way that everyone has the capacity to discover the way into "the life of things" without having to be in the Wye Valley. The implications of the ending of the poem go in a straight line to the students in reading the poem in Rievaulx Abbey. They become heirs to what Wordsworth means in the poem.

Understanding "Tintern Abbey" can certainly be done in a classroom, and is most often done that way, but the tactile dimension of being in a location that enhances the tone and mood of the poem links elements in the poem to the way we use our senses in the process of recollection. For the students it is the way that they absorb Rievaulx; their individual sense impressions of the scene's elements are felt in a variety of ways. A close awareness of their own process of gathering impressions matches Wordsworth's and provides them with a powerful way of entering the poem. How they come to understand the poem goes beyond the poem itself; they learn how to use experience to arrive at a richer meaning.

Since we change the schedule for the Kiplin Hall Program from time to time and alter the locations we visit, I have found that location counts. Discussing "Tintern Abbey" at Rievaulx carries a dimension of understanding that is similar to treating the poem at Fountains Abbey, which we visit on occasion. The quiet seclusion of the ruins can, at times, on an especially warm summer's day, approach an almost breathless intimacy with the environment. That glorious timelessness that can come in the rich brightness of a June afternoon provides a focus on the immediate moment, while in the mind's eye centuries of calm pleasure connect. Talking about "Tintern Abbey" at Fountains Abbey also allows for the sort of connections to the landscape possible at Rievaulx, and the students gain insight into the poem with tactile and visual elements as they absorb the scenes before them. The awareness of a deep past and the transitional effect on the physical aspects of the scene before them is brought home strongly in the ruins, and it is my hope that the sensual appeal of the landscape and its continuity leads each student to his or her own unique insights accompanied by their own understanding. Because I felt that Rievaulx Abbey and Fountains Abbey set up a resonance between the poem "Tintern Abbey" and various aspects in each location I was not in a hurry to change the schedule, but in time, I decided to experiment. Instead of going to an abbey for a reading and discussion we would go into a mountainous landscape in the Lake District without any buildings nearby. At the outset I expected a less animated discussion and had second thoughts about not going to Rievaulx Abbey, but I wanted to know if my concerns had substance.

Rievaulx Abbey or Langdale Pike

But oft, in lonely rooms, and 'mid
the din Of towns and cities, I have
owed to them In hours of
weariness, sensations sweet, Felt in
the blood, and felt along the heart;
And passing into my purer mind,
With tranquil restoration
(Wordsworth, *Tintern Abbey*, 25 – 30)

Figure 6: On the Ascent

Source: Kelley Holocker

After a demanding morning's mountain climb, we reached a resting place where
we would have lunch and a discussion of "Tintern Abbey." When we stopped rain
began in a steady, spirit draining way, saturating sandwiches and chiding
everyone's attention span. Nevertheless, I opened the discussion with a particular
emphasis on Wordsworth's mood in the early section of the poem. "Gloomy,"
"morose," "sad," "uneasy," and "escapist" were some of the words used by the
students to describe the speaker. A center of gravity on the mood developed
rapidly, and I found myself in the middle of a very rich and animated analysis of
the particulars of Wordsworth's nuanced depiction of the way that his current
mood in the poem moves him to thoughts about permanence and stability in life.

31

There were no abbey ruins where we were, but the environment of cold rain and wind enveloped us with the relentless power of time. Rain is commonplace here, the hiss of rain on rocks providing a soundtrack to the static feel of this isolated place. At Rievaulx, the abbey ruins acted as a touchstone for time's passing, here the physical aggravation supplied the connection. Wet through clothing and squelching footsteps amplified our shared perceptions of aloneness.

Is there anything worse than feeling the discomfort arising from the wet chill of rainwater dripping down your back, and knowing that you alone at this point in time are fully responsible for your own comfort and yourself? There was no option about moving except to do it one wet step at a time. The dripping crags echoed a dispassionate coldness that gave a focal point to our displaced sense of comfort. Each "plink" of water dripping into the surrounding puddles, and the way the rainwater oozed over rocks and into the mosses matched our dissolving spirits and weighed heavily on us. The immoveable bulk of the mountain and the enduring impassivity of the landscape evoked the alienation Wordsworth experienced at his lowest emotional point in the poem. The connection between the sharply sensed elements of dislocation and the yearning for stability to fend off a tumble literally and figuratively could not but be felt strongly. Literally because of the unstable footing on the mountain trail, and metaphorically because of a loss of purpose and meaning on the part of Wordsworth. The impassiveness of the natural environment and its effect on each of us demonstrated the power of nature in shaping our emotions and our responses to the natural world.

My initial concerns about the way in which changing the location of a discussion of "Tintern Abbey" proved to be wrong. The physical experiences on the mountain climb opened up the poem in ways I did not anticipate. While the landscapes around Tintern Abbey, Rievaulx Abbey and even Fountains Abbey share a common ground with hills surrounding the ruins and quiet meadows seemingly secure from the harshest forms of nature, their communicative value is of a different kind from mountain landscapes. The contemplativeness at Rievaulx brought on by the ruin in the landscape is sobering and thought provoking. A mood of rumination that shapes the association between the remaining decaying artifacts and ideas in the poem develops. Insight comes by joining thoughts about what is felt in the present, and what is known historically. As the historical narrative links us to perceptions of the ruins and how we feel about them now, in a very different age, perceptions of meaning emerge at a gentle pace.

On the mountain the sense of history and the past are embodied in the physical characteristics of the landscape. It is nature's work in the raw that we experience. The persistent wearing of time and the elements of wind and water on everything in view cannot be missed. Thinking comes viscerally. The sense of isolation in an environment that seems impassive and impervious to personal time and desires makes physically palpable what Wordsworth evokes in the passages where he outlines his desolation while in France. The relationship between what the students responded to in the midst of climbing a mountain, their perception of Wordsworth's mood as "Gloomy" "morose," "sad," "uneasy," and "escapist" in the early section of the poem came from their own deeply felt feelings at the moment. It is almost as though a certain dimension of tactile sensation that they were experiencing shaped their understanding of the words in the poem. Different as the source of feeling was in comparison to experiences at Rievaulx, the way that the students came to understand "Tintern Abbey" carried with it a knowledge that was physical in essence and linked to a particular landscape. Basically, it was an experience that enhanced understanding. As one very timid young woman confessed, "I was sure that I could not take another step at several points in the descent, but I knew I had to. I kept thinking of Wordsworth's words about seeing into the nature of things. I truly had enough of nature on the hike, but the more I zoned in on the words I came to a realization about my power of endurance. Against my physical discomfort I found a source of strength internally that urged me on. It was a glorious discovery of who I am."

Those shaping nuances of seemingly small aspects in a poem, the elements that lead to meaning and delight in a poem, emerged in a physical dimension with a strong legacy. Students remembered what they felt, but more in the Wordsworth tradition they well remembered how they felt and where they were. The process of this approach to understanding defies easy capture. How can a person measure the depth or range of another's feelings and sensations? Study guides, summaries, and analyses can point to significant ideas, stanza patterns, historical elements, and provide useful information, but the essential communicative value of a poem is largely embedded in our experiences. By giving students experiences that resonate in their lives and acting on their senses, what they encounter in particular poems becomes richer emotionally and physically fulfilling.

Devin Taylor expressed well the effects of hiking and poetry were having on him: "I looked at the natural world and thought about *Lines Composed a Few Miles Above Tintern Abbey*. I'd been exposed to Wordsworth before the trip; I'd taken Dr. Gillin's Romanticism course, and participated in class and mostly did the readings, but I had some problems with Wordsworth...I just didn't connect with him the same way I did with, say, the eccentricity of Blake and Coleridge or the formal and intellectual genius of Shelley. But on the Kiplin Hall trip, I actively learned that sort of deep ruminative state that produced such beautiful musings on the passing of time, and how that changes one's perspective of things. (Perhaps most importantly, I understood how one could achieve that state without laudanum or other substances). While hiking, I appreciated the beauty of Wordsworth's blank verse in that particular poem. I vowed that in my own writing I would make more of an effort to speak to some sort of truth: even if it is just a construct-as some allegt's such a powerful and beautiful one. I still need to recall that feeling somehow and convert it into verse. Perhaps its time for a hike."

Haworth and the Brontes

Wuthering' being a descriptive provincial adjective, descriptive of the atmospheric tumult to which its station is exposed in stormy times, indeed; one may guess the power of the north wind, blowing over the edge, by the excessive slant of a few slanted fir trees at the end of the house, and by a range of gaunt thorns all stretching their limbs one way, as if craving alms from the sun

(Emily Bronte, *Wuthering Heights*)

Figure 7: Haworth Moor

Source: Barbara Gillin

Not all days are spent in the mountains of the Lake District. Haworth and the Brontes' association with it and the moors to the west make it a valuable place to visit on foot. The roads leading to Haworth through Keighley and assorted small industrial, or former industrial villages provide a panorama of the industrial revolution and its aftermath. Vestiges of a world sporting confident buildings ornamented with turrets and friezes, grand entrances, and marble staircases are balanced against row after row of stone and brick houses joined side to side for blocks on end. The accumulated grime and mold on the buildings smolder with a feeling of loss, dejection, and time that has moved on to other things and places. A welter of human activity is reflected in the juxtaposition of automobiles incongruously set in places never designed for them. The small but trim walking paths of the nineteenth century carry the weight of contemporary autos parked pathetically on the path and partly on the narrow road creating a sense of social nonchalance. Accumulated grime and over a century and a half of weather staining give the row upon row of two up and two down houses a dispiriting air. Where clusters of shops huddled at cross roads give way to the scattered intrusion of twentieth-century largely single, free standing, box-shaped commercial buildings. Built for utility decades ago, the buildings are a jarring intrusion as the effects of time have removed any flash or sparkle, they might have had when new. Now they are a somber reminder of ordinary commercialism at its dreariest.

The outlines of the past are evident in the roads with their sharp turns and treacherous intersections, roads that were made for horse and foot traffic. Embankments furiously pushing back at the relentless shove of the earth, sag and seem on the verge of surrender. Given the dilapidated state of things that meet the eye it takes some imaginative will power to envision what these centers of 19th Century and early 20th century industry looked like when the future seemed assured. Buildings with decorative flourishes and made of stone, with grand entrances, and large windows bespeak a sense of place and assurance. Though now the decorative embellishments tip at comical angles, the brass fittings are tarnished, and the former grand entrances serve a variety of sub-divided shops, but what was monumental in the past seeps out. Buildings from more recent times embody function and speed. Fast food restaurants, convenience stores, petrol stations, repair shops, and used car dealers jostle each other in buildings and parking lots of indiscriminate shape and tedious design. As opposed to the stone buildings of the past the new ones indicate temporariness and a part-time commitment to anything beyond themselves. A multi-story council house in the style of faded Miami Beach hotels from the 50s, asserting its oddness and completely out of scale to all the other buildings, rounds out the incongruities of our passage through this soul sapping journey.

But then at the base of a fast-rising hill it is as if we have passed through a threshold into another realm. Cobbles jar the van as we ascend up what appears to be an impossibly steep angled main street. The street, the buildings and the church are all made of stone. Out of the van as we walk around everything seems made for durability, hard and resistant. St. Michael and All Angels, the very church where Patrick Bronte presided and his family attended services, is before us nudging the Black Bull Pub where Branwell spent too much time, and directly across the street from the Apothecary where Branwell purchased laudanum, ultimately to his destruction. The physically hard appearance of the village, the tree shrouded cemetery, and the narrow, twisted lanes, feel gothic, and on dark, cloudy days, elements of disturbing dreams, the sort of instinct captured by Emily Bronte:

> *The thick leaves in my murmur*
> *Are rustling like a dream,*
> *And all their myriad voices*
> *Instinct with spirit seem*
> (Emily Bronte, *The Night Wind,* 13 – 16)

Visual contrasts between the post-industrial landscape to the Lake District bring to mind the opening of Wordsworth's Prelude where he celebrates being free from the city and finds a blessing in the spirit enhancing breeze. The darkest elements of the 19th Century seem to haunt this place even on a sunny afternoon. The Bronte Parsonage is a trim exercise in grey stone offset partially by a well-tended front garden. A sort of grave scape captures two sides of the parsonage and the garden. Mature trees arch over the well-populated graveyard with its hundreds of stones and statuary cantered on slightly convulsed earth. Many young people are noted at grave markers, most of them dying as a result of contagious diseases. It is not hard to imagine restless souls lunging for brightness away from their early in life resting place. In the 19th Century Matthew Arnold, in Haworth Churchyard wrote movingly about this very graveyard, the centrality of nature in the lives of the Bronte children, and imagines their return to life,

> *Yearly awake to behold*
> *The opening summer, the sky,*
> *The shining moorland—to hear*
> *The drowsy bee, as of old,*
> *Hum o'er the thyme, the grouse*
> *Call from the heather in bloom!*
> *Sleep, or only for this*
> *Break your united repose*
> (117 – 124)

While the external atmosphere appears haunting the interior of the parsonage seems tight and confining. But being in the presence of the very table, in its stark simplicity, where each of the Bronte children wrote their works, creates a sympathetic response in the attentive visitor. Life in the Bronte Parsonage was restrictive and unconventional in many ways. The Reverend Bronte took his meals in his study where the children were not allowed, and the children were tended to by their aunt. The girls were discouraged from mixing with locals but encouraged to keep up on political and literary news from London. Branwell was his father's favorite and consequently given much attention by him. Each new level of failure by him as years moved on made life in the parsonage less certain for the surviving girls as they attempted to chart a way to survive.

The story of the Bronte Parsonage has been retold many times by various biographers so that it has almost become mythic to a degree. And the question arises, what is there about this place and its occupants that has so enthralled people for so long? The sense of their association with this very particular place and the connection to other literary luminaries such as Matthew Arnold, who among others of cultural note, respectfully visited here, makes somewhat palpable a connection to the period. Over the course of years many students on visiting this place have found a strong association between themselves and the world the Bronte sisters created in their fiction. The tree-shaded grounds of the parsonage evokes a gothic echo in the chiaroscuro play of intense light and dark, and seems a natural link to the exteriors in Wuthering Heights as well as Thornfield Hall in *Jane Eyre*. One memorable student was brought to tears just being in the actual place that her imagination had conjured in the past. In the days leading up to our visit her emotions and thoughts were riveted on Haworth and the Brontes. In a reverential tone she told me of her utter fascination with Emily, her life, and *Wuthering Heights*. Her dark hair, willowy way of moving, and deep, sensitive affection for literature made her seem to be a young woman out of the nineteenth century as she wound her way through the stone surrounded ally to the Parsonage. At the front door she had to take a minute to clear her tears of joy. With what seems to be a perpetual damp darkness on the outside of the parsonage makes even the mildly interested students aware of a time and place where young women were faced with considerable challenges in trying to make their way in the world of literature. The very physicality of place is a statement hard to miss.

Beyond the parsonage to the rear the earth rises sharply. At the top of the ridge a teasing glimmer of an expansive range of open ground can be seen. Penistone Hill lifts the sightline, and there is a temptation to look for Heathcliff and Catherine along the narrow paths through furze and heather. In the farthest distance it is possible to see a large tree and the outline of a building, Top Withens, the probable site of Emily's location of Wuthering Heights. Ponden Hall is believed by scholars to be the model used in Emily's description of Wuthering Heights, and Top Withens the imaginative site. Ponden Hall burned down years ago, but Top Withens endures as a curious ruin. Walking to Top Withens is a journey away from the twenty-first century. By degrees signs of the contemporary world, a farmhouse, a fence, a road, a wind turbine, fade as the moorland takes on visibly greater contours and vegetation. Scuttling down a small declivity brings us to a stream and a small stone bridge over it. Steep banks surround a small grassy place next to the stream. It was here that the Bronte children played games of their own devising, or watched the moorland animals, and listened to the birds. Wonderfully, the same kinds of experiences are still available. Lingering in this place and reading some of Emily's poetry fuses the effort to walk to this place with a sort of re-enactment of the source of the poems. Though not children, the students inevitably take their shoes off and wade into the chilly water. Watching them reminds me of links through time. The location probably excited the Bronte children in much the same way that the students are drawn to the water and splash about. It is as if time is side stepped. Afternoons, much like this one, were felt and enjoyed by the Bronte children. The movement of the stream and the vegetation on the banks are the same, nothing of the modern world has intruded into this place, and the feeling of timelessness casts a spell on us. Chelsea Garzione reminisced about her experience of this place in a note to me, "One part of the trip I will never forget is the Bronte parsonage. I felt a number of emotions on this particular day as we sat in the misty wet air at lunch time. We sat by a stream and I can clearly remember how powerful the silence was. I remember picturing Emily Bronte hiding in the shadows of the Moors and how she came to give birth to the characters Heathcliffe and Catherine. I don't think I will ever experience something like I did that day. It truly was a revelation of how passion for nature can translate into something completely different such as a character in a story." In her poetry Emily's soulful laments grew out of childhood and embrace the natural features of the landscape, combining adolescent darkness with the ever-evolving process of the moorland's mood-shaping beauty. During our discussion of Emily's poems several students react to the dark moods Emily creates. One young man indicates the way the landscape of the moor and the checkering effect of sunlight as clouds scuttle across the sky, "Makes me feel bright and dark in rapid succession. Emily must have experienced something like this often. It is a perfect link to the poems."

Moving on toward Top Withen's begins with an ascent of a steep bank, and on to a narrow path winding through the rolling landscape. Small direction markers written in Japanese at critical junctures attest to the universal appeal of the Bronte sisters. If many Japanese people did not come to Haworth there would be no signs, but they do, in sizable numbers. The particularity of this landscape I suspect is the primary reason why visitors from Japan make the effort to be here. Heathcliff and Catherine's passionate relationship can be understood at a certain level across cultures. But the way Emily Bronte weaves the natural rhythms of the moors to the trajectory of the lovers in their relationship sets Wuthering Heights apart from other novels of the time. The absorption of green gray and sepia colors of the landscape into each other, and the openness of a large expanse of land seeming to roll away on all sides, and pushed by wind that comes in bursts of varying intensity, combine to evoke a feel of timelessness, movement and stasis all at the same time. The "feel" of this place creates a difference, and perhaps that is why people travel here in what for some is a sort of pilgrimage. Our walk is less a pilgrimage than a way to absorb emotionally the specific physical sensations coming at our bodies. Each person cannot help to feel the sandy, rock-strewn path through their boots and up their legs. Air, brisk with what always seems to me to be a hint of rain, provides a refreshing wash as we slog along.

The final approach to Top Withens is very steep, and with only one tree blowing in the wind beside the ruin the barren extent of the moorland resonates with a mid-day timelessness. To the west the land undulates in a series of flowing, grassy ridges. Imagining Catherine and Heathcliff walking or running through the scene is easy, and captivating. That Emily wandered over the ridges and into the extensive open land, absorbing the impressions of a huge sky roiling with clouds, and ever-changing, communicates directly to me and to the students as I learned later. As a writer her habitual contemplation of this environment had to shape her sensibilities and sharpen her perception of natural details. What feels like a place unbounded in the midst of this landscape, even today, stands in contrast to the confines of the parsonage and the Haworth Village. Release from the social impingements and family duties had to enlarge her soul and the richness of her observation. Certainly, it figures into her poetry and *Wuthering Heights*.

The answer to the question I asked myself about why some people feel compelled to be in the landscape of the Haworth moors has become clearer over the years of my visits. We cannot be 19th Century people with their particular worldview, and their immediate sensibilities. The historical past moves farther away with each year. But the best of literature transcends time and place, and while Wuthering Heights is a first-rate novel in part because it speaks to us out of a particular time in the 19th Century, it also evokes wonder on a physical level. To be able to feel the scattered pathways across the moor is a tactile link to Emily's 19th Century world. The articulation between words and tactile sensations both stimulate and confirm a deeply imaginative awareness of particularities creating a kind of organic relationship between ourselves and the environment.

I believe that the reasons that brought me into the study of literature, and especially 19th Century English Literature, had to do with an open-ended fascination with the particularities of life in the 19th Century and the concerns of the writers. As a student I imaginatively put myself in the world of Wuthering Heights. I was creating links between the facts about the narrative as I learned them; the sensual suggestiveness and beguiling atmospherics of Emily's creation. It is this kind of link that escapes assessments and the metrical quantification of knowledge; it goes to the center of art. As a teacher it is also the thing I want to communicate to students. For the students on the Kiplin Hall Program the physical realities of Haworth and the moors helps to generate those dimensions that go beyond isolated facts. The rift between Catherine and Heathcliff's unique childhood freedom as they shed the confines of civilization against the inevitable loss of freedom rises up by our return to Haworth Village. Farm houses and barns, fences and roads serve as reminders that a walk on the moors is ending. How small and compact the village seems. Uncomfortable with the prospect of resuming her duties in the parsonage, Emily must have felt the smallness and limiting quality of her home against the emotionally liberating landscape surrounding Top Withens. A pleasant surge of recognition gives me another element of understanding something more about Emily.

One particular student, Sarah Snyder, developed a passion about the Brontes before participating in the Kiplin Hall Program, and her time in Haworth became a revelation to her. Her recollection is clear, "A trip to Haworth, where the Brontë's lived and wrote, was life-altering. I still remember the day we ventured to Top Withens, the possible setting for Emily's Wuthering Heights. The moors stretched before me in their unique beauty, and I could not stop thinking about my shoes. Clad in sturdy hiking boots, worn in with weeks of walking prior to our trip, I still slipped and lost my footing on jagged rocks and sunk in puddles of mud. How did Charlotte, Emily, and Anne hike this rugged country? From all accounts, they had dainty shoes nothing like the boots of modern times. It was in that moment, completely connected to the physical environment, that it struck me how revolutionary the Brontë sisters were. They were passionate and spirited women who did not fit in with societal standards, and the landscape of the moors helped shape their creative sensibilities. Being able to hike in Haworth was invaluable to not only my understanding of these women but to the research and development of my senior thesis." Sarah's life changing sense of the Bronte women has proven to have further reverberations. On a trip revisiting Top Withen's with her fiancé she told me of the many recollections that welled up from her earlier visit with the Kiplin Hall group.

Her latest visit built on many of those memories and her increased knowledge of the Bronte novels andpoetry, but a very special added dimension came when her fiancé proposed to her at Top Withens, a truly romantic, life changing event! She accepted.

Whitby Abbey to Robin Hood's Bay

I never saw him once with his hands joined—Unless it was a case of eyes to heaven.And the quick sniff and test of fingertips. After he'd passed them through a sick beast's water. Oh, Caedmon was the real thing all right.
(Seamus Heaney, Whitby-Sur-Moyla)

Figure 8: Cleveland Way to Robin Hood's Bay

Source: Barbara Gillin

It needs to be a clear day to fully enjoy the sea-scape at Whitby. Going to the sea always carries the idea of freshness and reinvigoration along with a dramatic exposition of the edge and intersection of things. Where the sea meets the beach nature's contending forces push and pull with each other sculpting alternating smooth and jagged lines. Traveling in an easterly direction provides tantalizing peeks of the North Sea from the undulating roadway. On sunny days the vista seems an endless stretch of reflected sea and sun. Entering Whitby from the West Cliff shows off the town and harbor snuggled between the sharply rising cliffs, after passing by a confident looking series of eighteenth and nineteenth century buildings devoted to visitors as hotels.

Neatly ordered crescent buildings recall a time when Whitby, and indeed, a large number of coastal towns became resorts for the fashionable. The buildings seem to be well maintained and I always have the feeling that their owners are waiting with expectation and hope that holiday seekers will arrive here as opposed to going to Ibiza or some other hot weather resorts as is the general fashion today. The neatness of garden and grass areas, and the lack of visible trash, points to a civic sense of pride and optimism. The descent into the heart of the town is through a labyrinth of alleys and byways. Houses built into the cliff show resourcefulness and creativity in their perching presence, and the charm of smallness and the human scale in opposition to the tendency in contemporary housing toward conformity and largeness. While the roofs throughout the town are made from orange tile in a Mediterranean barrel style the visual effect is comforting and intriguing. The roof-lines are near in height, but the pitch and angle of each roof challenges me to see more on the narrow and irregular streets. Bram Stoker used Whitby as the haunted setting for his novel Dracula, and his descriptions of locations in and around the town remain accurate to a surprising degree.

Whitby in Dracula

> *The harbor lies below me, with, on the far side, one long granite wall stretching out into the sea, with a curve outwards at the end of it in the middle of which is a lighthouse. A heavy sea-wall runs along the outside of it...Outside the harbor on this side there rises for about a half mile a great reef, the sharpe edge of which runs straight out from behind the south lighthouse. At the end of it is a buoy with a bell, which swings in bad weather, and sends a mournful sound on the wind. They have a legend here that when a ship is lost bells are heard out at sea.*

(Bram Stoker, Dracula)

Figure 9: Whitby Abbey

Source: Kelley Holocker

The ghost of the nineteenth century lives on in alleys and walkways. Moving toward the East Cliff now leads to a confrontation with a mighty flight of stone steps. At the top Caedmon's Cross appears and is anchored to a graveyard here made noteworthy by Bram Stoker. The juxtaposition of Caedmon's Cross and its association with marking the place where the man credited with being England's first poet and the ordered world Caedmon celebrated in his Hymn, with Dracula in all of its gothic darkness and fearfulness is somewhat jarring. But seeing the ruins of Whitby Abbey is a reminder of great age and the layers of history, cultural shifts, fashion, and geology in this remarkable place. Looking out at the sea from the abbey my imagination prompts me to search for Captain Cook's ship, or Viking longboats, or sailing ships from past centuries. Out beyond the horizon lies Scandinavia. The winds of winter must be fierce here. On this day neither ships nor winter are in evidence on the sea, but it feels natural to imagine many things. Perhaps that is why so many explorers and adventurers in England's past came to the border between sea and land and discovered the urge to go to the horizon and beyond. Undulating in rhythmical regularity the sea teases us by letting us feel its considerable power and its seductive allurement to join the flow.

The grounds of Whitby Abbey stand in sharp contrast to Rievaulx Abbey. Rievaulx Abbey is stately and made secure by the surrounding hills and verdant meadows. It seems to be a place in the heart of things. Whitby Abbey is almost defiant. Perched on the highest ground of the East Cliff it can be seen for miles in all directions. Winds, almost gentle at times, are constant and refreshing, though during the winter they must be fierce. It is grandly exposed on all sides. It is hard to miss the symbolic and religious value of its site even today. Everyone must look up to see it. Before it became a ruin, it must have provided comfort and inspiration to the town's people and the sailors either leaving or arriving. In its current state it still commands attention and dominates the town below with provocative endurance, in spite of the depredations of time and war.

The walk along the top of the shoreline cliffs is well worn, and easily followed. Serious hikers, old age pensioners, and day-out strollers move at varied paces, but share the same urge to move, as if by walking they can absorb the contours of the landscape and the power of the rolling sea below. Caedmon must have walked the same pathway and perhaps it was on a day like this that he found inspiration for his hymn. The vastness of the sea with its perpetual crashing of waves against the steep cliffs is timeless, how appropriate that Caedmon sang about the creation of time in his hymn. The stratification between God's place in creation and mankind's, as Caedmon records, appears visible during the walk. Looking forward, the expansive vista of sky slowly becomes shrouded by clouds from the west, the croplands and meadows leading to a sharply defined end point at the cliff's brittle edge, and the sea below harmonize their separateness and confirm a continuity of purpose. Order in the immediate world is visible and seems to confirm what Caedmon knew from Genesis. What it is that moves a person to create a poem has a long history, but I feel that the land and sea-scape along this ancient path had to speak to him.

Throughout the years we have been making this walk students have enthusiastically expressed enjoyment about the luxury of walking freely forward instead of hiking up mountains. Bodies move differently here. With the sun bolstering spirits the physical joy in moving comes as a supplemental pleasure. Progress to Robin Hood's Bay is steady, the afternoon moves on and can be measured by the shifting of sunlight, and the pulsating echo measuring the crashing return of the tide below. One student remembered his day this way, "The most emotional moment of the trip was walking along the seaside cliffs from Whitby to Robin Hood's Bay."

Roosting birds' flair out of their cliff nests filling the air with their riotous calls, and ever so gracefully they catch the updrafts and settle back as we pass. Today's journey brings to mind all the years of my teaching and a flood of memories. Walking seems to prompt inward thoughts, and as one thought excites another, I find myself in a reverie about teaching.

Reveries and daydreams were in many ways the best part of my schooling. Something a teacher would say, or a story, or a physical sensation delightfully instigated my speculations and attention and I was off into my own thoughts. I could remove myself from any situation by imagining the way it must have felt to live in ancient Rome or Greece, early America or medieval Europe, or how it must appear to experience the world from the point of view of an ant. As the walk to Robin Hood's Bay continues, the conventional awkwardness in my body shifts to a more fluid motion. The minor abrasions from my backpack and boots seem to fade as I move in the landscape with a sense of well-being and connectedness. The rise and fall of the farmland seems to copy the flowing of the sea below the cliffs. My breathing is measured and easy, the earth is checkered with mud and compacted topsoil. Moving forward is without hurry or a sense of obligation; it is elemental.

A human body treading across a landscape much traversed for millennia; it is a thought that takes my attention because of its simplicity and utter accuracy. The act of walking is an assertion of being and an appropriate representation of our humanity. Taking each footstep is an act of faith that our body will function to carry us, and the sum of much early development in our lives as we learned to take that first step away from crawling. Our individuality is shaped and reinforced as we develop our own moving cadence. Musculature and body shape are sculpted in part by how we move and by how much.

Watching students in front of me and behind is different as I emerge from my speculations and thoughts. They move as individuals and as a group, or more accurately, several small groups. Some move with a jaunty, energetic bounce, others flow in an ambling rhythm, while a small group seems to be laboring, but talking animatedly. A few seem to be lost to their own concerns and take time to stop and look at the sea and the cliffs. At irregular intervals students move from one group to another in a flow, like the streaming intersection of waves beneath us. A sociologist might make much of the patterns evident among the group, and have lots to say, but my interest is in the connection to what I had been thinking about literature and literary study. We all share a common purpose: to walk the cliffs between Whitby and Robin Hood's Bay, the primary purpose is the walk itself, and absorbing what we can from the environment.

Though the terrain is the same for each of us, we experience the meaning of our movement individually. Who we are, our ages, our life experiences support unique points of view and understanding? The same book yields a panoply of meaning threaded together by the text itself, so too does the landscape bind us and separate us.

Robin Hood's Bay is a delightful warren of houses, pathways, alleys, shops, and a confrontation with the sea. Eye-catching houses kilted by age and the relentless weathering of winds and sea spray set off the cleverness of builders who constructed the houses embedded in the cliffs, and give testimony to human endurance, will power, and creative engagement with natural forms. Life had to be harder and more challenging here in the past given its remoteness, but people made their way. I have the sense that now there are many holiday or weekend visitors for whom the town is largely a place of quiet beauty. However, to be from here and making a living now must be as difficult as it was in the past. The Victorian Hotels at the top of the town, though still lively and active also echo a time whose heyday is over. Fashionable holidays here a hundred years ago were probably the envy of middle-class people when a week at the seaside was a dream. Now, with relatively inexpensive flights to inexpensive destinations on the Mediterranean Sea, what was the heart's longing is now ignored particularly by younger people. Robin Hood's Bay today is unique since it is the destination for people hiking across England in what is known as the "Coast to Coast." Beginning at St. Bees on the Irish Sea stalwart individuals cross through the Lake District and its most trying mountain trails, then across the Pennine Mountains and the rolling countryside of North Yorkshire, right past Kiplin Hall and then on to the long descent across the Yorkshire Moors to the sea. It interests me as to why people take up the challenge and put themselves through the one-hundred-and-ninety-mile course.

Walking from Whitby has made us all hot and sweaty, and the sandy beach just beyond the sea wall is too inviting to pass up, so students start stripping off outer layers of clothing and walk into the fifty-five-degree water of the North Sea. Inching ever so delicately at first, shivering in the cool breeze and cold water, the tense facial expressions of the first few adventurous students, more or less relax into exhilarated shouts of excitement as they proclaim success in the day's hike. Other members of the group splash in motivated, I think, by a combination of peer pressure and emotional abandon. Several of the girls have come prepared by wearing bathing suits under layers of fleece, while the men take to the sea in their boxers. People on the beach smile at the antics and good humor of the students. A middle-aged woman steps toward me and says," Too bloody cold for me! You Americans must be used to cold water." I tell her "No they are just young and having a cultural experience." She looks at me doubtfully. At home I feel sure they would not go into sea water this cold, but it is England and we are here.

The cliff walk from Whitby to Robin Hood's Bay can be accessed by following the main street on the East Cliff to the base of the stairs leading to St. Mary's Church and graveyard. After ascending the stairs go forward into a cul-de-sac where buses (coaches) use as a turn around. An access point appears to the left between St. Mary's and a farmhouse, and is noted by a sign post.

Meals at the Kiplin Study Centre

There is a joy in every spot made known by times of old New to the feet,
although the tale a hundred times be told

(John Keats, *Lines Written in the Highlands After a Visit to Burns's Country,* 7 – 8)

Figure 10: Kiplin Hall Study Centre

Source: Courtney Fitzgibbon

With the long day skirting the seashore complete, we head back to Kiplin Hall with thoughts of food in the forefront of our thoughts. As a way of keeping costs to a minimum we prepare our own meals. This means keeping resupplied with groceries and all the necessities for the preparation of meals. Barbara, an instinctive organizer, has developed a useful and effective way of cutting our time in super markets down to no more than fifteen minutes. Given that there needs to be groceries for twenty people, being quick in the supermarket is not an easy chore to complete. In our early days there were no supermarkets in the area. We would go into what would be a "convenience store" sized market in the USA and just about clear the shelves of groceries. Local people would shop with a personal sized basket; we would show up at the checkout counter with six to eight shopping carts filled to the brim and beyond. Bafflement was the most common expression on the faces of regular customers. People would ask if we had a very large family, in a way, I explained, we do, but the kids are almost all the same age. I did explain but not until they seemed uncertain about what to think. A small tradition developed as some pensioners near the cash register started taking bets about what the final cost would be for our food bill. We were an economic boon to the village, and a source of entertainment for some of its inhabitants.

In short order going to the butcher, the green grocers, the bakery and the like gave way to the more efficient Tesco Supermarket chain. The new supermarket had everything in one stop. It is an old story, and we saw it live itself out as the individual stores could not compete with the large, well-supplied, and efficient supermarket, and they closed. Storefronts were empty in town and people were out of their living. The loss of interacting with shop-keepers, with their attention to serving customers and the gentle, pleasant friction of connecting with them on a regular basis is more than a cultural change; it is a diminishment of how we interact as people. There is no doubt that Tesco makes our time in England easier; it feels like supermarkets here in the USA and makes for quick work of shopping, but the little bounce of pleasure of being recognized as "the Yank" by shop-keepers and knowing what we needed was gone. The more or less facelessness replacing the quirky and at times the long windedness of the shopkeepers and patrons, seemed to be at one with the way loss of contact with individuals paralleled the growing loss of contact with the natural world.

On arriving at the Kiplin Hall Study Center there is a scattering of individuals in several directions. Some get directly to their writing assignments, others seek a nap, others rush to the showers, while still others go to the kitchen to get the evening meal ready. Four students at a time help prepare, cook, and serve the meal. The emphasis is on nutrition and meeting the variety of eating habits. A standard meal involving a serving of meat, beef, lamb, ham, or chicken works for the majority, but vegetarians of various sorts, those who only eat vegetables, those who eat vegetables and fish, those who eat no fish, no dairy, no eggs, and so forth, also need to be served. Fortunately, most of the non-standard eaters want to prepare their own food, and so the kitchen becomes a scene of fervent activity.

Lessons in food preparation evolve as necessity dictates, and something remarkable happens. Experiential learning of a different sort takes place as students, some of whom have never done kitchen work, learn how to make a meal and serve it on time. Barbara orchestrates the coordination of students on duty and the preparation of each evening meal. Students who are not on duty filter into the kitchen and offer to help. Others come in to set up an impromptu cheese board, and the conversation begins. Events of the day are recounted and questions about the poetry and the lives of the writer's percolate.

Crosshatched in the conversation are personal stories, and personal reactions to things going on in the lives of students. What goes on in their lives is at times disconcerting and sad. The pressures they are under carrying the weight of family discord, divorce, the fallout from drug or alcohol addictions, and their own sense of dislocation in their sense of a world where security on both a national and personal level is uncertain. They understand that they are privileged since they are in college, but what comes after for them is vague and unclear. It could be said that it was ever so, but there is a gnawing edge of anger at the political fecklessness of leaders and the push toward conformity and regulation, narrowing their perceptions in their ironic tone.

I often point out that the very poets and writers we are studying had to face very uncertain times in their lives in an environment that was severe in its punishments. During these informal moments there is much learning going on. I gain privilege to the world of eighteen to twenty-two-year olds, their culture, fears, concerns, and hopes. The students get a chance to discover each other on a level that they would not have on campus. Many students report that the people they most enjoyed in the program were people they would not have socialized with at home. The shared purpose of delivering a meal to the group made them work together and discover qualities about them they would not have recognized otherwise.

What I learn from them colors what I do on campus. Back in the classroom I no longer see them as heirs to my experiences and aspirations when I was an undergraduate. For way too many years I have made assumptions about the lives of the students I have taught that do not meet the mark. I fully believed that if I worked hard and steadily kept acquiring knowledge things would work out. At a certain level I do still believe this, but as an English Professor in a job market that has never been bright in my career I know and feel the disparities between conventional beliefs and the harsh realities of the marketplace. For twelve years I served as the Chairman of the English Department and during that time I led searches for new faculty members or replacements. At the annual Modern Language Association Meeting where most of the interviews for hiring took place, I often felt ill winding through the lobbies of the hotels populated by young scholars very anxiously waiting to be called for their chance at a job. My particular discomfort came from my knowledge that only a fraction of the young scholars would get the opportunity to become faculty members. Unfairness is never absent in our world, but how we handle it makes a difference.

Helm Crag

> *Fair trains of imagery before me*
> *rise Accompanied by feelings of*
> *delight*
> *Pure, or with no unpleasing sadness mixed*
> (Wordsworth, *Home at Grasmere*, 756-758)

Figure 11: Helm Crag

Source Kelley Holocker

The fallout from the strong sense of literary insecurity evident in conversations with students makes me think about the way that literature can work in their lives. As we set out on another day to climb a challenging ascent with many associations to Wordsworth and his life in Grasmere, Helm Crag, thoughts about what I am doing in leading students in this place, and what its value is undergirds my thoughts and perceptions, to some degree. On campus, in class, I often ask students what they remember from their favorite course from the previous semester, and I joke about giving them a quiz on that favorite material. Invariably they shrink into their seats uncomfortably realizing that they do not really remember a great range of specifics, which, of course, is my point. College is not just about gaining information, there are lots of ways to get information, the real value in going through the process of college has to do with experience, and how experience shapes our unique perspective on the world. Developing that unique perspective is at the center of my aim as a teacher, and it does not fit into a neatly circumscribed metric. My desire is to create their interest in where poems lead and hope that they will extend themselves to grapple with what they come to understand from the poems, challenging conventional thinking, and discovering a certainty within themselves that resonates with what has been written.

The drive to Grasmere where Helm Crag is located takes us along England's route 66, a stretch that flows through distinct landscapes in the traverse over the Pennine Mountains. The highway itself is a driving challenge. The road goes from single lane to dual carriage-ways, with access roads butting in often at odd angles. Since we drive the route early in the morning on sunny days the landscapes in front of us are captured and illuminated by the still rising sun. Where the road rises the sky-scape, usually with roiling clouds, seems to embrace us. The farmlands anciently marked by scattered stone walls embody stability and resignation to the constant effects of the often wet, windy weather. I often wonder about what life is like on these isolated farms. Unexpectedly there are llamas being raised among sheep and cows. A few bare-boned cafes compete with barns and livestock pens on the periphery of the road, as trailer trucks, (lorries), busses, cars, and farm equipment bound with a sort of competitive surge to get ahead of each other, particularly before the road returns to a single lane. In the vastness of the ever-opening countryside it is easy to get caught up in speed. The transition from farmyards and pastures to moor is abrupt and dramatic. Stretches of green, punctuated by rock walls, withers into the sepia of low growth vegetation and a stark outline of the terrain. To the west the ribbon of road unfurls in swooping undulations into Cumbria and the mountains of the Lake District begin to loom into view. More often than not richly lush cloud banks hover over the mountain tops and stratify the sky with what looks like frosting on a wedding cake, impressive and enticing.

Turning off the A66 at Threlkeld opens into St. John in the Vale. The road, barely more than the width of two cars winds through one of the most beautiful valleys I have travelled. The terrain at the valley's base rolls under old growth trees in part. While pastures slide to the base of the mountains and in their greenness seem to climb the lower reaches before being checked by scree and boulders. Ancient looking stone-walls seem to shimmy up the fells marking out fields that have maintained sheep for perhaps thousands of years. Sharp turns and a road that goes up and down as much as it shifts from side to side wobbles to a B road that more or less follows the traditional road from Grasmere to Keswick.

As an American the road feels tight, but the hanging evergreen tree limbs and the first sighting of a lake, Thirlmere, the tightness transforms into a sense of snugness amid the sharply rising mountain-scape. We skirt the edge of Helvellyn's base where I know we will face a distinctive challenge in the next week. To the right I point out the mountain we will climb today, Helm Crag, and the students look up and do not say much. I take their response as a sign that they are having some thoughts about what they conceived we would do and what we were actually doing. Soon the mood is lightened. The smooth ascent over Dunmail Raise leads to the revelation of Grasmere. Surrounded by mountains and edged with a lake containing a distinctive island, the village looks like a scene from a fairytale, especially with the sun shining defiantly among bursts of clouds.

The rapidly shifting interplay of light and dark in the ascending morning mist creates a mixed perception of something that is really there and something that seems evanescent. The effect is enchanting; the quintessence of The Lakes. After parking the vans, the students' energy levels rise rapidly. There is much chatter about how high the mountain is and how long it will take to ascend, as well as excited talk of missing hats, socks, and chocolate. Inevitably there is need for stamps, cash, looking in shops, but we move on, fortunately the sunlight portion of the days is long at this time of year, so frenetic rushing is gloriously absent. As we walk toward Helm Crag students generally ask me many questions about Wordsworth and what life might have been like for him in this place. I tell them anecdotes and stories that I have gathered over the years of reading. In this place of remarkable beauty today they are saddened by a story related by Wordsworth in his Recollections about a terrible snow storm that roared into this valley cutting inhabitants off from any kind of communication. The ice and snow lasted much longer than usual, and a farmer and his family perished in the process of trying to reach Grasmere for food. The parents perished first and so did the children from starvation. It is a grim story and a sobering one for the students, but a reminder of life's unpredictability and difficulty.

Ignoring the painful and tragic in life is to hobble individuals by limiting the range of their emotions, the depth of their compassion, and the clarity of their powers to understand. The recent academic concern over a dimension of political correctness, where some students do not wish to read required material that might prove to be offensive, yet want to be considered members of a class, is reason to think about the implications of their wishes. Our world is violent enough, and sensitivity to violence I see as a good response, but to try to isolate information that causes discomfort, particularly from literature courses, is to warp reality and give the impression that by wishing something to be true it will be. For students to know about the tragic stories connected with the beautiful and elevating vistas of the Lake District as recorded by Wordsworth, I hope tempers any superficial response they might have. Wordsworth tells us:

Fair seed-time had my soul, and I grew up
Foster'd alike by beauty and by fear;
(305 – 306)

Throughout the Prelude he reiterates the shaping influence of these two forces, beauty "and" fear, not "or." Wisdom for our time.

Passing through a gate we begin moving upward, at first somewhat gradually through a few switchbacks, and then very sharply as we take on stone steps set into the mountain alongside a stone wall. For about two hundred yards we seem to have entered a stone world shrouded by thorn trees in full bloom. The unevenness of the steps, along with the possibility of slipping from the trickle of water spreading out over the rocks puts me on high alert; I am not alone. Breathing becomes somewhat labored quickly, and the fleece that seemed perfectly comfortable a few minutes earlier now is unbearable as a wash of sweat gushes through the fabric. The compact group at the bottom of the mountain is now spread out into distinct smaller groups. Since I go forward and take the lead, I try to keep the front movers from dashing ahead disheartening students less fit. When we began the Kiplin Hall Program I felt very comfortable in almost jogging through this portion of the mountain. Time has moved on and my body has lost a shocking level of nimbleness.

Reflecting on what I used to feel and what I do now becomes a sort of internal reverie for me. As a graduate student when I first climbed Helm Crag with Barbara I distinctly recall feeling a searing sensation in my lungs and chest as I aimed at muscling my way upwards, with a sure sense of bravado and showing off. I believed that I could simply keep pushing myself and ascend to the top in a kind of willful fury, until my quivering legs buckled and locked themselves into calf and thigh cramps. Dropping down on an outcropping of rock overlooking the Vale of Grasmere, feeling chastened and foolish, I just stared and stared at the pastoral scene below. The lush greens of woods and fields melded into a seductive arabesque by the radiant sun reflected off Grasmere Lake, and the background stretch of fells and sliver of Windermere opened a sense of infinity. Though weary and winded I felt my breath taken from the emotional effect of so much palpable beauty: a combination of physical depletion and aesthetic shock. I believed that I could smell the far-off fir trees on the other side of Grasmere; the clean freshness of their imagined fragrance lifted my spirits, and my body seemed to melt as muscle fibers relaxed. With my spirit reanimated I was ready to continue the ascent but with a new emotional centering. With nature as a constant gauge, I realized that we test our experience against it. Wordsworth was on to something.

As the group of students wends its way upward now, I can feel what they are experiencing, and I believe that I understand what they are doing, but with a substantially different perspective from my initial experience all those years ago. Each stretch of their legs, tentative in search of a firm foothold, then the lift and strain as their bodies wobble up, the grab for a rock or tree branch for stability, like toddlers taking their first step into independent movement, is a reenactment of what everyone must face in making this hike, and also a transition into an individually unique realm of experience. How like life. The step in search of stability, and the reach for a pull forward, and the will for endurance under stress fit a pattern.

When Wordsworth roamed these mountains, he had to trust the belief in what he was doing as a poet. His forward motion as an artist, based on the experiences of his past is deeply intriguing. How to achieve the confidence in his vision of literature? Could he have understood the effect of his vision? I have come to think that the answers to my questions reside in what we are doing today. The physical demands on my body are punishing at times, and my determination to overcome the temptation to stop gets increasingly stronger as I age, but desire pulls me upward. Past ascents have confirmed to me, not only that I can do it, but that there is a soul-enriching fullness that comes from continuing toward the summit. My trust is that the students today will share an inarticulate bond with each other as they experience the climb and come to feel its personal meaning.

Invariably, a small group gathers at the front, panting to show their strength and their eagerness. Oh, do I know the feeling! Behind them in ever smaller groups the looks of puzzlement and pain show up on the passing faces as I watch them hunker on. "Are we near the top?" becomes a refrain. When I say, "No," a strong realization that their bodies ache and might fail them unfurls in their faces and is made obvious in their body movements. The outcropping of rock where I had that ever so blessed time to recover all those years ago is just before us, and so I tell the students that it is time for a rest and lunch: the exhale of gratitude is audible. As lunch progresses, I ask them to take out their Wordsworth books and direct them to "Home at Grasmere." Remarkably, over the years that we have been climbing Helm Crag the weather on the way up has always been bright and dry. With the panorama of Grasmere and its surrounding before us, and an arresting silence hanging in the air, I point out features in the landscape and their relevance to Wordsworth. It was at the southeastern edge of Grasmere where William and Dorothy first made their entrance into the Vale of Grasmere from the Ambleside road. It was the end of the year and the beginning of a significant milestone in their lives, and English Poetry.

As I read passages from the "Home at Grasmere" I point out natural elements from the poem that can still be seen. The fir tree grove that Wordsworth notes in his description of life in Grasmere in 1800 can be seen to the left of the lake:

> *Not less than half way up yon mountain's*
> *side, Behold a dusky spot, a grove of Firs*
> *That seems still smaller than it is: this*
> *grove Is haunted—by what ghost? A*
> *gentle spirit Of memory faithful to the*
> *call of love*
>
> (Wordsworth, *The Recluse,* 384 – 388)

The ordinariness of life in this obscure place becomes extraordinary because, as he indicates, it was threatened by the growing incursions of the industrial revolution. Its uniqueness is still under a threat as the drift of modern culture is toward homogeneity. Wordsworth's directing of the reader's senses to the village activities forces a consideration of elements in life not included in the poetry of the past. The harsh language of the shepherd and the communal struggle to eke out an existence in a secluded and remarkably beautiful setting is set against the privileged position of Wordsworth as a narrator, who has chosen to join this world, and rejected the fashionable world of London and city life. The durability of the natural elements visible before us, and their portrayal in the poem, proves to be a signal moment for the students. Their personal reactions begin, generally in a limited degree, in this resting place as we have time to talk, but the real impact comes later as they write about what they have absorbed from the combination of intense physical exertion and the links between the poetry and the landscape.

A journal entry by a woman begins with the observation, "That the perspective from the mountainside provided a sort of buffer from the world below with all of its activity and where I sit. My personal sense of solitude was intensified by the silence in the sunlight." The reframing of the circumstances in which the poem is read and thought about opens up a thinking and internal sensing place where emotional ties, almost like synapses in the brain, form a distinct web of connections. Their joy at understanding the selections from the long poem informs how they feel in addition to what they feel. The conscious shaping of the "how" is most important. Descriptive poems can feel potted and limited: pretty pictures in pretty words. Because the students have had to negotiate the physical demands of hiking to this point, their awareness of how they feel is personally keen. With that awareness in mind, and in their strained muscles, they come to a clearer understanding of how the poem works, and what Wordsworth is doing in his poetry. Physical strain with its narrow focus on attaining a specific goal helps to concentrate their acceptance of the unconventional in the poetry.

The chill following the rest urges a re-engagement with our climb, and so we move on and up. With the nearly vertical series of stone steps behind us, the trail widens into a welcome roll. The crunch and shuffle in the loose stones and gravel sounds hypnotic as our bodies warm again but reminds us of imminent blisters and other aches. Some students move with a balletic lightness of foot and body, others, like me, move in halting, staccato-like steps often slipping and sliding, supplemented by a low-level embarrassment. After a series of ups and downs the trail bows to the right and opens onto a deceptive green stretch of grass pocked by rocks. Because of increased erosion, especially in recent years, the trail is now outlined in part by gravel and stone baffles in an attempt to hold the mountain together. In my early association with this mountain there were relatively few people hiking. Though I am doubtful that visitors come to the Lake District, as they did in the nineteenth century, as a result of reading Wordsworth, the legacy that he established in awakening people's awareness of the healing power of Nature lives on as numbers of people seek refuge from a post industrial world, which increasingly leaves little room for privacy. The grassy stretch does not look all that steep, but in short order our calves flame and cavalcades of dripping sweat confirm the way the eye can trick the brain.

Not all students are in the same physical condition and inevitably the distance between the first and last person increases as the terrain becomes more difficult and reserves of energy and strength are depleted. Nothing is more dispiriting than to be at the back of a group feeling incapable of moving on and somewhat embarrassed or ashamed as the front of the group moves upward. From our very first year Barbara has insisted that the front group must stop and wait for everyone else to catch up, and then pause to gather back our strength and stoke our determination. No one objects to pausing as we slog through this stretch. Tears are not uncommon. It might sound like planned cruelty, but in tearful moments and the conversations we have in those moments, elemental levels of honesty and primal feeling surface.

Megan, a student, commented in her journal, "I found the hiking to be strenuous, but because I was an athlete and loved to push myself physically, I discovered that I could expand my boundaries. My connection to the mountain in association with the poems we read brought me joy and confidence." Barbara is masterful in the way she coaxes reluctant students upwards and forwards. She points out to them that she is old, and if she can keep going so can they. At times she has held the hands of students who were faltering, the physical contact seems to comfort and reassure them, and they take strength from her to go on. It happens often. The physical and emotional distress force the students to understand what they perceive as their limits. For all students who have reached this point they realize that they are on their own, isolated and sometimes deeply cold and wet. At these nadir points, invariably the group offers encouragement and urges their classmates to keep trying after they have rested, and they do. The emotional thread of compassion and understanding that weave through these moments happen in the context of mutual effort: talking about compassion and experiencing it are very different things.

At the top of the grassy portion of the climb there is a ridge between a peak and the summit. From the ridge the mountain falls off dramatically opening vistas of the ancient road, Dunmail Raise, and the base of Helvellyn. The next stage of the climb is to the summit and it involves climbing hand over hand among the sharply rocky mountain-scape. Before continuing we pause to read and consider passages from Wordsworth's Home at Grasmere where he expresses the source of his work:

> *Nor aught of blinder vacancy, scooped out*
> *By help of dreams—can breed such fear*
> *and awe As falls upon us often when we*
> *look*
> *Into our Minds, into the Mind of*
> *Man— My haunt, and the main*
> *region of my song Beauty—a living*
> *Presence of the earth, Surpassing*
> *the most fair ideal Forms*
> *Which craft of delicate spirits hath*
> *composed From earth's materials—waits*
> *upon my steps*
>
> (Wordsworth *Home at Grasmere,* 790-798)

The link between the external world and the sense of our interior life that Wordsworth notes is palpable in this moment. A student points out that, "It is impossible to miss what Wordsworth says about 'Beauty–a living presence.' I now understand that he is referring to the essence of beauty within the context of all that is palpable, like where we are." Reading and thinking about poetry in this place gives focus to the richness in the air, and the glow from the emerging awareness that we have all come to this point together. The link is as emotional as it is physical; it is how the physical and emotional join together. On sunny days, it is a luxury to stretch out on the last patch of grass and face southward toward the unraveled landscape. I often imagine vacationers on tropical islands, cool drinks in hand and a shimmering pool before them, seeking a perfect tan. Dressed in saturated shorts, fleece, clunky boots and soaking socks as we are, looks to be the antithesis of style and pleasure, but having reached this point on our own efforts and volition gives us a sense of having earned what we each feel individually. "Radiant" comes close to evoking the way sunlight seems to lift the atmosphere into the cobalt reaches of the upper sky. Fulfillment of our goal to reach the summit is near at hand, and the tarry smell of sheep droppings, ubiquitous here, snaps me out of my reverie. So, we push on.

The peak is not visible, but that is no matter as all our attention is riveted on what is directly in front of us. A labyrinth of rocks has us continually looking for safe places to plant our increasingly banged up feet while looking forward in quick snatches, like an over caffeinated chess player. Using our hands and arms as well as our feet, moving crab-like, brings a kind of giddy laughter to some while others are daunted by fears of falling. My walking sticks become a nuisance in this section of the mountain, and as I try to join Barbara, who is coaching reluctant students forward, I become the object lesson in awkwardness by catching my shins on every available rock, along with spasmodic lurches in all directions. The students follow Barbara's advice and avert their eyes from my rattle-trap movements.

Arriving at the summit is transformative. I am always gratified by the way that students who had the most difficult time hiking up find an excitement that is communicated by laughter and often tears. With the wind slashing at each of us, like a rebuff to go away, the group-wide awareness of accomplishment makes everyone feel curiously relaxed. The uncertainty for many who have never even thought of climbing a mountain finds relief and is replaced by an exalted understanding of their capabilities. Belief in themselves and a sharpened understanding how the will can be directed toward achieving what seemed insurmountable will come to them as letters from former students in the past attest: but not now. We learn in a process of unfolding. Sometimes it takes years before we truly understand what our experiences mean, and so it is with regard to what we feel our way toward.

It is dangerous to take too seriously the perception of personal invincibleness at the top of a mountain, but as the fears, trepidation, and physical strain dissipate, misgivings individually and as a group have been overcome. The whooping and laughter among the students intensifies their joy and their desire to save the moment in pictures of themselves at the summit. Physical confirmation needs to be enacted, and communicating this meaningful moment needs to be shared. When we began the program, the pictures taken had to be processed and printed, something that took some time. Now the pictures they take are immediately sent to friends and families back home. By the time we descend to the mountain's base they will have received messages from home expressing congratulations: we live in a very different world. Technologically this is obvious, but are we so different at the core? In writing about this landscape in the early Nineteenth Century Wordsworth aimed at capturing the scenes before us and engaging the reader's senses in the hope of evoking strong emotions that would communicate his reverence for the natural world and lead us to contemplate our place in the world. The manifestation of his physical involvement and his emotional reactions to the evanescence of his acute sensations find material form in the poems. Today, as we all struggled to the top of Helm Crag, each person had experiences of his or her own, accomplishing the goal leads to what seems like a human need to capture and savor the moment and then communicate it. Of course, Wordsworth's skill as a poet is the significant difference between him and us, but the essential pattern is parallel. For the students it will become clear when they return home that while family and friends will acknowledge the accomplishment of their mountain climb today, they will not fully understand the experience. It is truly a "You had to be there moment." It is in the experience itself that meaning resides. Descriptions, pictures, text messages will not convey fully what is felt. I noticed one student sitting contemplatively on a ledge looking out toward Dunmail Raise, the road into Grasmere, and the one we travelled on earlier. He said he was imagining Wordsworth as he described himself in the Prelude when he was anticipating glee going home for the Christmas holiday, and he climbed a crag to look for the horses that would bring him home. During that home visit his father unexpectedly died. He recounts the emotional tie between the prospect of joy and the dread he experienced in connection with the elements of the scene." I expanded on his thoughts by citing some of the elements, the single sheep, the blasted tree, and the wind on the stone-wall. Wordsworth, I pointed out, says that these elements stayed strong in his memory and he revisited the unique emotions associated with his recollection and its associated images. "I have experienced things today that I will be thinking about for a long time, I hope. Wordsworth becomes more familiar the more I move and feel this place." As I walked away from him to gather the group and begin the descent, I felt sure that the student had come to realize a deeper sense of pathos between Wordsworth's memory of the beak December afternoon and all of its particular elements, and the student's own realization of the way the wind, cool air, and bright sunshine that he experienced on the climb today would become a source of insight into himself.

It took several hours to climb to the summit but going down is surprisingly fast. While I suggest to the students that the descent can provide a useful period of time to reflect on the landscapes that alter with the angles of descent, as well as the shifting of sunlight and the encroachment of clouds from the west, but many, excited by summiting their first mountain, bound down the trail with abandon. Part of me envies their shock absorbing joints and youthful cartilage. Descending I feel my age in the unsteadiness of my legs as they tend to lock into the angled slope, jolting the rest of me like a stiff legged argument. Curiously, the keen awareness of my physical abilities in the past compared to now is not deeply distressing. It is the natural way of the world and my time in it. Compensation comes in the way that my intensely alert, eye riveting descent, bracketed by a concern for injury, provides me with time to reflect on my mortality in this extraordinary landscape on a remarkably bright day. In spite of setbacks in life it is a privilege just to be here, and the particular joy in sharing my own love of the landscape and Wordsworth's poetry with another fine group of undergraduates. The warming effect of the late afternoon sun is surpassed by the growing internal warmth of satisfaction and emotional fulfillment as I hear the chirp and twitter of birds signaling the tree line and the nearing base of the mountain.

The poetry we talked about today meant something very different to me when first I read Wordsworth as a student. His evocation of the landscapes I understood with reference to the natural world I came from, his world had to be imagined. Centered in his landscape today brings home to me how much I fell short in my imaginings, and yet limited as my initial perceptions were, they were not inaccurate in their essence. I know that I understood the way the natural world is rife with sensual delight, and the way that senses can shape our understanding of our place in the world. Most of all I recall the power of delight and joy arising from the physical effort of walking, running, and climbing in the natural world. As a student, particularly as a graduate student, I should have been thinking about the way Wordsworth was influenced by other writers, and how he influenced others to follow, or what his critical perspectives were. Dutiful as I was, I did consider those aspects of his work, but it was the works themselves that really spoke to me. Excitement generated by the portrayals of interactions with nature sparked my imagination and led to an abiding love of the poems. The effect on my life was and is profound. I knew that I needed to find a life of the mind where poetry figured prominently. Consideration about the practical areas of life seemed to be something for another day. A full reckoning of how things came together is a story for another time. But what became central in my aims as a teacher came to me as an undergraduate when my goal was first to teach in a high school, and later as a graduate student whose goal morphed into a different kind of classroom. Answers and good leads in life to the perennial great questions in life could be found in poetry, certainly not a new thought, but a cornerstone of belief in my teaching. Bringing students to their unique awareness of how significant literature can be in their lives connects the beginning of my career to now, and I live in hope that they will pass on what I have discovered.

Approaching the gate that we all passed through this morning as we began our ascent up Helm Crag reveals itself to our welcoming eyes. Some hours earlier a degree of uncertainty could be read in the expressions of some of the students; deep breaths, checking of backpack straps, retying of shoelaces, and some nervous energy shaken off in the movement from one foot to the other while waiting for everyone to assemble. Now like strollers on the Champs D'Elysees a confident feeling of belonging reigns throughout the group. Recounting their feelings at different segments of the hike permeate several conversations I cannot help to overhear. Having achieved a set goal, ascending the mountain, has given everyone a significant boost in self worth and self-satisfaction. One girl good humoredly offered her reaction, "It was the first time I encountered hand-over-hand scrambling. I forced myself to do it and I am surprised at myself. I did more than I imagined successfully." I take pleasure in listening to how they were sure they could not walk another step only to find that they could, and a good deal more. A few venture off the general track of conversation and ask questions about Wordsworth and his life here and the poetry. There is a group wide agreement that the landscapes are richly inspiring in themselves, and I understand what they say as an indication that they have come away with perceptions of things they have not experienced before nor felt precisely. As we gain a paved road and the footing is more secure, we drop into a rhythm as we walk toward Grasmere. The loosely synchronized amble of our bodies after various levels of physical and emotional struggle, with the now regular rise and fall of our breathing, is matched by a shared emotional bond, like the cadence of the poems we have been reading. We are on the same wavelength; we have experienced a locus to which we can return in our individual memories in the future.

Beginning at the village green in Grasmere, follow the Easedale Road, opposite Samuel Read's Bookstore. While remaining alert for automobiles follow the road away from the center of Grasmere past a youth hostel on the left. Continue across the meadow before you to a small cluster of farm buildings. Turn right, go through a gate, and then upwards.

Time to Look and Think

> *O joy! That in our*
> *embers is something*
> *that doth live,*
> *That nature yet*
> *remembers What was*
> *so fugitive!*

(Wordsworth, *Intimations of Immortality from Recollections of Early Childhood*,
133 – 136)

Grasmere as Wordsworth knew it is still discernible insofar as the essential layout of the village and its buildings are concerned. The village is small today and was much smaller in Wordsworth's time. It is relatively easy to imagine shops for the butcher, the baker, and the proverbial candlestick maker. As a tourist destination, which Grasmere has clearly become, the shops hawk backpacks in an astonishing variety, hats for all occasions, socks enough to supply an army, waterproof jackets, pants, and gravel crushing boots. In all fairness the weather in the Lakes is very changeable; a gloriously promising morning can sink into an afternoon of lashing winds and side-wards rain. As much as we are the very people for whom the wares are aimed, and no matter that I think there is a good degree of humor in the awkwardness of feeling the commercialization of this lovely village along with the gratitude that comes from knowing that I can replace my broken shoelace without complication. Contradictions in life do abound. Grasmere is a village that became somewhat sanctified in the nineteenth century by the popularity of Wordsworth's poetry and the way that Wordsworth cultivated a growing mythic air about the village and the district. People made their way to the Lake District for holidays since it held out the lure of an alternative to the polluted cities ravaged by the steady industrialization of the country. Breathing the purer air in the simplicity of villages reminiscent of a popularly perceived simpler time began a process that burgeons today. Though the roads in the Lake District largely follow routes carved out centuries earlier, making travel frustrating because of traffic jams and a limited amount of parking, people still come in ever greater numbers.

At the edge of a small park in the center of Grasmere, there is a bus shelter, and on one of its walls there is an inscription noting that Queen Elizabeth came to this very spot to dedicate the structure. I imagine that the queen's appearance must have caused quite a stir locally, with everyone beaming with pride, and anticipation about some enduring good. The queen's appearance to dedicate a bus shelter perhaps measuring twelve by four strikes me as being very British. It is comical on one hand, and kind, and thoughtful on the other. Creating a celebration for a bus stop shelter suggests catastrophic backwardness and a particularly narrow world view and ironically silly, but taking time to travel to this relatively remote area of England, and acknowledging the way that this structure will make life just a bit more comfortable by her presence also shows an endorsement of civility and fellow feeling. The cultural gap between what I see and what I understand is always opening new crevasses. How very much like the way that literature works on us. The description of the familiar and our reflexive responses to it gets turned, sometimes ever so gently like a ballerina shifting her weight and teetering gracefully balancing between falling and controlling the moment. The uncanny awareness that a line or phrase in a poem creates in us a response that can resonate for a lifetime, makes the ordinary extraordinary and fuses delight with uncertainty.

Watching the students as they disperse to various tea and ice-cream shops, I find our American ways indistinguishable from the native English. The emerging international culture, I note to myself sardonically, seems to be based in eating and shopping. As Barbara and I sit down at an outdoor café ourselves for tea and scones one of the students catches my eye as he stands near us with a look not quite blank, more of tentative uncertainty. Asked if he would like to join us he nods his head forward quickly, but then qualifies what I take to be his perception of assertiveness on his part and an intrusion into the private time between Barbara and myself, by briefly jerking his head backwards and raising his hands in a gesture of negation. We assure him that he is welcome and as he begins to be seated two other students, seeing space at the table ask to join in as well. Tea and fresh scones have reached sacramental status in my estimation, especially after a vigorous day of climbing. With what appears to be the everlasting summer sun in England, daylight at this time of day is like a prolonged yawn, warming us just enough and the prospect of hot tea in sight I know that this is a cherished moment. The chatter of the students amplifies my spirits and I cannot help to smile, a smile that momentarily distracts the students as they wonder why.

The table talk moves from a recounting of difficult moments on the mountain earlier in the day, to questions about literature. Parsing our movements, detailing the nuances of effort in the climb, and delight in the satisfaction of accomplishment, I point out, have a direct parallel to the way poetry works. One student slightly bedraggled by the mountain climb brushes crumbs from her mouth with the back of her hand in a sort of swashbuckling sweep, something I suspect she does not do ordinarily given her physical delicacy and what I have perceived as her personal level of sophistication. Then she asks a rapid-fire litany of questions about Wordsworth and how people in his time understood him, and what he was about being a poet in a poor, hard working environment.

Sensing the chance to gain the center of attention, another student, trying hard to impress us all with his clear-sighted concern only for art and issues of the mind asserts that biography is not as important as the poems themselves. A third student looking slightly forlorn wonders aloud whether poetry matters in the world at large. The jousting is largely gentle and good-natured and follows a track I can easily trace back to other groups of students. The questions and concerns are phrased somewhat differently, but the basic thread links the past and the present: poetry and physical experience in the natural world are our touchstones. I ask them if they discovered anything about themselves from today's climb that might connect with poetry and especially Wordsworth's.

Momentarily, the air goes out of the conversation, and the students lurch into seminar mode as their backs straighten and mouths tense as if a dead fish were dropped on the table before them. Assured that I was not quizzing them, lightness returns to the conversation and they tell how the depiction of William and Dorothy's entrance into this very village, and perhaps walking on the very flagstones before us, makes the description a living thing. What for most people might have been a pleasant stroll in a striking landscape, becomes for the Wordsworth's a declaration of a new life? Details that many might not have noted permeate the descriptive passages, and by writing about his reactions and aspirations the vaporizing moment is captured and preserved for us. The act of writing where the evanescent is given form and substance, they conclude, is more than a legacy; it is a way of opening ourselves to the human condition. The comparison to the world of 1800 becomes interesting to speculate about as we sit in the physical environment of that time and adds yet another layer to meaning and understanding.

It would be hard to believe that people in 1800 could imagine our world and the way we conduct ourselves in it. With tea and scones consumed our conversation ends on a somewhat plangent note. A growing self conscious awareness of how this lovely village has become defined by tourists, where superficiality supersedes substance in the form of Wordsworth pencils, fridge magnets, bookmarks and the like, we feel a little tainted, like walking through a stand of poison ivy while wearing shorts: vulnerable with a sense that a price must likely be paid.

On the other hand, life in this place in the past was very hard and often harsh. The appearance of cultural coherence might be something of an illusion that we fall into. Post-modern scholars have opened several avenues of approach to this phenomenon but talking with students in this context brings theory into a physical presence. I do believe that the destabilizing effect on the students' preconceptions will turn to good use when they return to the classroom next semester.

Discussions like this happen often enough without scheduling or prompting. It is the more or less a one to one relationship that happens in the context of these impromptu discussions that makes a strong, and, I hope, lasting impression on the students. In my regular classes on campus I strive to make each lesson have more than a single focus on the literature we treat. Telling about the biographical highlights of a particular author and recounting dramatic or comical aspects of their lives or circumstances is my way of putting the literature into a life frame bordered by the web of personal connections each author had. Today has been a success enriching both students in what they have accomplished and for me for having led them throughout the day without serious friction. I am so grateful to be able to have the privilege!

Since we are so far north the daylight hours are long, and as we make preparations to leave, the sun, still high in the sky at 6 PM, illuminates the fells on the eastern edge of Grasmere with a radiance reminiscent of Wordsworth's words from the "Intimations Ode," "celestial light." I would love to linger here near the village green and watch the presence of this now vibrant light turn to a slowly fading glance that will continue up the rise above Dove Cottage, and feel the subtle evening chill replace the dream like warmth surrounding me now, but we have a ninety minute drive ahead of us back to Kiplin Hall.

Ordinarily, both Barbara and I do not drink caffeine in tea or coffee. We both feel that the rhythm of our days is balanced by refraining from stimulants in caffeine. Life is jagged enough at times. While leading the program though both of us drink caffeinated tea, or on some day's coffee, simply because after a long drive to the days' trailhead, hiking for several hours, and driving back to Kiplin Hall the stimulation is useful for safety reasons. When I drink caffeine after a long absence, the effect is delightfully shocking. Alertness to my surrounding emerges with precision and particularity, a wash of well-being clears the inside of my head. However, like everything else in life there is a price to be paid.

We have learned where we can stop for tea on the way, but tea has a fairly quick effect on me: I do feel sharper, my reflexes are livelier, but the need to urinate can come on with a cramping vengeance. For the majority of the drive there are no rest stops, no cafes, no petrol stations, and no accessible woods. The dilemma is almost comical, except that the discomfort is trenchant. Safety belts serve an obviously important function, but the pressure from the lap portion of the safety belt on a full bladder, with no way of decently serving the internal physical signals for discharge can be miserable. Travelling the A66 across the Pennine Mountains takes us through scenery remarkable for its starkness that melds with gradually intruding greenery; as arresting as the landscapes are, I am a cauldron of mental and physical tension. The brief but unmistakable twinge in my lower torso begins to block my physical farsightedness into the opening landscape unfolding through the windshield with a bifurcated attention to the road and the rising unease within. I try to trick myself by calculating how far we have to go, thinking that if I know how much time is left, I can convince myself that I can hold on.

Grabbing the shoulder harness to slacken the pressure on my lap momentarily helps, but down deep I feel degrees of evolving panic irresistibly rising. Getting involved in the car conversation proves to be a useful distraction, for a while. Desperately scanning the surroundings for cover that I know is not there, and not going to be there I begin to imagine alternatives. Should I pull off and stop? But then what? I cannot very well urinate in full view of the students not to mention drivers along the road. Besides, it is probably against the law. Suppose I was arrested for public urination. That sort of thing is not going to be greeted with favor back home. Perhaps it is a firing offense. What to do?

With about twelve miles to go I begin the squirm, moving back and forth in the seat seeking a shift in pressure. Almost home, but a stop-light brings the vaguely comforting rhythm to a sharp halt. Why do stop-lights seem endless when there is urgency to move on? Two miles to go, I feel light headed with the prospect of impending relief. A hay truck here, potting along at about 20 miles per hour, life is unfair! The gate is in sight, rumbling through I park and flee the van like a man escaping from a burning building. My burn is all internal though. No one notices my situation; how could they? My personal drama is over for now, but I know that we will travel that road again in the same circumstances. Is it really odd that the events of the day have mixed unique highs with the ordinary in a mélange of personal reflection, where sharply distinctive moods shape such emotional disparities?

The White Heifer

A very little humoring of their prejudices, and some courtesy of language and demeanor on the part of Englishmen, would work wonders, even as it is, with the public mind of the Americans

(Coleridge, *Table Talk*)

While the day and especially the ride back have set me up for a quiet evening, living with students between the ages of 18 to 22 demands still more. It is evening, about nine-thirty, and the students are ready to visit the local village of Scorton and the White Heifer Pub. Known to locals as the "effer," the pub has been a pub since the seventeenth century. While Barbara and I do not encourage drinking alcohol, we do permit it within certain boundaries. We accompany the students to the pub since we feel responsible for them, and as much as we can we want to make sure that there is no discord among them, and the local village. Since most of the students are not of legal age in America being able to order and consume a drink in public is a sort of milestone. Bitter is the common drink of choice and many of the students who want to "fit in" try it and invariably one proves to be enough. I am not sure if it is age or culture that has American students preferring sweet drinks, but they seem to. Generally, there are more women than men in the Kiplin Hall Program; consequently, more girls arrive at the pub with us. This is a delight for the local young men and something less than delightful for local young women who sense the competition keenly.

Fortunately, the welcoming spirit in the pub allows for a pleasant intermingling of the groups. Talk of sports is always the core of much pub discussion, and the subject of baseball arose. Magically, before we knew it people from the village showed up with baseball bats, gloves, and soft balls. Why they had so much equipment was a mystery. Have local people been waiting since the end of world War II when there was an airbase near the village, to play again what might have been a past shared experience? No matter, at the moment our vanity was on the line.. We Americans played with enthusiasm and gentleness, dominating the game easily. We felt happy at the end and somewhat smug since we all could throw and hit fairly easily. The next evening, we were challenged to a football match (soccer). The English men and women literally ran circles around us until they put in replacements, eight and ten-year olds. We looked even more foolish, but the spirit of fun was on us and we laughed at our fumbling ways. The camaraderie felt genuine and rounded out a good "English Moment."

City of York

> *How often in the overflowing Streets?*
> *Have I gone forward with the Crowd, and said?*
> *Unto myself, the face of everyone*
> *That passes me by is a mystery*
>
> (Wordsworth, *The Prelude*, 7. 594-597)

The next day takes us into a different direction physically and emotionally. The City of York is just under an hour's drive from Kiplin Hall. Going to York provides a day out from hiking and the physical exertion that goes with it. It is an ancient city, multidimensional in its appeal. On my first driving trip to York, I was very eager to spend time in the Minster in the hope of absorbing the rich medieval atmosphere embedded, as I believed, in the very stone-work itself. The A19 traverses a largely flat plain, and the road with its many straightaways, seemed to conspire with my eagerness to get to the city. I kept searching the horizon for what I was sure would be the Minster rising above the hedgerows. Instead I found myself in a maze of roundabouts, rocketing drivers, and the outer reaches of York's suburbs. Sifting through the remarkable amount of traffic brought us through tree-lined streets of impressively grand houses, which carried an air of grace and gentility in their brickwork and wrought iron fences. While many have been turned into guest-houses, they generally share a common connection of being well maintained, suggesting vitality, as knots of people walked along the sidewalks purposefully. Parking on the streets was clearly out of the question, so finding a car park just at the edge of the old city came like a rainstorm in a drought-stricken area, unexpected but gratefully received.

Pay and Display parking machines have been used in England for many years. The principle of selecting how much time one intended to stay parked and paying a specific amount for the service seems reasonable to me. However, the coins in England tend to be large and weighty compared to American currency. Getting enough coins to pay for three vans is not something to take lightly, literally. Barbara and I make a point of gathering a variety of coins in good numbers so we will not be faced with searching for a place where paper currency can be exchanged for coins. Like most all of towns and cities in England York is perpetually faced with making life for its inhabitants reasonably uncomplicated, while attempting to limit the ways that automobiles tend to take over increasingly large portions of geography. Parking is at a premium and cost of parking as a consequence keeps rising. I begin to feel somewhat self-conscious as I keep inserting coin after coin in the Pay and Display machine; the people huddled around me, anxious to get their ticket and be on their way, patiently wait as I empty two pockets and a small plastic bag of pounds, halfpounds, and two pound coins. Like a man receiving a reprieve from the governor, I collect the last ticket and feebly wave all the tickets in the air, to a few cheers and sighs from my fellow coin haulers, and patient standbys. This, I realize, is a truly English moment. People in France would never keep the queue, and we Americans would not likely show such remarkable patience.

Our plan is to let the students take a day on their own, to give them time away from us, and to explore on their own. But first we agree to walk to a location where we can all meet at a prescribed time. Immediately out of the parking lot we walked along the river Ouse, tree-lined and animated with rowers, pleasure boat traffic, and sightseeing ferries. I can see in the way the students move that they are absorbing the energy from our surroundings. Their steps are quick and deliberate; their talk is vibrant, as if they are trying to capture the flow of things around them. Rising up the stairs from the river walk to the bridge level opens up a ricochet of sounds. Roaring busses, screeching taxis, sputtering scooters, lumbering lorries, and above all the overwhelming sound of changes being rung from the Minster envelope and embracing us with an almost electric charge. After hiking yesterday in the freedom of the mountains, waiting for the little green man on the crossing signal granting us permission to cross seems somewhat fussy and tidy. To do otherwise would be suicidal. Ringing bells give dimension and vibrancy to the feeling of awe as we stand before the Minster and try to take in its magnificence. Playing off the broad expanse of the east wall, the sunlight enriches the tactile intricacies of vertical and horizontal lines of the wall. The eye cannot help to travel upwards with the sweep of the stone toward heaven. In spite of our vast technological superiority the emotional power focused in this structure fused coherence into the culture of its time and still speaks to us with its dominating presence.

Since childhood I have always felt enraptured by historical sites. I find myself staring at and absorbing my immediate surroundings without looking for words or the interference of comparisons. In my imagination I can hear the medieval masons hammering stone with a metallic resonance, shattered stone ricocheting, the shouts among the workers, and feel the tang of fast running sweat streaming down dust clogged faces. The long building process must have been trying I suppose. How many setbacks and discouragements must there have been for those working on the Minster and for those watching the life-long building process? As I speculate about the past, I hope that among the students there are some who open up their senses and embed what is available here.

At the east porch of the Minster, I tell the students that we will meet here at five o'clock. Always the professor I go on to relate how it was in this spot that drama begins in England with the production of Morality and Mystery Plays. As I go on giving a brief history of the process by which elements of the Mass migrated outside, several students begin to shift from foot to foot, and I take their respectful hint, send them off, and wish them well for the day. Walking along the cobbles in the Shambles, the medieval portion of the city, I have to alter the way I walk to accommodate the lurch and stretch demanded by each step. Slow is good. The narrow streets fill quickly with Saturday shoppers and tourists set on finding the things that will give the day something tangible.

A kind of mental dilation makes me think about the pattern of what has been going on in this very place for a thousand years or more. Before the Romans came people lived here and they carried on their lives in patterns not entirely different from our own. They collected market goods, met friends, and enjoyed time away from work. Then there were the Romans, the Angles, the Vikings, the English, and now a cross section of native English and a broad assortment of people from many lands.

Others have walked along these streets with similar intentions; trying to make a living and lead their lives as well as possible. Being surrounded by medieval buildings I feel that I can touch the past, the fractured timbers and cracked brickwork serve as a locus for my speculations about how the aspirations and hopes of people in various historical times were overridden or destroyed by the political conflicts and social abrasions of their day. I wonder what it felt like to be under the rule of outside forces with all the frustrations and resentments that were part of that reality.

The seemingly intractable difficulties and fears of our own time, in this place, seem merely to be a part of a long human story. Forces coming from circumstances, luck, human will power, sustained thinking, and effort all seem to play an unending role in shaping our lives, the mosaic of the human story is vastly complex, fascinating, and for me reassuring. I believe that as humans we are up to the moral and ethical demands that result from technological wizardry as well as corrosive ideologies. Life, I think, has always presented much to be feared, and people have often acted against their best interests, but there is much that is to be cherished and enjoyed in life. Beauty and a sense of the past enriches where we are now culturally and mitigates the sinking sense that everything can be reduced to quantification, and therefore predictable.

Much of our contemporary culture in America promotes the idea that the moment is all, a performance culture. What is in now is it; it is meaning in itself. A rising sense of well-being, like early morning ground fog lifting to the rising sun, excites my sense of place, and in the recesses of my mind I know that this is one of the personal moments of perception I try hard to harness and communicate to students in my classes, not just the feeling, but the certainty of a connection with the past that transcends superficial elements of the immediate. Literature is the lifeline in the process, making others and other times felt and knowable.

It is odd how walking around a city can be much more tiring than hiking in mountains, but so it is for me. The kaleidoscopic fracturing of sunlight against deep shadows, the voices of passersby, a mixture of urgency, laughter, commonness, and inquisitiveness bathe me into a lassitude that ends by my sitting on a well-worn bench and observing the passing parade of people. Seeing myself reflected in a shop window reminds me of my age; for the moment in my imagination, I have become one of those men often seen on park benches watching, and watching. It is a sobering moment and makes me evermore grateful that I can engage with students. The flash of a full-on smile and an excited wave from one of the students amplified by two of her classmates breaks my reverie, and like a bee sting makes me focus on the immediate. As the young women excitedly brandish their finds from the day's shopping. I share in their good-humored silliness, my plangent stare of a few moments earlier replaced by the latch of purpose. I am back in the moment, but I also know that time works its way, and I will have to confront its advance on me.

I wonder about the way the students are experiencing their time in this ancient city. So many people I have known looked forward with joy toward retirement and a change of life. It is not that I am a workaholic, but as a teacher everything I do, and have done, I think of in connection to the classroom. When I read, widely for the most part, I think about how I can use the material or examples in what I read for class. Many have said to me that when I retire, I will be free to read whatever I like, when I like. That is attractive to a degree, but the idea of not being able to share what I learn with young students fades the image of great, unfettered freedom like a newspaper dissolving in a puddle.

As I wait with Barbara for the students to gather for the ride back to Kiplin Hall, a few students smilingly talk about a day off and the pleasures of shopping without wearing hiking boots and smelling more civilized, but two others talk in measured and contemplative tones about their fascination with the Minster and the medieval labyrinth of streets, alleys, and the way the past can be felt simply being among such old buildings. "The feeling," one adds, "gives you a sense of going backwards, thinking of the past, and what kind of meaning for my life comes from a different historical perspective. Washington College is old by American standards but seems like an adolescent by comparison. There is a lot I need to think about." He is right of course, and I am grateful for his self-developed perceptiveness. My day in the city was focused on time and its meaning for me at this point in my life. The medieval buildings, streets, and alleyways, old as they are, provide the framework for contemporary life that pulsates with energy and its own purpose. The students seem to have bridged the gap between the medieval world and our own without disruption. I am sure they were aware of the same sights I saw, and moved by the palpable sense of the past, and I hope that they will take with them a city experience that is both different in the historical sense and connected to fundamental patterns of civilization. Wordsworth notes, "Getting and spending we lay waste our powers." Emphasizing our need to learn from the rhythms of nature, and not limit ourselves to understanding life as a commercial enterprise. My belief is that the experiences the students are having will lead to that sort of understanding.

Teaching Matters

Figure 12: Green Head Ghyll

Source: Barbara Gillin

Teaching is hard work, the strain and stress of gaining control over the material to be taught is a constant nag because ideas about literature alter and grow in depth and range. Sorting out what students need, particular kinds of attention, adjusting to the personality of each class, and shaping what I want to have happen, among a number of other elements, demands agility and constant thought. Wearing yes, but when things go well, such exhilaration and moments of purpose! In college it was necessary for me to work to pay my way. During those years, I had many jobs and I learned graphically what I did not want to do in my life. Paths toward a solid middle-class life, and more, were open, but I found that learning, just for the sake of gaining knowledge, was more satisfying and meaningful for me. Many of my friends, whom I still cherish, counseled practical ways of securing a position and job in the business world. Something inside resisted, not because I was lazy, but because I wanted more substance in things that mattered to being a human. Science was provocative and fascinating regarding the way the world is formed, but the humanities engaged my emotions as well as my imagination and intellect, and teaching seemed to promise a life that I could imagine for myself. The impractical dimensions of a life as a teacher would manifest themselves in time, but the core of my sense of value in teaching remained firm.

So here I find myself on a bright Saturday in York with a group of students with a variety of personalities and interests, yet bound by our relationship in a program designed to open their awareness of a number of poets, but more importantly, their apprehension of bigger pictures. Learning how to live and for what meaning are core elements in the big philosophical questions confronting us, and by coming to the threads of the humanities in our time together, I hope that those threads will serve as lifelong connections to what we do here and also to meeting the challenges that will befall them in life.

As it is time to return to Kiplin Hall, we reanimate each van and set off through the tightly narrow streets of York to the wider lanes as we emerge into the countryside. The gently rolling landscape has a hypnotic effect on all of us in the van. We are on an "A" road which is the designation given to roads that represented the first foray into long distance driving in England after World War II and the earlier departure of the Romans. I try to keep the speed to about fifty-five miles per hour, and I am passed by other motorists frequently. As cars, vans, and trucks roar by me the tension in my body focuses on my hands as I strangle the steering wheel in the hope that we will not be blown off the road. Traffic often hurtling at me in the opposite lane at speeds well in excess of the limit keeps me riveted in my attention to what goes on around me. This is an unintended benefit after a tiring afternoon; grogginess is not an option. The trip from York is much shorter than the commute from the Lakes so our arrival in Northallerton comes up reasonably quickly and provides us with the sense of coming home since Northallerton is the closest town to Kiplin Hall. Saturday is market day here as it has been probably since the middle ages. During the week the residents move with an alert purposefulness as they go about their business, but today at this time there seems to be a weary fullness and sense of checked motion as kiosks are being dis-assembled, the street cleaners sweeping up shards of lettuce, paper candy wrappers, and cigarette butts. The scene is commonplace and timeless. Much of life moves in the same way I think. People want to lead productive and fulfilling lives in a secure and friendly environment. So much of the money boosterism in America in our time touts the lure of unfettered wealth, and the notion that everyone can become a billionaire, and more damaging, that everyone ought to be striving to accomplish money goals primarily.

These thoughts seem to be a piece of what I contemplated in York earlier in the day about the importance of literature and the humanities. A nagging sense of who I am and what the meaning of what I do as a teacher has tucked itself in the furrows of my brain and keeps emerging like bubbles in boiling water. My concern about the way young people are moving toward a sliced and diced world punctuated by measured competition on a variety of life fronts is broad, and also very particular. I am not holding up my views of teaching and education as a model for the ages; I see myself in the lineage of people who have had a fundamental belief in the value of learning for the purpose of knowing, in the hope of understanding our role and purpose as human beings. Teachers I have

72

had and writers whom I admire share a bond in their dedication to pushing knowledge and experience to a point where a clearer perspective on who we are reveals itself. Liberal arts colleges have been places where active and, often informal, conversations about books and ideas shared a belief that intellectual matters were crucial to the "work" of education..

Like most young and serious faculty members, the early years demanded much in regard to cultivating a broad range of knowledge across many literary periods as in my case. Reading up to the point of actually leaving for class in the subtle terror that I would go blank and speechless with nothing to say on a given subject was characteristic. The number of different courses I became responsible to teach kept me actively engaged in reading widely and continuously. Participating in committee meetings and volunteering to guide students for their senior obligation, office hour meetings, and a number of other distractions and intrusions were bedrock. Even though the college had no means to support scholarly work there was the constant awareness that professional responsibilities had to be met. Being a professor carried much in the way of institutional expectations, but there was a clear feeling that we were all in it together. Personally, there was much to be sacrificed; my salary was grotesque by most standards and raises, when they came, were continually less than increases in the cost of living. A middle-class life seemed to be aspirational.

For my wife it meant derailing her own career and giving up many common places like a house of our own and a reliable automobile; in general there was an air of genteel poverty of sorts among the faculty accompanied by the certainty that what we were engaged in was for a greater good. I thank God often for Barbara's vision, determination, and willingness to work toward our shared responsibility to each other. Her dedication to the students she taught and her phenomenal ability to adapt to fast paced changes, have given me much to look up to. Our efforts would provide perspective on the ever-rising materialism and superficiality of contemporary culture. Society would be served by our dedication to keeping the best of what men and women have thought and written through the ages and making students aware of the rich heritage they were in the process of inheriting. It was far from an easy existence, but it allowed time to think about the implications of what I read and time for family matters. Professionally it was what I most wanted: students willing to be taught and a belief that teaching mattered.

Some students talk about wanting to become professors, but a larger number, I believe, look down on us as odd-ball losers who get enthusiastic about things that are just not cool or monetarily rewarding. The most popular majors these days promise rewarding careers in various commercial enterprises. The killer job replaces the slog of academic life. What the shift away from seeing an academic life as potentially rewarding and fulfilling, in addition to serving social basics, means that it is not clear at this point; hence my dark thoughts on this otherwise bright day. In contemplating my misgivings, fears, and understanding today I also believe in the recesses of my being that dedication to a life of the mind and service to others will prevail in spite of forces aligned against good sense and what I understand and have experienced about the value in teaching. As we approach Kiplin Hall talk about the day and the expectation about tomorrow animate the students in the van and we emerge into the Study Centre in good spirits.

A New Beginning

The budding twigs spread out their fan,
To catch the breezy air;
And I must think, do all I can,
That there was pleasure there
(Wordsworth, *Lines Written in Early Spring*, 16 – 20)

Figure 13: White Moss Common

Source: Kelley Holocker

Bright mornings are a blessing from God in England. No matter how tiring the previous day was the crispness in the early light, the sun high well before 6 AM because of how far north we are, and bracing air, shedding dew energizes me and I feel excited about the new day. When I get the chance, I run into the countryside along back lanes shrouded by hedgerows. The chirp of birds makes keen my listening to the absence of intrusive noises. The rumble and roar of traffic like an ominous thunderstorm in the distance serves as the background of every city and suburb I have experienced. Tires with their adhesive peeling, the swish of cars, and the splutter of badly tuned trucks spin out to our ears and distract us from the nuanced variety of bird-calls. We adapt to what we cannot control, and in the process, we lose something of ourselves. Hearing birds without the thrum of twenty-first century distractions connects me to a swell of quiet joy and optimism. In the rush of wind through the hedgerows I feel washed, and this morning's run links me to the way poetry speaks to me. Drifting over the rolling landscape I hardly perceive my muscles working. I am moving but my attention finds focus on something abstract. My breathing is steady, and the percussive sound of my own footsteps has given way to shapes of thoughts suffused by deep feeling. Gratitude centers me in my imaginative reverie, and I feel fully revived from the caustic thoughts of yesterday.

The metallic striking of the clock in the courtyard tower as I arrive back at the Study Centre returns me to clock time and things to be done today. Mornings in the kitchen as Barbara and I describe the day's plans, and students preparing breakfast and lunch reminds me of an episode of the Keystone Cops. Movement is very limited when twenty people stake out precious space and work on sandwich building, fruit gathering, drinks, and an assortment of sweets. With the fragrance of coffee pulsing in the air laden with the bubbling of oatmeal, the crackle of frying eggs and sizzle of bacon by the pound there is a parallel acceleration of anticipation. Today we will travel to the farthest point in the Lake District, Langdale Pike. During breakfast I explain that packing extra water and extra food is fundamental since we will likely be encountering many challenges. The trail up demands strong will power, much endurance, and concentration. The atmosphere in the breakfast room cools and the slightly nervous banter about what is coming up drifts off as students in rapid succession excitedly ask how hard the hike will be, how long is it, what if it rains, has anyone ever gotten lost? I have no desire to scare them but at the same time I must make it clear that the climb today is a serious one demanding much from them physically and emotionally. Repeating the basics, that gloves, a hat and extra fleece, everything in their packs stored in plastic bags along with the Wordsworth book and their notebook, additional water, and additional food I could see was making their eyes slowly grow wide and lips slightly more tense. They seemed to understand that today's climb would be different.

The Way to Langdale Pike

> *'T was summer, and the sun had mounted high:*
> *Southward the landscape indistinctly glared*
> *Through a pale stream; but all the northern downs,*
> *In clearest air ascending, showed far off*
> *A surface dappled o'er with shadows flung*
> *From brooding clouds*
>
> (Wordsworth, *The Excursion*, 1 – 6)

Figure 14: On the Way to Langdale Pike

Source: Kelley Holocker

Getting out the door and into the vans should be an easy move, but it never is. At the last minute, someone calls out that they forgot their lunch, or their jacket, or any number of items. So, the door is unlocked, things are retrieved, and just as I am ready to lock the door inevitably someone needs to use the bathroom. In the early days of the program, I used to get frustrated and I remember my face clenching into disapproval, now after many years, where I have been the one who needs to go back for something, I have become remarkably patient, at least most of the time. On two past occasions in my rush toward efficiency and keeping to the schedule I have discovered on arrival at our destination that I had forgotten lunch for Barbara and myself, as well on two occasions, I forgot my waterproof jacket. Fasting through lunch is one thing but not having a waterproof in the Lake District can be dangerous. On those two occasions our journey to the trailhead was delayed by my having to purchase a jacket, an expensive mistake. The danger in not having a waterproof is connected to the effect of exposure, a very unpleasant interruption to the day.

On an ascent of Helvellyn several years ago as rain began to fall, I noticed that one young man, eager I think to show his maleness, continued walking in a tee shirt when everyone else was clad in layers of fleece and goretex. I caught up to him and said that it was prudent to put a jacket on. His face somewhere between embarrassment and a cold look of pain signaled that there was a complication I was not noticing. He sheepishly told me that he forgot his jacket and his fleece. I could not let him go on; the real danger was immediately apparent to me if not him. We were more than halfway up the mountain, and he expressed how ashamed he would be if he became the cause of the groups' having to descend.

Fortunately, the other students were shrouded in hats and hoods and could not hear the discussion we were having, and their own concerns were on the deteriorating footing as the rain intensified. I had an extra fleece with me, and I reasoned to myself that if I kept moving, I would generate enough body heat with two fleeces on to weather the storm. So, I gave the now shivering student my waterproof jacket. I told him to walk steadily and not to stop so he could keep generating heat. Ascending further I realized that the plan for myself was dissolving rapidly as my fleeces absorbed rainwater and held it against my rapidly cooling torso. The other students looked at me quizzically as I shook among them. Nearing the longed-for summit, I felt the rain lessen by degrees and then cease. At the summit I stripped the fleeces off and squeezed them out as the students hooted good naturedly at my pasty white body. Putting the cold wet fleeces back on took all my determination in the windy, sharped edged surroundings.

Descending from a summit, I have found, is always a substantially cooler experience than ascending. All the students, including the young man who forgot important clothing, were in high spirits from achieving the goal of summiting, and I tried to insinuate myself into their happy mood. They seemed not to notice my continual shivering; they thought that the speed of my descent was a kind of race challenge to see who could reach the base first. I did nothing to divert their perceptions. At several points in our downward trek I felt a peculiar kind of lethargy, I just wanted to sit down and roll up my body, I was very deeply cold. Having proper clothing came home to me in a way I will never forget. The student who precipitated the event was fine, though awkward among his classmates for a while since his attempt at hyper masculinity became an ongoing joke.

Thoughts about past ascents up Langdale Pike filter through my mind as we make the long drive to the mountain's base. I know that it will be a long day of driving and hiking. To break up the way we travel to the Lakes we take a diversion away from the A66 and wind our way through the Eden Valley, and pass through Kirkby Stephen along the way. Aside from pastures and hedge-rows the road to Kirkby Stephen is uncluttered in its rolling flow. As we travel, I wonder about the way that this very road seems ancient since there are no visible, likely alternatives, and surely people lived here in the long past. As opposed to the gritty decay of the post-industrial towns we have driven through the fields and stone-walls bordering the road are naturally complimentary. A student in the back of the van recites "The farmer in the dell" as a farmhouse rises up as we crest a steep hill. All of us in the van laugh since, I assume, we all have been thinking about the territory we have been travelling through.

The approach to Kirkby Stephen is gradual with a few repair shops just opening for the day's work, roundabouts slow us into the tempo of the town center. The shops are active, and another nursery rhyme, "The butcher, the baker, and the candlestick maker" slips into my mind as various people go about their morning's business. Market Day is today, and the small-town square is fluttering with activity. Notable is the number of people dressed in hiking gear, boots, heavy socks, anaracks, and backpacks. I learned later that Kirkby Stephen is a major stopping point for people hiking the Coast to Coast, a trek from St. Bees on the west coast of England to Robin Hood's Bay on the East. Since we encountered trekkers at Robin Hood's Bay at the end of their country wide walk, seeing people after what is reputed to be the most difficult part of the Coast to Coast provided a living glimpse into people's temperament as they made their way east. To my eye the hikers seemed to be in good spirits and energized, probably because they knew that the physical demands ahead would be of a different kind. Comparisons with what we had ahead were natural and I felt wary and enthused at the same time. I knew that Langdale was physically much more difficult than the mountains we have ascended so far, and elements of safety and the students' well-being are always on my mind, but I also felt a surge of energy at the prospect of being able to lead students to a new level of accomplishment. I was like taking students into a poem they have not contemplated before.

As always, everyone needed to take time out for a bathroom break and in my continual search over the years for an appropriate location and easy access to the needed facilities the Morrison store in Kendal fit the wish list. It is a clean grocery store, parking is easy, and coffee and tea can be had. Customers hardly give us a second glance, though we are noisy, largely in shorts, and obviously American. After a brief stay, we are on our way. The Lake District mountains rise up dramatically on the nearing horizon. Cloudless days bring views that are riveting and emotionally warm and energizing, on cloudy days views of the mountains pulse into view with a cold indifference. Today shrouds of mist lace their way up various slopes and the sunlight accentuates the richly variegated green landscape that drifts in and out of view.

In the vans, we do not allow individual iPods, headsets, or ear buds. Our aim is to have people in the vans talk to each other. It takes a day or two for students to get used to the idea of time without their playlists. The crush on many of them is so strong that we arranged for a compromise. Each student in a van can play his or her favorite music so all can hear. I thought I had a wide range of tolerance for a number of things, but the music some students play is withering. They hear something in what they play that has no resonance for me, try as I may. In fairness we give everyone a turn each day, and I often find my incomprehension and revulsion to their choices of music overwhelming. Some students are shattered as well, but since everyone gets a turn, they are reluctant to speak out, and I understand. We are living in close quarters and if compassion breaks down, there could be a severe backlash within the group. A young man who seemed older than his years and distinguished by a notable range of reading in English Literature creating respect for himself in the group, was particularly fond of opera music. When his turn came to play his favorites, he set up his collection of Puccini. Groans and gasps went around the van as the music began, but he just turned and stared at his classmates, eyes unwaveringly firm in determination and incredulity, and simply stated the obvious, that it was his turn. Over the weeks in the van he took to singing along with the patter songs from Gilbert and Sullivan. His rendition of "I Am a Pirate King," became a favorite even among those who railed at this music initially. I am not sure if he won many fans for Puccini, but everyone knew the pirate song.

The approach road to Ambleside allows for enticingly quick flashes of Windermere from breaks in the stone-wall bordering the road. Entering Ambleside requires quick reflexes and even faster driving decisions. Somehow the van, large by English standards, seems even bulkier and more lumbering as I steadfastly attempt to ferret our way through the narrow streets avoiding the oncoming surge of quickly moving vehicles. Up to this point the road has been a tight fit with many sharp curves, but the last leg of our drive to Langdale Pike is very English. To my outsider's eye the essential road is merely a paved version of original paths, probably carved by early Britons or the Romans. Stonewalls, beautiful in their craggy asymmetry, seem lethal at thirty miles per hour. I feel my eyes darting continuously to the left while at the same time trying to keep focused on the twisting, irregularly paved road before me. At the tightest turns hefty-sized trucks or massive coaches looking like steroid enhanced insects almost on cue appear. Survival instincts make me stop with a lurch and the sound of grumbling gravel severs us up to the very edge of vehicular mayhem.

In moments like these a sort of pas de deux develops with backing and angling on the part of the vehicles involved and nervous energy sparking from my fingertips. The dance flourishes over several miles of the road. Behind the wheel my body moves rhythmically to the evolving challenges. My elbows snap to my ribs as I squeeze the steering wheel while my feet do a two-step, slamming the clutch into the floor and the brake to full resistance. The halting advances allow for momentary glances at the scenery surrounding us. All that makes travelling the road an exercise in terror; it also makes a superb connection to a largely bygone era.

The road is a small intrusion on pastoral scenes right out of 19th Century guide-books. The meadows are rich with wildflowers, the sky untroubled, and it is easy to imagine a human scaled life in this particularly remote area. It is the area that Wordsworth set The Excursion. Over the years I have often thought how wonderful it would be to stay here and spend time wandering farther afield. The thick woods, ancient looking in the number of very large, durable looking trees, enchants my speculations. The contrast between the sun-warmed fields, wispy as the early morning dew draws upward, and the deep shadows along the edge of ponds covered in part by cattails and water lilies makes me yearn to stop and linger. I know of course that my thoughts are not for today, perhaps someday, but not today.

As lovely and promising as the day is experience has taught me that the weather can change very abruptly, and often does. Today is a case in point. The drive has been long and the near-misses with stone-walls and other vehicles on the road have brought everyone in the van away from drifting into sleep and to full- and at-time eye-popping attention. A small descent away from the tree line gives us the first look at Langdale Pike in something like its terrifying glory. Silhouetted against a momentary deep blue sky the rock face looms with the air of defiance. It seems too grand and high, the very shape of the pike pointing to the heavens. It seems to say, "Don't think about trying." Immediately the students, bending to look out through the windshield, get the message.

Silence takes over the interior of the van. Then the questions come at me like a hailstorm, pelting each answer I give with another question. "Is that where we are going?" "You are joking with us." "I don't think I can do it; I feel ill." "What if we don't make it?" "Can I stay in the van?" The rising tension takes a bounce deeper as the sky opens and a lash of heavy rain descends in a fury of rooftop pinging and a waterfall flow off the windshield. Immediately the conversation takes another turn as comments from the students take on an air of hopeful relief. "I guess we will have to do something else today." "Gee, too bad we have come this far, it was a nice ride." I remind them that when we began the program, I told them that we would face difficult weather from time to time, and that we would forge on. To a person they seem to have stopped breathing. Down deep I share their misgivings about the way the weather seems implacable and confrontational, but I know that weather systems can be fast moving here, and the mottled clouds in the distance give me hope that the deluge will be short-lived.

To get to Langdale Pike from Ambleside by car, take the A593 from Ambleside toward Skelwith Bridge and bear right at Skelwith Bridge onto the B5343. Follow on, bearing right at Wainwright's Inn, past the Langdale Resort, and wind yourself to a small Pay and Display Car Park opposite the Stickle Barn Pub. Walk the lane between the Stickle Barn Pub and New Hotel to a gate, just to the right of the Stickle Barn. Once through the gate the Stickle Ghyll will be to the right, and after a gravelly path stone steps begin. The trail is clearly evident. Another option is to turn left after going through the gate with Dungeon Ghyll on the left for a short distance and follow the trail with Dungeon Ghyll on the right. Though I have taken both trails, I prefer the straight-ahead trail with the dramatic waterfalls of Stickle Ghyll on the right. During the ascent to Stickle Tarn the roar of Stickle Ghyll seems refreshing and dramatic. The banks of the tarn offer a useful place to sit and reflect on the panorama.

Langdale Pike

> *But he had felt the power*
> *Of Nature, and already was prepared,*
> *By his intense conceptions, to receive*
> *Deeply the lesson deep of love which he,*
> *Whom Nature, by whatever means, has taught*
> *To feel intensely, cannot but receive.*
>   (Wordsworth, *The Excursion*, 191 – 196)

Figure 15: Langdale Pike

Source: Kelley Holocker

Our arrival at the base of Langdale Pike is also the end of the road, literally. A farm calmly situated just to the west of the car park is the punctuation mark signaling the end of the torturous way we have come. My spirits rise as we climb out of the vans; the rain has stopped. Good spirits animate relief that rain is out of the picture, at least for now, and shifting of shoes to boots, and searches through backpacks with the occasional shriek of "I forgot gloves, or my hat, or my book" sliced into the humid air. Laughter is the dominating sound and I find myself absorbing it and what it

82

signifies. English people have often commented on what they perceive to be an American tendency to laugh a good deal.

Stereotypes take flight from perceptions, and I suspect our penchant for laughing and being noisy is accurate to some degree. This moment of laughter comes out of nervousness and the joy of anticipation, and I love being in it. We are bound by the agelessness of human laughter. In a place defined by natural elements of wind, water, stone, and sky joy in our laughter is a complement to our location, and an elevation of sharpened awareness. Gratitude for what I know will be memorable in the peculiarity of the moment overtakes me and I step away from the group to let the full impact eddy into my emotions and memory. I realize it is a transcendent moment; it is both felt and understood immediately. What kind of number does this rate or deserve? The devotees of quantifying everything come to mind, and I really wonder how what I am experiencing can be given a number that means anything valuable. A case for a number might be made, but the superficiality of reducing everything to a numerical quantity seems even more distant and superficial. An age that is in love with numbers will torture every experience into a factor, but the truth of the experience escapes the numerical lock surely. I realize that in what I feel so intensely now is an outcropping of trust.

The students are vulnerable at this moment; they face a daunting challenge in gathering their courage to begin the ascent of the mountain that soars above us, but they trust me, and my judgment. The realization is heartening, but there is no time to bathe in the elation I feel. The general mood is festive among the students, but the expressions on some faces suggest that I need to talk reassuringly about what we are about to do.

A pub, The Sticklebarn, is our immediate destination where we will make last minute checks of equipment, and instructions. I tell them that while the rain has stopped, it is likely to come back, but not to worry since we have clothing that will serve us well. Using our ascent up Helm Crag as an example I point out that reaching the summit of that mountain seemed too difficult at the base, but that we all made it to the top in good form. Helm Crag, I point out, was about one third of the height of Langdale Pike, that we are not going to race to the summit, and that by steady determination we can push through the strain of climbing. One foot after another consistently is our way for the day. Taking off some of the layers of clothing now is useful I suggest as I look at the assembled group looking like a line of people waiting to get on the Trans-Siberian Express in mid-winter bulked up and hunkered under piles of extra clothing, instead of hikers in mid-June. Doubtful looks greet my suggestion, so off we go. Two hundred yards later, several sweltering students ask to stop so they can peel away a fleece or two.

To our right, there is a very fast moving and forceful ghyll, or stream, the water pounding down the last few hundred yards with the full gravitational force of the mountain emerging in a thunderous explosion of spray, cooling the air. What leaves the students slack jawed is the sight of a group of about fifteen children about twelve years old in the water. I have seen this kind of activity in the past, yet it still commands my attention as well. Wearing wet suits and helmets the children are fixing a rope to the top of a waterfall about twenty feet high. Most seem oblivious to the crashing water around them, though a few appear cold, their body language betraying their wish to be doing something else as they hang back and at the edge of the rocky water pool. We all stop to take in what the children are doing. Their goal is to climb up the waterfall and continue upwards to Stickle Tarn, the source of the ghyll. Half astonished and half cynical, one student notes that scaling the mountain among middle-school-aged kids would never happen in the USA; there would be endless lawsuits and criticism that the task was abusive.

We push on leaving the young students to their task, but a conversation about cultural differences rises as throughout the line of students I can hear them discussing how children in England seem to grow up faster in many ways and take on responsibilities earlier in their lives. They talk about seeing children walking to school a good distance from their school, and how they are faced with a schooling that pushes them hard. The consequences of failure in English society carry a lifelong effect. Even success in school, from what they have learned from evening discussions with university students in the pub, is no guarantee of stability. Most local graduates have to string several part-time jobs together to make their way. The reality of life in England contrasts sharply with the American dream, even the new downsized version. The source of current anxiety in America about the value of higher education and the worth of a college degree is directly related to finding a job. Stoked by politicians and internet hucksters, people's fears, especially parents', are excited by what appears to be the uselessness of certain areas of study, particularly the humanities. While it has been true, and remains true, that college graduates have better job prospects than non-graduates the current social and political unsettling is tied to the dramatically different economic uncertainty we find ourselves in. The fears and concerns are understandable, but in comparison to the reality here in England we seem to be in good stead.

Early difficult footing among the collection of jagged stones gives way to gravelly sections punctuated by steps shaped out of neatly placed rocks. Jokes about the ultimate Stairmaster break out, as do copious amounts of sweat. Within a few hundred yards everyone's clothing blossoms in shadows of sweat. The sound of shuffling feet is overcome by heavy breathing sawing into the sound of nearby running water. I try to keep track of those students who struggled on other ascents. Every hundred yards becomes a resting point. Some very fit students are eager to keep going, but as we established on the Helm Crag ascent, we wait for everyone to come together, and we move as a group.

In all the treks up Langdale Pike, the same falling out occurs. About two thirds of the students show signs of weariness but are still able to push on. The other third falls into smaller groups of two or three at a time who are approaching a breaking point. By keeping everyone together and taking time out for a true rest, the lagging students regain momentum I think from the realization that even the most fit students are struggling as well. The rest stops also give me the opportunity to point out elements in the landscape below us. Wordsworth set portions of his important poem "The Excursion" in the valley below us. He was very careful about the location of his poems, and his extraordinary rambles up and down the mountain group we are in gave him a range of emotional and physical substance to draw on. The view below us at this point makes our vans, clearly visible, seem like miniature toys. Glancing upward shows a cacophony of boulders bordered by a quickly clouding sky.

Switchbacks make the way up less steep, but in spite of that movement quickly devolves into a grueling slog. Every two switches become sites for catching our breath. Wet-faced and sweat-soaked, the students are quiet, the easy joviality earlier in the climb dropping away steadily. Barbara and I talk with them and assure them that they can keep going, and that the effort will be worth it. Some nod, but generally a resolved quietness glows from the steaming rest. I remind them that Wordsworth wrote and set much of The Excursion in this very landscape, and that the demands of that long poem parallel the physical difficulty we are encountering. Following the switchbacks, the trail borders the roaring and slamming waters of Stickle Ghyll, the edge outlining a steep declivity to the left.

Recent heavy rains have swollen the ghyll to an aggressive extent. Struggle in various degrees is universal in our group now, and before us is what, at first glance, seems to be a trail blocking, smooth boulder about twenty feet high. Years ago, in my first encounter with this interdict I looked around in the hope of finding another way to continue on. I remember that impulse clearly. What I discovered though is that by confronting the boulder and thinking about how I could take it on directly I found a way, in fact two distinct ways. As the students assemble here now their facial expressions mimic my own first response. With slumping shoulders and tightening lips in irritation the students' body language is aimed at me. I tell them to find a way up on over the rock. The smooth surface provides no apparent hand or foot holds, and after several failed attempts to get a start, a vertical fissure becomes the center of attention to one young woman and she wedges her hands crosswise into the fissure and with all her strength she pulls her body up about a foot. In her second try she figured out that she needs a foot plant as well as a hand-hold. She simply jammed the edge of her boot into the crevice and pulled with her hands. Hand over hand, and foot after foot she progresses as if it was the most natural thing to do. She found a way for all, and she did it with grace. Everyone was lining up to follow her, when another young woman found an even easier, though less dramatic way up the right side.

Finding a way becomes a metaphor for us. In the car park earlier, several students were doubtful that we could find our way up the mountain. I told them that the closer you get the clearer the way becomes, so it is in life. Life issues, seemingly insurmountable, can be overcome with clear thinking and resolve. Somewhat refreshed by the time taken in sorting out how to proceed upward, the students now are thinking about lunch. Pointing to an overhang of rock I tell them that not far beyond that point we will stop for lunch and a class. But first we need to cross Stickle Ghyll, which is furiously cascading down, continuing its carving a steep gorge in the rock-face of the mountain.

We began the morning's climb in a spirit of trust; at this perilous juncture trust is put into action. Boulders, some submerged, others kilted at varying angles, with no two facing the same direction, and the thumping water aggressively culling the undersides of the rocks, make crossing, at first sight and first impulse, impossible. Furrows in the foreheads of a few students betray their uncertainty, but as we all have discovered on the hike so far, we can overcome obstacles, and we can trust each other. A young man takes on the responsibility of crossing first with the intention of establishing a human chain across the ghyll. Tentatively at first, he makes sure there is no rocking in the foot plants, and gradually lifts himself onto a stable rock looking for the next step. Our eyes are laser like in their attention to his every movement, our shared breathing shallow. Nearing the other shore, he skips quickly over the last three rocks, turns toward us and takes a bow. Cheers explode. A young woman announces that she will step to the middle and serve as a relay person, taking the hand of the next person en route and delivering that person to the young man established on the other side. Not everyone has the same degree of balance and sureness. In spite of reservations stemming from uncertainty rising up from the stomach and off the nerve endings in hands, one by one all the students make their way across. For all it is a fine moment, but for some it is a defining experience. Out of their vulnerability, the most uncertain of students had to find the courage within to overcome their very real fears and sense of inadequacy to act on the trust that has been emerging.

With the crossing accomplished in a deeper sense of trust, there is an uplift in spirits, and an eagerness to surmount the overhang that promises to be the entryway to lunch. The last two hundred yards to that point is a hand over hand pull among monoliths ranging from twenty to fifty feet in height and width. They seem like gigantic sugar cubes left over from the time when titans roamed the earth. Our progress is slow, footing is continually uncertain, and having to use our hands and arms adds new strain to the process. Trying to keep eye contact with everyone, I stop frequently holding everyone back. I know we are very close to our destination for lunch at Stickle Tarn but knowing that the climb has been especially taxing my primary concerns are about safety and making sure that the prospect of a break does not cause someone to act too quickly and be hurt. As I wait, four people, three men and a woman, all elderly, approach me stepping quickly and precisely in their movements. They courteously walk past each student with words of encouragement to them. The lead man stops to talk with me. Smilingly he says it is a fine thing to see so many young people hiking this difficult mountain. I ask him why he is here today hiking as well. He tells me that he is celebrating his eightieth birthday with three of his friends who have all passed their eightieth birthdays. At first, I think that he is joking with me, and he picks up my skeptical look, and in good humor he assures me that he is telling the truth. When his companions reach me, they verify that they are all octogenarians. What a club, I think!

When the students finish struggling up the last series of twists and turns in the trail, I point out a grassy rise, and suggest that they sit down so we can have lunch and a class. They rummage around, trying to find a spot clear of sheep droppings, and in time either find it or don't care and sit down anyway. Once seated I point out the group of three hikers now pushing up upward toward the summit and tell them that they are all over eighty years old. Recognizing their own fatigue, their reactions range from questioning why anyone that old would do what they are doing, to genuine admiration. The physical challenges they are experiencing heighten the understanding of what the elderly hikers are performing, and I hear in some of their voices, as they speak honestly about the three hikers, a reflection on how their lives have been insulated from the mental and physical toughness shown by the three.

Today, in spite of the threat of rain in the air, is for the moment sunny enough to make sitting in the grass a pleasure especially as everyone is talkative and feeling the headiness of having come so far under their own power. Peanut butter and jelly sandwiches once again taste like celestial food, and apple juice is the very nectar of the gods. Among us we carry an ample amount of food for our own lunch and a more than ample amount of various kinds of potato chips, many boxes of cookies, and an armload of chocolate. I do not recall ever bringing food back with us. Appetites have expanded, but the amount of physical exertion keeps us from expanding. They are scrupulous about making sure that nothing we bring with us stays there. Papers and food debris are collected into our backpacks, and I admire their concerns for the environment. With the sun peeking out I begin a class on some of Wordsworth's lyrics and I ask them to take time to feel the peculiarities of the scene before us by considering each of their senses.

The tarn reflecting the blue seeping into the sky as it gradually clears suggests links, connections and above all process. What we see is unfolding in the play of shadow, light, wind and girded under by the clean smell of air without the all too common freight of noxious chemicals. Each moment presents a slightly different offering to the senses. The students take in what is around us without comment, but with a shared sense of community evident in the way they look at each other in a self- conscious attempt to suppress smiles. The moment is poignant. Each of us feels the remarkably austere beauty of Stickle Tarn surrounded by haunting peaks and the mottled glare from a rock wall opposite, but to talk about it would bring the moment down. We will talk about it, but later. Just before we departed, one student offered a Wordsworth insight by alluding to *The eye it cannot choose but see;*

> *We cannot bid the ear be still*
> *Our bodies feel, where'er they be,*
> *Against or with our will*
> (Wordsworth, *Expostulation and Reply*, 17 – 20)

He captures the moment with a fine assist from Wordsworth.

We are roughly about two thirds up the mountain, and I cannot help to reflect on memories from the past connected to this very place. On our first ascent in 1970 Barbara and I made it to this point, aspiring to go to the summit, but we knew we had to catch the last bus stopping at the New Hotel at the base of the mountain. As I think about that time now, I inwardly chuckle at how incredibly inexperienced and naive we were. We had a day off from class and we wanted to go as far into the mountains as we could. Since the road runs out at the base of Langdale Pike, and the reputation of the mountain was that it presented many challenges, it seemed natural that we would find a way to get there. We did, the bus provided our way out for the day. Fortunately for us the day was almost uncharacteristically consistently dry and bright; we had no foul weather jackets. Since that time, we have taken students here and successfully made it to the top every year, but it was never easy. Perhaps there is no reason why things happen the way they do, but ascending this mountain, and getting back down is almost a study in the uncanny. Life's unpredictability takes no account of our plans. Engaging with vicissitudes and finding a way through is experiential and can provide an important element of strength to our endeavors.

Several years ago, when we arrived sweating and panting to this spot, rain dropped into the atmosphere and welted us as it lashed from what seemed all sides. Like today our immediate goal was to have lunch, so in the midst of a mountain hurricane we stopped to eat our sandwiches. Between the flailing wind and gushing rain sandwiches crumbled, what could be eaten having turned into mush. Anguished looks were universal as plans for a restful lunch washed away. Feeling a certain kind of discomfort that only being cold and wet can cause I nevertheless said that the rain would not last and that it was best to continue on lest we get chilled standing around. Various mutinies came to mind as I cajoled them to decouple their feet from the soaking ground and move on. Remarkably they did. Weathered as we were, and with a full third of the mountain yet to be climbed a kind of silliness grew as we moved on, and in our rain-induced misery we laughed out loud at the situation. Our squelching foot-steps provided the soundtrack for a relatively short segment leading up to a rock scramble.

A burst of confidence came as we looked down on where we had sucked up our lunch; we had ascended very quickly, and this sparked hope. Threading through the maze of moss-covered rocks and boulders glazed with rainwater put us all into slow motion. The angle of ascent grew steadily steeper and slipperier. Little shin nicks, elbow slams and a certain amount of oxygen debt tested our will and resolve to continue. Caught between embarrassment and a sinking of their physical confidence two girls were very close to tears. They did not want to become the ones who gave up, yet they were in a situation totally new to them. Most of their walking was around shopping malls. Participating in the program so far was opening up experiences that were proving to be a shock to the parameters of their existence and at this point I could see in their frightened eyes and plaintive voices real fear.

While others rested, Barbara and I sat with the women to calm them down by reassuring them that they could make it to the top, and that the physical discomfort they were feeling was being felt by all. They were in a unique situation in their lives. Going back at this point they surmised would likely generate resentment from their classmates, especially after enduring what they had so far, so that was not a good option. They were reasonably fit and with an act of will they could find the internal resources needed to move on. The other dimension was that given the very real difficulty to complete what we had scheduled would show them the strength of their own fortitude. Climbing the mountain was a choice, completing the climb in the midst of unexpected difficulties was a life changer. I told them that making it to the summit would not change the world, but it would change how they saw themselves in it. Biting their lips, they composed themselves as Barbara said she would climb with them. Sniffling briskly, they stood up and launched themselves upward. The distance of the scramble is not long, perhaps three hundred yards but it is sapping physically and mentally. I admired their fortitude.

The bouldering ends on a ridge just below the last push up to the summit, a hand over hand section. Landing at last on the ridge in the anticipation of relief we were greeted by 40-mile-per-hour winds roaring from the northwest. Cold was immediate and stinging. Wincing upward I pointed to a gaggle of rock outcroppings and indicated that we should move in that direction. Though there was only about two hundred yards to go, the immediate reaction to the menacing rock face was that there was no way to go upward. Added to the trepidation was the elevation. Behind us was a significant drop, sheer in its clarity, of at least a thousand feet. Winds whipping at us brought no comfort either. Always the professor I indicated that like many times in life where we feel we are in a hopeless situation, there is a way onward. I told them that each person should look for a handhold then, a foot plant, keeping focused on what is directly in front of them. The mood of each member of the group brightened as they forged on. The two girls who had difficulty in the bouldering section seemed assured as they each broke a quick smile and a nod of their heads. I stayed behind them offering encouragement. Happily, for me they did not need it, they powered up as if they had been doing this sort of climb for years.

As I crested the summit, I could hear the celebratory yelps, cheers and laughter. Blasting winds and cold air seemed not to make any difference to them; they were joyous. Exuberance was infectious. We all shared a moment we earned by our efforts of will and physical exertion. The open looks in the eyes of each student attested to me the honesty in the moment as well as the soul-yielding lack of restraint and reserve. We were one, and I hoped that the poignancy of what we were sharing would fuse into their memories and remain a lasting influence on them in their lives.

Echoes from Past Ascents of Langdale Pike

Among the hills the echoes play
A never-ending song

(Wordsworth, *The Idle Shephard-Boys,* 2 -3)

Figure 16: Summit: Langdale Pike

Source: Barbara Gillin

Recollections about that climb today are with me today, but my focus is on the students. Inevitably one of the young men in the group challenges others to dip into the tarn. The challenge is met full well. Before I have time to tell them that the water is frigidly cold, since we are high up in the mountain, in they go. Immediately, visceral shrieks of surprise echo from the mountain wall in front of us by the women who jump in first followed somewhat more cautiously by the men. Once in, a new test challenge seemed to be who can stay in the longest? A woman who up to this point had been generally quiet and more or less in the middle of the pack as we hiked, splashed her way well out in the tarn. She seemed oblivious to the cold, which by this time successfully chased everyone else out. After some cheers in recognition of her steadfastness, the students—many with their mouths opened—just stared at her nonchalance and ease of her swan-like movements in the water. I was as mesmerized as the others, but the shocking possibility that she might cramp up and need help registered in my brain, so I urged her to join us on shore. A fear-induced scenario came to mind: A You tube movie of how in her distress, the proverbial maiden in distress, I launched myself into the water to help her, but hypothermia overtook me and essentially, I expired, spoiling the day. End of movie. I have no illusions about heroics. Ever so grateful as she emerged from the water, I asked her if she did cold water swimming often, and she gleefully said, "Never!"

As the students more or less dried themselves, put on their clothes, and shouldered their backpacks they seemed refreshed to their bones as they hustled to assemble themselves. We advanced, as other groups had done in years past, into the bouldering section. One year in my desire to try to find a less arduous way up I kept to the left of the boulders, that always proved to be tedious and energy sapping, where sections of scree splayed down the mountain face. Because I kept looking back to make sure everyone was moving well and shouting to them to keep a good distance apart from each other lest they dislodge a rock and send it tumbling at a person below, I inadvertently found myself, and the leading members of the group into the scree field. I could see a clear gap ahead and pointed myself in that direction, better to keep the upward momentum going than to shuffle back into the boulder field. Calling back and below I told them that should a rock or some of the scree come lose shout "rock" as loud as they could.

The angle of ascent was very steep, but the handholds were secure since there were many bulky rocks to grab. Just as I neared to ridge, I heard a penetrating "ohhh" slap my ears. I urged those near me to continue to the ridge, and I went down to see what happened, my heart racing and my hands shaking in trepidation, hoping and skidding in the scree. My wife was comforting a woman who as it turned out had a misstep, lost her balance and skidded down about ten feet in the scree. Clearly upset and in some pain from the cuts on her hands and arms from the grating she received on the scree she began to cry. Using materials from our first aid kit we were able to clean her wounds and bandage them. The pain of her fall served as the platform of her embarrassment and accentuated a number of her fears. In spite of the somewhat precarious place where we were located, we talked for a while until she felt ready to go on. Though she was in pain from the abrasions, she regained her good humor and showed determination to finish the ascent by straightening up, took a couple of deep breaths and climbed on as if she did this sort of thing every day.

Seeing her bandaged hands and bloodied shirt gave pause to all the students who were waiting on the ridge just below the summit. The momentary immobility of the group, some staring, others averting their eyes, gave way to some gentle ribbing about scoring an eight out of ten, as if she had been competing in a gymnastic event. Climbing to this point was tiring, but a new dimension of alertness informed every move as we climbed the last section to the summit.

Of course, achieving the summit is only half the story; there is the descent as well. This mountain has always had its complications for me and for various groups through the years. The view from the summit is stunning, to the north Nab Scar and the Fairfield range can be seen very clearly, as well as Helvellyn. To the east the long stretch of Windermere reaches itself across much of the horizon, to the south and west the forbidding outline of ScaFell Pike, England's highest mountain broods in the mist. The landscape is treeless, trees having been used for ships and assorted other building materials as well as fuel in ages past. As austere as the mountain-scape is it is not without a degree of warmth and human connection. The mottled greenness, especially in full sunlight, in contrast to the aggressive shadows in their vertical plunge to the foot of each mountain invites lingering gazes and soft daydreams. Peaks arching into each other in a snug border-line, between us and the rest of the world enhance the desire for a leisurely stay. As fatigue from the ascent enters our muscles and stiffens our bones though, the flirtation with rest disappears as a blast of cold air rips through the group. Keeping in mind our past experiences on Langdale Pike I think to myself, sardonically, that everything is on schedule. What complications are brewing for us? I point out the direction we will follow along the drop toward Dungeon Ghyll. We will need to go down and then up sharply.

At this very point years ago, the reasonably mild weather embracing us on the ascent shifted ever so quickly; within a few minutes the reach of the horizon shrunk to seeing only a few feet around us. At first, I thought that it was a low cloud and that it would pass, so I urged everyone to hunker down for a while. After about a half hour I noticed one person, then another begin to shiver. Eyes of the students were on me; words were not necessary to understand that they were unsettled and cold. I told them that they must sit and stay together as I went back to find the trail, we came up on so that we could retrace our steps to the way we came instead of continuing on with our planned route. I had a generally good sense of where the ridgeline was at the top of a very steep descent. My confidence evaporated briskly as I went to the point where I felt sure I would find the trail only to discover that nothing was familiar. I could see my feet but not much beyond, and as I rummaged around the feel of the ground tilting outwardly reminded me that the precipice was sharp and likely unforgiving if it were to be stepped over.

Squatting down, I tried to swing my right leg in an arc in the hope that I would discover secure ground to begin a descent. Disorientation coupled with rising fear made my attempt to stake out a clear way to return the way we came impossible. Sitting on the ground gave me time to think about the danger of trying to guide twelve people down through the boulder field we had ascended. I knew we had to move since we were all becoming very chilled, but moving on the top of a mountain carried significantly more problems than at the bottom. By this time, I too was very cold and keenly aware of my responsibilities. Experience was the bedrock underlying what began to emerge in my mind. I knew that if we followed a course to the south-west we could take a very long way around the other mountains in the Langdale group. Compass in hand, I felt like a traveller from an earlier era, but grateful for the help it offered. Sorting the direction was one thing actually following a way out came with the very real possibility of tripping or sliding on the rocks we would have to descend among and barely see, then there were the bogs. Bogs checker the surroundings. With the students and myself already very cold, the prospect of soaking up bog water and the ever-attendant slime darkened my diminishing optimism. There was no reasonable alternative though; we had to move on. This became the holiest of days in the history of the Kiplin Hall Program; prayers flooded my thoughts and pushed to the forefront of my mind. To the students I reported the inadvisability of trying to descend the way we came, we must take a long, but much safer, in my estimation, way down. Uncomfortable as they were, they steeled themselves against the shrieks of cold wind wrapping around us, penetrating their jackets and fleeces, and understood the situation we were in. Miraculously, with no way of my knowing how many prayers of various sorts and expressions of hope were uttered, though I had a strong impression that there were many, a strong gust of wind washed the mist away and we all could see the mountain-scape clearly. Fearing that the view would not last for long I demanded that we line up in single file in the direction of "Haystack," another peak to our south west. I took a compass reading in case the mist descended again, in the hope that we could move in a straight line. With bogs everywhere we had to splash our way through them to keep on course. The broken glass shock of cold water made for quick steps, and while the squelch and suck of our boots wobbled the line, we continued on, prompted by a greater fear and significant cold. The mist returned on and off for several hours as we stumbled our way down. Gradations of perceived temperature changes became the topic of conversation along the line as each of us, I believe, harbored thoughts of warmth and dryness. Ever so slowly we made our way down among some sheer cliffs and a magnificent amount of mud. As we reached the base of the mountain, timorous sunlight insinuated itself into the slowly dissipating gloom. The upsurge in good spirits that attended the near completion of our earlier hikes was replaced by a plangent weariness.

The exhaust of fried food reeking from the Stickle Barn Pub transported everyone's thinking about how cold they were to the prospect of hot food. Before long we were warming ourselves in gratitude before a wood fire. Not much had to be said about how difficult our situation had been, nor of the very real danger. The group proved its worth by acting intelligently and carefully. For myself, I felt the weight of responsibility like an anvil on my back. Experience played a vital role in having alternatives and knowing the jeopardy that had befallen us. Wordsworth in his writings about the Lake District notes the number of times shepherds inadvertently walked off mountain ridges in mists that disorientated their otherwise fine sense of direction. Knowing that I did the right things to get everyone down safely brought some consolation, but a chill of what could have happened rifled through me. The experience at the summit of Langdale Pike on that day lives with me on every hike we take.

Yet Another

And the breeze, murmuring indivisibly,
Preserved its solemn murmur most distinct
From many a note of many a waterfall,
And brook's chatter

(Coleridge, *Lines Written at Elbingerode,* 9-12)

As challenging as being lost in mist was, there is yet another complicated memory fringed with discomfort and pain associated with Langdale Pike. It was a difficult group ascent, largely because one member of the group, a young woman, could not climb at the same pace as the others. We spent an inordinate amount of time making our way up. She labored at every stage of the early portions of the ascent, through the switchbacks in particular. Each leg of each switchback is about fifty to seventy yards in length. The young woman had to stop at each turn to catch her breath. Those in the front of the line were growing impatient, and good will was leaching away with each stop. Barbara and I were aware of the growing tension, so Barbara suggested that I take the lead group up, and she would stay with the woman who was having difficulty. We followed the plan. The lead group reached the summit well in advance of the last few members of the group and the woman who was laboring. She was very happy with herself for having achieved a level of success she would not have imagined before the trip. I shared in her glee and felt proud of her. She was a very large woman and before the trip I suggested that she spend much time walking and exercising to get her body ready for the daily strain. The difficulty she showed in reaching the summit suggested to me that she probably did not do much. But she did reach the goal, good for her. With recollections of time at the top in the frightening mist on an earlier climb, I was antsy to get moving, though the students were having a grand time taking pictures and gazing out at the view, especially to the east where Lake Windermere could be seen in dazzling clarity. With the last group's arrival, as well as the young woman, we spent more time than I would have liked at the summit so that the last arrivals could collect themselves and take in the remarkable views.

With my fleece hat, gloves and jacket collar hiked up to cover my ears, I looked like a leftover from last winter, not someone out for a climb in mid-June, but I was cold and getting colder from being still for so long. Barbara signaled that everyone was ready to descend and gratitude welled up within me. In spite of some mid-ascent tension, the group was functioning well at this point, and the way before us was clear. I intended, and hoped, that we would descend without any serious complications as we had in the past. The woman who had so much difficulty during the ascent, Ibelieved, would get down with much less strain, and things would be fine. I conjured these reassuring thoughts thinking that we were due for a smooth descent. The security of my self-congratulations was throttled by a slowly rising pelting sound all around us accompanied by a strong roaring wind. Hail lashing directly at our faces, limited our view, and stung like a hive of bees. And the wind, it temporarily stopped us in our tracks. Gone was the sun and clear skies in an amazingly short space of time. A mournful "OOOH" rose in unison from the group. Scouring hail made progress very slow. Each of us devised ways of blinking, sheltering our faces, and peeking to see our way forward and down. My thoughts were truly in the moment as my concern especially for the young woman who was having so much difficulty earlier in the day made my stomach clench. We were descending more or less parallel to the Dungeon Ghyll. The upper sections are surprisingly steep in several locations. Footing is on exposed rock and fragmented boulders. In dry weather, care had to be taken, a slip could be tragic in these sections. Today, with everything wet and a covering of ice from the hail fast building, I could feel the tension within myself and tried to imagine what the students were feeling, as my hands clenched into fists.

Each person picked his or her way, progressing at a glacial pace. Glacial seems appropriate and ironic at the same time. The woman having difficulty on the climb was suffering much more at this point. My waterproof jacket proved not to be, and I was soaked through, and feeling deeply chilled. As each member of the group came toward me and went on, I could see that they too were drenched, though their faces remained impassive. Barbara was with the woman at the back of the group and I knew that her progress was going to be very slow making the other members of the group colder as they would have to wait for her. I gathered the lead group together and told them that they should continue on, the trail was very obvious from the point where we were. They were to wait at the Stickle Barn Pub for us. Like birds freed from a cage confinement they strode off immediately in a small burst of energy. As I watched them descend the increasing coldness in my body made me want to join them. However, I waited for Barbara and the woman to reach me.

The woman seeing the others descending at a soldier's pace began crying. Her mud-soaked boots, saturated clothing, and trembling begged for sympathy and commiseration. Both feelings I had for her in excess, but sympathy was not going to get her down. Nothing but her own will power and resolve would work. There were no mountain services with brawny men able to pick her up and carry her down. Given the weather conditions a helicopter rescue was out of the question. She had never done anything remotely connected to the kind of physical activity we were doing, even though students are told before the program begins that they have to be in good physical shape to succeed in the hikes. Nevertheless, we had to move. Looking downward in the direction where I knew the trail led, I longed to be where I could not see. My body was rebelling; my shaking hands served as a counterpoint to the twitching in my upper body and the shiver in my legs. My feet were wet to numbness. I did not know where my limit would be, but I suspected that I was nearing that unwanted discovery rapidly. Discomfort and exasperation caused by inertia flared anger into my chest; I could feel my self-control slipping. Fortunately, I did not say anything, held back primarily by the insistence of the still shredding hail. Fighting to make eye contact with the woman in the hope of getting her to move on I blinked away some melted hail in my eyes and caught sight of her clearly as she sat down in the fast running water underfoot. She was giving up with no sense of what she was doing. Looking at her in the mud and water melted my exasperation and momentary anger. In obvious pain and giving in to the maliciousness of our circumstances she was abandoning hope. Barbara quickly ordered her to stand up, stop crying, and move on.

The commanding tone of Barbara's voice seemed to reach deep into the student's sensibilities, and she did what she was told to do. I had renewed visions of sustained movement downward to dry warmth. Hope rose.

My fantasy dissipated in no time. The woman was up but barely moving. Barbara and I took turns staying next to her or leading her by pointing to each place she needed to place her foot. Foot by foot and step by step, we were coming down. Water soaked creases spider webbed her jacket, her legs mud splattered to the knees, and bedraggled hair falling out from her hood gave her the air of bewilderment. After an hour the pelting hail switched to a driving rain. By now I could see a bench that was placed some years ago in memory of a longtime resident of the area. Many times, in the past we had passed that bench in warm sunny weather, and for a few moments I lost myself to daydreams about warm and hot days we have spent on this mountain. The severe discomfort and combination of frustration at the slowness of our progress and my heartfelt sympathy for the woman led to reflections about the way different emotions strain to wrench us in one direction or the other at the same time. Thoughts about the sense of feeling and how sensation creates emotional states became a way of detaching myself from what I was feeling, both sensually and emotionally at this time, and opened a way of understanding something essential about learning. Simply put, it had to feel right. Just as we talk in terms of "gut feelings" or "being rubbed the wrong way," really knowing something carried an emotional commitment. For now, I just wished that I could feel less wet and cold.

I could not deny my real feelings of enervating cold in my bones and anger at the cause of them, and my fundamental concern for this woman who was pushing the limits of all that she had ever experienced physically, and as far as I could discern, emotionally as well. I really wanted to just leave her on one hand because of my own pain, yet for moral, ethical, and emotional reasons I could never do that. The ache in my deeply cold legs by this point settled into my knees and made each step an exclamation point of pain acknowledging yet another completed step. Dungeon Ghyll's consistent roar deflected my self-centered thoughts for a while. How wonderful it is, I thought, that distractions can subdue our anxieties. The change of focus shifted my languishing hope to a brighter place. Throughout the descent each of us slipped many times; it was impossible not to with hail-glazed rocks higher up and moss laden stones partially submerged by the now constantly falling rain threatening every foot plant. Elbows, knees, and shins provided target points to be bashed at each slip and fall. "Oh," "Ow," "Aah," rose into the saturated air like a chorus reduced to guttural noises.

Bracken! Entering into a stand of bracken brought some relief since the ground was spongy with thick moss in contrast to the rock embedded trail above and where we were. The splashing base of Dungeon Ghyll announced itself clearly and the border of the water could be seen, hope as I had never experienced it rose within me; we would end the descent.

Two hours had passed since I sent the rest of the students down and in the last stretch of the trail I recounted the climb, and especially the descent. Shamed at my thoughts of anger for being held up so long by this student who was by now walking steadily on the largely even trail, I thought about her and what she had accomplished. At the moment I was too cold and wet to talk or even think clearly, I just wanted to get indoors. Throughout the ordeal Barbara was a rock. She spoke calmly and encouragingly to the woman and convinced her that she would succeed. Her care was genuine, and her own discomfort was never an issue. She held her hand and coaxed her on. Several times in my own cold frustration I asked her if she was ok, or if she wanted to descend and I would stay with the student. Her clear-faced look enhanced by a stare was unmistakable. She suggested that I might want to go down, but she was remaining. Arriving at the base of the mountain she showed no outward signs of cold, in contrast to my jitterbug movements with my body in full rebellion.

The group that descended earlier was well warmed by this time, and joyful for our arrival. I sat by the open-hearth fire for over an hour absorbing as much heat as I could in my slowly steaming and drying clothes. My reflections were on the woman. I did not want to talk; I needed to think. Conditions this day for the group were worse than I had ever experienced. The surprise slashing of hail welted our faces to the point where trying to see provoked a disorienting loss of balance. Picking our way through the scattered boulders and icing as we moved, on a descending incline that is challenging in good weather, was unique in my experience, and frightening. The young woman had to be terrified given her inexperience, yet she found something deep within herself to goad her onwards. Much of the way down her face contorted in rictus she was flat out, beyond her entire realm of previous emotional and physical experience. She was courageous. The courage that she mustered was connected to circumstances. Surely she would never forget her climb today for all of the physical pain, but more importantly, I believe that she would also know that her discovery of fortitude and courage in the face of significant difficulty will continue to shape her existence. During the rest of her college career, when I would meet her on campus, she acknowledged the life changing experience that came to her on Langdale Pike. Her success made me feel very proud of her and disgraced at my own self concern for warmth and relief.

Langdale Pike Today

> *But this I feel,*
> *That from thyself it is that thou must give,*
> *Else never canst receive*
> *(The Prelude*, 11. 332 – 334)

Figure 17: Stickle Tarn

Source: Kelley Holocker

Recollections of events on Langdale Pike flood my mind as we continue on this year, on a day that has been largely uneventful, at least within the borders of the conventional. One third of the mountain to go! This group is fit and able to ferry through the boulder field efficiently. The distinctive rock outcroppings leading to the summit invite us to grab on and rise up. Pulling myself up from the last hand-grip the calmness of things on the summit pleasantly surprised me. No gale force winds to greet us, and the sky is clear in all directions. Discarding their backpacks some students ramble around the peak, some students take pictures, while others sit down or stretch out in the sunlight now at its fullness. Chocolate bars and cookies appear to the delight of all. A few disheveled students near me high in the knowledge that we have ascended very quickly, the fastest of any group I have led, gives them a certain swagger. At dinner the night before I told the group about the difficulties, we have encountered in the past on Langdale Pike. The stories sobered them, as I hoped they would. It is a difficult mountain. Now they are sure I had been making up the stories, particularly the changeableness of the weather. Their good-humored cockiness I saw as the certainty of youth. I did indicate to them that we were only half way through the climb, and it was best not to feel overly secure.

Setting out on the descent, it seemed leisurely in comparison to other departures in the past. I allowed myself to be optimistic about the conclusion of our climb. A new series of switchbacks added since last year makes our initial way down smoother and quicker. We fall into a sort of bouncing rhythm as we hop and shuffle in the gravelly surface. But then the "tick, tick, ticking, on my hood was the first announcement of rain, followed quickly by belligerent winds pushing at us from behind. I stared hard at the students I spoke with on the summit. One fellow fighting to keep his balance as the wind twisted his steps acknowledged that we in fact did have half way to go. Then, he smiled. I smiled, too. What was a generally clear day devolved into a steady, driving rain. As we made our way down and around the mountain the wind was less severe, but the rain was relentless. Our steps slowed as we sought for footings that were stable. At three points the trail is very narrow, there are drops of several hundred feet. Not surprisingly, a little fear has a way of sharpening everyone's focus and attention. Every slide on the rock face earns grimaces and involuntary shouts, but we keep moving. By the time we step onto the first in a series of bogs we are drenched by the steady downpour. For some unaccountable reason I always think that if my feet are dry, I am dry. Not so. Water has insinuated itself beneath my jacket uncomfortably draining in cold rivulets down my back, and inattention on my part causes me to walk directly on to a bog sinking me up to my knees.

My blunder was missed by no one; whoops and laughter spring into the rain-soaked sky. I am abashed but glad for the light moment against the dreary afternoon, even at my expense. Getting out of the bog hole provoked a scene worthy of an act from clown college. The ooze in the bog hole held me fast, the more I tried to raise one leg the more the other sank farther down. Seeing my predicament two students took hold of my arms and pulled me out. It was a slow, mud-churning process. The students were not much bigger than I, and their whole-hearted efforts to help me led to a series of interrelated lunges, grabs, and falls culminating in a high tide sit down in the sepia colored water. A deep uneasiness that my boots would be sucked off into the muck worried me in the process because I knew I could not hike the rest of the way barefooted. With two students down from the blowback of my release I emerged out of the muck like some ancient mythic figure emerging from the primeval slime ready to be washed by the still cascading rain into new powers.

My feet were not only wet they were wallowing in mud within my boots. Onwards again with flatulent boots as the mud sucked rhythmically inside and outside of my sodden boots as I walked. Becoming the mud-swamped fool changed the mood among the students, they cared less about getting wetter or muddier. Our movements grew easy, a lightness within each of us made the track downward less arduous, and the bond among us did not have to be spoken of; it was felt in that moment and understood in the context of the moment. Slogging on developed into an irritating chore and as I looked to my left toward the steadfastness of the mountain's girth I was searching for a response that would tie the multitude of nagging muscle aches and the wetness of my body into a revelation that would bring clarity in an overarching meaning. I stared and stared, moving like a beslimed robot descending with a pounding stamp, but the mountain gave up no clues. Scanning my memory for appropriate lines from Wordsworth that might capture the indifference I was experiencing failed to lift the seeping dread at the edge of my perceptions. I wanted clarity now, right now. That was my error. What I was seeking was not entirely logical, yet I was insisting on intruding my own more or less logical template to arrive at a meaning I could record and understand immediately. It was not until later that the very hollowness of my emotions and hope at that point in my descent on the mountain revealed meaning. I was about contemplating feelings and emotions that led to the understanding that we are not in control, and that we make meaning in the process of doing and recollecting.

After years of challenges on Langdale Pike, our arrival at the Stickle Barn Pub once again was welcome and reassuring. Drying out in front of an open fire after a day of cold, soaking winds is a delight in itself. This was not the first time, but the pleasure in gathering in the warmth gradually emerged and led to a calming of my spirits. It was late in the day and if we were to follow our plan, we would arrive back at the Kiplin Hall Study Centre very late in the evening and then begin preparing a meal. That was not an inspirational prospect. Barbara was ahead of me, not unusual, and she suggested stopping on the way back at Ing, a very small village with the Watermill Inn, which is noted for its variety of home brewed ales and good food. Barbara and I discovered the inn several years ago during an exploratory drive through the lakes in search of places that might be useful for the program. My spirits brightened immediately at the prospect of bringing the students to the inn since the inn was very old and it maintained what I would call a characteristic look of traditional English country pubs: exposed beams, stone walls, slate floors, and rustic tables and chairs.

With these thoughts in mind, I searched the faces of the students who were sampling local ales, recounting the days' events, and animatedly talking at greater volume as the full effect of warmth and beer took hold of their spirits. Watching their faces breaking into smiles highlighted by mud stains and bedraggled hair made me thankful for them. Like students from earlier groups these students have found something that bridges their initial differences, oddities, and personality quirks. "I never thought I would ever climb a mountain, and never, ever would I have climbed Langdale Pike," came from a girl who once described her greatest physical exertion as walking from one end of the Annapolis Mall to the other. "Did you see how far we sank into the bog," came from one of the young fellows who yanked me out of the bog, in a tone that hinted at a remarkable feat of dexterity. The surface chatter continued along much the same line, but in spite of all that they endured today the conversation moved to the future as several students asked, in a mixture of eagerness and apprehension, what the next climb would be like. I told them to trust in the ability they demonstrated today physically and willfully. There would be higher mountains, but none as challenging as Langdale Pike. Food is the central desire of all as we approach The Watermill Inn. I do not generally drink, though I do like beer. The very aura of this traditional pub instigates my desire for one of their ales, but with driving responsibilities on me, I banish the thought. Tables can only accommodate four people, and the students slowly drift to tables in a way that suggests a sociology experiment. Who will sit where and with whom temporally usurps the longing for hot food until everyone just settles in? The result is that there is no odd man out. During the week I noticed how students who were awkward around classmates they did not know steadily found links to establish new relationships. Here, they, individually, shed reservations and open themselves to others they probably would not have talked to on campus. The day's events prove fertile in generating conversation. The temptation to drink more than they should is wide open since the group members are scattered all over the pub, but without any chiding from me or Barbara they are sensible in their use of alcohol. I am relieved and heartened. Americans are probably fairly scarce in this little village, and local people in the pub begin conversations with several students. The students tell of the day's climb, and the local's express admiration for their accomplishment. Perhaps inevitably the conversations turn to American politics, and the students are shocked at how much they know about things that they have only a glancing knowledge about. By nine o'clock it is time to depart for the Study Centre. The drive seems magical as we travel through the Eden Valley as the sun sets amid a kaleidoscope of shifting colors brilliantly illuminating the isolated landscape.

Retracing the road to Ambleside took us through some of the more enchanting landscapes in the Lake District. The road winds sharply around meadows variegated in a riot of green hues, early evening mists rising from low ground near scattered woods looking ancient in the chiaroscuro interplay of shadow and diminishing light, and irregular stone walls caressing the roadside. Forced to drive at a very slow rate allows me to snatch glances at the scenery we are passing through, the effect is like a series of snapshots, a perfect form for capturing the world stilled out of time. Reaching Clapper Gate Bridge brings us almost to a stand-still, the stone bridge in defiance of any attempt at speed is narrow and steeply- arched, it also signals the outer edge of Ambleside. The Romans lived here as the center of their mining interests, and since that time the town serves as a center of local commerce and activity.

It has always interested me, to a degree, how so many outdoor gear shops could survive. If you are searching for ice axes looking like Viking relics, crampons medieval looking in their ferocious gleam, pitons, ropes in assorted colors and lengths, head-gear of all sorts, not to mention backpacks large enough to serve as a spare room, boots in an elaborate range of weights and thicknesses, and jackets advertised to ward off rain while keeping you dry, not sure how that happens with human sweat that is contiguous with activity. Ambleside is a riot of merchandising, and visitors seem to absorb the look of the outdoors adventurer. Along the narrow sidewalks people show themselves off with newly off-the-rack clothing ready to be tested in the nearest pub. I find my own growing smugness ironic since I have purchased equipment and clothing in Ambleside. I have been inebriated today by the students' self-assurance and their residual feelings of accomplishment. As I consider my superficial and sardonic reaction to the commercial dimension of the town, I know that the shops and the community depend on tourists for their survival. I also feel duly humiliated in a calibrated way since I know that there are true mountaineers in this region whose accomplishments are heroic. Our accomplishments together today are of a different scale, not lacking merit, but perspective is important.

Green Head Ghyll

Around that boisterous brook
The mountains have all opened out themselves
And made a hidden valley of their own.
No habitation can be seen

(Wordsworth, *Michael*, 6 – 9)

Figure 18: Haworth Moor

Source: Green Head Ghyll

Perhaps the most tangible connection between ourselves and the world that Wordsworth inhabited and wrote about appears in the poem, "Michael: A Pastoral." The poem describes the later life of a shepherd, Michael, his wife and son and the nature of their existence in a remote fell area of the Lakes. The emphasis Wordsworth gives to the physical environment makes elements of the landscape almost into characters. Green valleys, streams, rocks, and fields, the air itself, animate Michael's history. Vivid is the particularities from the introductory depiction of the steep climb that greets the walker after leaving the public road. He goes on from there to portray the way that a remote valley, not visible from the pathway, opens out and leads to a heap of semi stacked stones. The stones are the remains of a sheep fold never completed, and a unifying symbol in the poem. Every year we leave the public road and retrace Wordsworth's steps to the sheep fold, and there we read the poem and talk about our impressions.

The early stage of the hike is exactly as Wordsworth describes it in the poem: very steep and breathtaking. As we ascend, I reach deep in my lungs for air. I can hear the sound of others behind me huffing and stumbling on the loose rocks. I stop often for my own survival and to allow everyone else to catch up. Breathless and percolating sweat I explain that the trail will taper off into a gradual ascent. No one speaks but the looks from under pulled down hats warding off the bright sun suggest skepticism. "No, really, "I try to assure them, "it will get easier. After ascending about five hundred yards we take a long break. I tell them that if they look across the valley, they can see Helm Crag and gage how high we are. As they gaze, I can see by the lean of their bodies and the squaring of shoulders a rising confidence. Lines from Michael came to my mind here:

> *But they*
> *Who journey thither find them selves alone?*
> *With a few sheep, with rocks and stones and kites*
> *That overhead are sailing in the sky.*
> *It is in truth an utter solitude;*
> *Michael*

(Wordsworth, 9 – 14)

As demanding as the hike has been so far, they have come through with much less difficulty than when we climbed Helm Crag to just about the same height. The conversation brightens away from aches and pains as their confidence instigates them to look forward knowing that they can do more than they realized. Experience makes a difference, broadening their perspective, and the sense of themselves. The trail narrows to about two feet wide, with a drop off to the left of about a hundred feet as we enter a stand of bracken lush at this time of year with its delicate tips wrestling and arching with the temperate breeze. The walking is easy and abetted by the cooling effect of the breeze in our faces. The last stage to the sheepfold requires careful stepping over and around moss laden rocks and many rills of mountain run off.

By the time we reach the sheep fold everyone welcomes the opportunity to sit in the sun warmed stones, have lunch, and a class. The amount of chocolate we eat becomes the topic of conversation at first. It is true. Chocolate is different in England from chocolate in the USA, coupled with the way that calories are vaporized by our physical activity, it is easy to rationalize our indulgence. Disclaimers abound, mostly from the women, who declare their aversion to sugar and junk food in general, but with diminishing guilt, they keep eating Cadbury Bars. I read "Michael" with them,, each person reading a verse paragraph, and I always notice in my peripheral vision students looking around them at the reach of the surrounding mountains upward, and the birds gliding in the updrafts from the valley, as well as Green Head Ghyll itself tumbling and splashing only feet from us. When I finish and give them time to take in the storyline in the poem, speculation about Wordsworth's aims leads to a discussion of passages, especially about the pathos connected to the pull of the land and the pull of parenthood, but the main thread of our talk is the way that nothing has changed in the landscape in two hundred years since Wordsworth came here and wrote the poem. Wordsworth refers to the sound of the Ghyll several times in the poem, listening to it right now makes a powerful link. The sheep perched on the mountain side, the clouds drifting overhead, and the birds chirping all serve to bring particular elements in the poem directly to us. The physicality of where we are, in the very sheep fold depicted by Wordsworth, enhances the emotional power of the narrative line in the poem. Over the years of coming here students in their conversations with me seem to remember this experience most vividly. One young man confessed that he had never felt the unique interrelation between a physical place and a poem with such intensity before. "Sitting in the sheepfold, feeling the stacked rocks against his back, and looking at the descending valley," he noted, "brought together a myriad of sensations that underscored the poem's emotional meaning." Inevitably students talk about the value of specific places in poetry; they come to feel and understand the immediate sensual power of where we are in conjunction with the effort it took to arrive here. I tell them that the physicality of the moment is parallel to the mental effort in reading and thinking about a demanding poem. Students return to the idea frequently during our time together.

In the early days of the program, we would descend from the sheep fold and make a relatively easy day of it, sometimes combining the climb with a visit to Beatrice Potter's house, Hill Top Farm, in Near Sawry. But for the last five years we have taken on what initially seems like a fairly small challenge to climb the slope of the mountain leading upward from the sheepfold to Heron Pike at the top, not visible from the vantage point at the bottom where we begin. From the sheepfold the slope looks deliciously soft and gentle. As we prepare to begin, I tell them that there is a sizable gap between the appearance of what we can see and the reality of climbing it. My advice to the students is to stop about every fifty yards to make sure everyone is together. Stoked by the newly gained confidence in knowing that they have already climbed at least as high as Helm Crag, one of the students starting to begin the ascent, over her shoulder says in a tone bordering on arrogant, "Surely we can do better than fifty yards at a go."

The first section lays into a somewhat more vertical wall. At the first stop we are all together and talk about burning legs and muddy hands from grasping hand holds filters through the group. Buy our next pause everyone is sweating through his or her clothes. Even though it is breezy we are all down to shorts and tee shirts. More of the students look upwards searching for the top. I tell them that there are a series of false peaks, eight of them, and that the top cannot be seen until we are almost there. "Maybe we should go down" offers one woman who announces that she has a newly discovered fear of heights. The fact that she has not said anything about a fear of heights on earlier climbs suggests to me that she is probably fatigued under the considerable strain of this ascent. For a while I sat with her and bluntly indicated that going down from this point is much more difficult and dangerous since the descent is very steep and the grass is soaked, slipping was not something she wanted to take on. Tearing up she grows angry with me as she recognizes the logic in what I have pointed out to her. "You really can do this I counsel," in a calm tone off set by her outrage knowing that the group has moved up the mountain side. I take her back pack from her to lighten her burden and urge her to catch up to the others. As she nears her classmates, they speak in encouraging ways about how much they need her to continue on. Two of the men insist on taking her backpack from me and share the load willingly. She composes herself and begins talking with the others. I know at this point she will make it to the top. There really was no other option. I suspect she had doubts about what I told her concerning the danger of changing direction and going down the way we came. Nevertheless, she advanced.

The fifty-yard pauses embraced us and were quickly cherished by all as we climbed higher. The strain tore at the fittest with a sharp burn and the least fit with an almost overwhelming sense of hopelessness. Since we needed to use our leg strength in a consistent rise at a fifty-degree angle there was considerable strain on them. Grabbing onto knots of grass, or the increasing number of rocks, we were taxing our bodies at a higher level than in the earlier climbs. At each of the false peaks we took time to rest and simply look at the ever-expanding, remarkable views to the west. We could see down on the peak of Helm Crag. One woman noted that she could not have imagined that when we summited on Helm Crag, she would successfully climb Langdale Pike, and do what we were doing at this moment. Comments about the way the mountains are stark, without trees, and yet comforting in their rich greenness laced into speculations about how climbing, as hard as it was, made sensing the landscape so much richer. The physical experience of confronting each climb was a personal challenge, and a direct way of knowing the landscape. Thoughts about Michael and the harshness of his everyday life surfaced and were greeted with nodding heads. Understanding the poem with our muscles quivering and near to cramping we could feel the poem and understand the distance between ourselves, and the way we live, and Michael's solitary existence. At the end of the poem Wordsworth exhorts the reader to think about the loss of Michael's way of life and what it means to us. Sounds of Green Head Ghyll haunt the atmosphere and enter into our sensibilities along with Wordsworth's lament.

The woman who baulked earlier is calm though with her drooping mouth and heavy eyes I can tell that she is on the border of anguish and rage. But I leave her alone so she can work out the last portion of the climb on her own terms, as we are nearing an actual trail to Heron Pike. Sensing that the last false peak surmounted will bring our goal into view, several students push themselves to be first on top. Normally, I would ask them to stay with us, but their energetic burst might just be enough to inspire others to push through the last segment. At the top of the last rise, just below Heron Pike, the woman who had so much difficulty on the climb is shouting with glee about how she made it. Her exuberance brings smiles to all and all-around congratulations. I cannot but help to believe that much has been learned sensually today beyond the thoughtful conversation about "Michael" earlier. A grinning Sofia told me, "My body was not completely exhausted as I had assumed it would be, and my mind was more awake than at any other part of the day, it was a truly spiritual moment for me. I know I will remember the climb." Relieved to be at the top myself, I think back to other ascents completed through the years.

Past Ascents to Michael's Sheepfold

*Hence, he had learned the meaning of all
winds Of blasts of every tone: and
oftentimes
When others heeded not, He heard the
south Make subterraneous music*

(Wordsworth, *Michael*, 48 – 51)

Figure 19: Class at Green Head Ghyll

Source: Barbara Gillin

109

During the years of the program, there have always been injuries, most all fairly small. We have taken students to the local hospital for severe sunburn, a suspected broken finger which turned out not to be broken, colds, and an over dosage of medication. I always seem to be successful in banging my legs and hands, cutting them in the process. Once I was blown off balance by a powerful gust of wind, fell directly on my right knee and tore up my meniscus. That took an operation to set things right. Barbara hurt her ankle substantially in climbing Scafell Pike, but more on that later. The worst accident occurred in 2014 to Barbara at Michael's sheep fold.

At the sheepfold, we were casually having lunch, when I heard a modest thump behind me. My daughter Courtney shouted, "Oh No!" Courtney then flashed past me as I struggled to understand what happened, and as I turned around, I could see Barbara stretched out on the rocky ground. Before I could get to her Courtney, after rolling Barbara over, cried out, "She's dead!" Blood was scattered over her face, and she did not respond to us. Initially I felt inert: I could not comprehend how this could be. "My life was over," raced through my mind and I felt entirely lost in that moment. I tried to revive her by talking to her and rubbing her hand. Fortunately, one of the students, and older student, was a qualified EMT. She urged the students to soak spare socks or gloves in the cold water of Green Head Ghyll and bring them to her. Dede pointed out that Barbara's lips were moving and breathing steadily so she was alive the actual movement of time from Barbara's fall to this point was about a minute, but it felt as though I was in a free float out of time. The first flicker of Barbara's eyes yanked me out of the free float with a slam. Courtney and Dede cleaned Barbara's face and placed the socks laden with cold water on Barbara's forehead where a large bloody lump was developing. Because we were in a valley none of the mobile phones worked. We were in an isolated area where I cannot remember seeing any other people in the past. Seemingly out of nowhere an English fellow appeared saying that he saw Barbara fall, and that he was aware that we could not get mobile reception. He said that he had a powerful mobile phone and that he would go up the mountain-side and call Mountain Rescue.

Consciousness of time was vague for me, but I think that about fifteen minutes after the Englishman's call a helicopter appeared over the mountain crest to the north. The helicopter circled for several minutes before descending to the base of the valley we were in. After a half hour we could see a team of rescue workers making their way to us. Immediately the first man to arrive introduced himself and said that they had to go to the base of the valley since there was not a place to land, and he apologized for taking so long. Among the six on the team there was a doctor, four other men, and a woman. The doctor examined Barbara and said to me that she needed to be brought to a hospital as soon as possible. His concerns were for broken bones and head trauma. The helicopter they came in was not powerful enough to extract her by a dropped cable, but he knew that the British Air Corps was nearby on a training day. When Barbara heard the conversation, she immediately nixed the idea of being hoisted out on a litter attached to a cable. She was sure that given the wind in the valley she would be transformed into a pendulum swinging in arcs guaranteed to make her sick. "Prince William might be the pilot," one of the rescuers added. With all due respect Barbara was firm in her refusal to go out by air.

The lead rescuer rolled up his mouth as he looked at Barbara, smacked his lips and said that she was not that big and looked light, so the team would carry her out. While the leader called for an ambulance to meet us at the base of the valley the team members arranged themselves around the litter and secured her on it. Going down the trail was an exercise in care. The trail is very narrow, about two feet wide, and the drop off to the right was sharp and substantial, about fifty feet. As the team carefully made its way downward, occasionally one of the rescuers would slip, let go of the litter, slowly re-ascend the slope, and take hold of the litter again. The descent was slow but remarkably efficient and careful. The ambulance was waiting for Barbara, and the woman who was part of the team explained that they were trying to find a hospital that had room for Barbara. The closest one in Lancashire was full, but the hospital in Barrow had space, and that is where they planned to take her.

Barbara seemed to be stable at this point much to my immediate relief, but there were a series of intertwining complications that had to be worked out quickly. I was determined to go to the hospital with Barbara, but I needed to get the students back to Kiplin Hall. There was no purpose in my mind about having everyone go and wait at the hospital. The students were upset enough. We all travelled in three vans, Barbara driving one of them and Courtney the other. I needed someone to drive Barbara's van. Dede was the obvious choice since she was old enough legally to drive a rented car; the driver had to be over twenty-five according to our rental contract, and she was. When I told Dede her eyes enlarged, she gulped hard, and looked at me fully to see if I were joking. The instantaneous, serious expression washing over her face showed me that she understood what I was asking her to do. Her voice lightened as she said she would do her best, but had little experience driving a standard shift van, and no experience driving on the left side of the roadway.

Having a driver boosted my returning sense of control, but she needed to be insured. Courtney was ahead of me in thinking about insurance and she had raised the college person responsible for making those arrangements. Courtney handed me the mobile phone, the college contact person gave me the telephone number of the insurer in England, and within five minutes the insurer confirmed that Dede could drive and be insured, but he would have to have her driver's license. He was seventy miles away in a direction opposite from where the hospital was. Spirits sank. My momentary despair was lightened by Courtney who asked the insurer if she were to send a photographic copy of the license via her mobile phone, would that be acceptable? He said sure. Technology can really be useful, and the flurry of obstacles falls away.

The woman rescuer wrote out directions for me to the hospital but suggested that I use a GPS since it was getting dark in the mountains and the way to the hospital was complicated. Our GPS had given up working for us days earlier, but I felt sure that with a map and directions things would work out. But first I needed to find a meal for the students. Scouring Ambleside for a restaurant that could take nineteen people proved useless. Between the pull of concern for Barbara's condition and my obligation to the students I began to feel rattled. In a last try I asked at a pub if bar meals were available, and with a "Yes" we were in faster than an English downpour. The students knew I wanted to leave, and they took over organizing themselves, and insisted that I go. Courtney and Dede would make the long drive back with a group of students dedicated to turning a tumultuous day into a day memorable for selflessness, cooperation, and re-assurance. I could not have asked for a more cooperative group of people.

Starting from the village green in the center of Grasmere, go north on Broadgate which merges with Swan lane after the park and playground. Cross over the A591, the Swan Inn will be on the right, and ascend the paved road bearing left. A small sign indicates a paved lane which rises sharply, Greenhead Ghyll will be on the left. At the end of the paved lane there is a gate, go through staying to the right of Greenhead Ghyll. With Green Head Ghyll on the left climb the steps at a sharp angle that lead to a small grassy patch with a bench. Continue on, the angle of ascent becomes less daunting. About a hundred yards from the bench there is a fork in the trail. Stay left. Follow on until you come to the ruins of a sheep fold made famous by Wordsworth.

Continuing on From Green Head Ghyll to Rydal Mount

If with old love of you dear Hills! I
share New love of many a rival
image brought
From far, forgive the wanderings of my thought

(Wordsworth, *Composed at Rydal On May Morning 1838*, 1 – 3)

Figure 20: Ascending Helvellyn

Source: Courtney Fitzgibbon

From the top of Heron Point, the trail leading southward to Nab Scar takes a series of dips and rises. At each high point the length of Windermere appears to float into the distant background, and clouds hover in the illumination of the setting sun. The perpetual wind adds a dramatic quality to each vista and makes the lower level woods seem protected and secure. The descent from Nab Scar winds through a good number of switchbacks put there to limit the knee-grinding effect of a straighter line, as well as helping to limit erosion. Conversation from the students weaves in and out of speculations on how much harder it is to descend a mountain

113

than climbing it. Aches, twists, and slips aside we descend into the grounds of Rydal Mount, Wordsworth's home. The house is fairly large, but certainly not grand. Wordsworth lived in it when he had achieved literary distinction and gained an international reputation. Many important literary figures visited him at Rydal Mount; young girls on holiday during the Victorian Period snipped roses from the front hedge often enough that the hedge had to be replaced.

We tour Rydal Mount every year, sometimes early in the day before a climb, and on other days after we have completed a climb. Today, we come at the end of our climb and the students, instead of looking for a place to sit and rest, are eager to visit the interior of the house, and walk the considerable grounds. Barbara and I first visited Rydal Mount in 1970 when we were graduate students enrolled in the first Rydal Mount Summer School. Recollections come back to us in abundance from that first visit; it was during our time here that we first imagined bringing students to the Lake District when we secured teaching positions. It seemed like a great stretch of our combined imaginations then that our dream would be realized in time, but here we are, again! When students, a few at a time, filter out of Rydal Mount their animation about being in the place where Wordsworth wrote so many significant poems gladdens me. The students are taken by the site of the house, looking out into a quintessential Lake District view of trees, flowers and Windermere, but they are moved by the story related to Dora's Field and the death of Wordsworth's beloved daughter. I have them read the sonnet Surprised by Joy while we stand in the garden and ask them to walk down the hill to the field named by Wordsworth for her. When they return, moved by the poignancy of the sentiments expressed in the poem we discuss the way we often almost ignore the present as we look to the future without realizing what is of prime importance. Among the many hopes I have for the program I do not want to make Wordsworth into a totally revered figure, removed from us in some sort of sanctuary, quite the opposite. The sonnet, the place, and the Hiking in the mountains as they have done today and arriving at Rydal Mount foot sore, make the human link with what were similar days for Wordsworth all that more tangible. The connections between the physical exertion of ordinary life for Wordsworth and its necessity as a condition of the frame from which he created and wrote can be felt as well as known. Raw elements of nature seeming to challenge us earlier in the day, in the enclosed, rolling landscape of Rydal mount's grounds, are transmuted. The civilized aspects of the profuse, overflowing of flower gardens rich in variety and color, the carefully terraced walks, and the singular trees ancient in their appearance lead to a mood with a noticeably calming effect on the students as they wander through the grounds. We talk about the differences.

Though the grounds of Rydal Mount appear "natural" as opposed to the formal, geometrically designed gardens seen in eighteenth-century great houses, they were arranged by Wordsworth to give the impression of "naturalness." Wordsworth was an avid landscape gardener indeed the cultivation and care of gardens has been and is a major thread in English culture. A male student talks in an open and unguarded way about the different way he feels within the grounds, as opposed to the feelings at the top of Nab Scar. "The calm within the grounds allows for a careful consideration ofparticular feelings," offers another student. "The wind and the view from the top of our climb today was exciting and somewhat frightening," says another. There is general agreement among all regarding their observations and thoughts. In time the conversation winds its way into the specific feelings that arise in different landscapes, and how poetry can capture those feelings for particular ends. "The landscape of Greenhead Ghyll seems like a fairy tale in a way to me because I live in the suburbs," offers Jennifer, "but in reality, Wordsworth was reflecting on things that were perfectly normal to him. And he made poetry out of it." As their teacher I cannot help but to indicate that in the Prelude, Wordsworth develops the idea that his life as a poet was predicated on beauty and fear. Most of the students have a limited knowledge of the Prelude, but with our firsthand experiences and discussion today I feel sure they have much to build on in understanding Wordsworth. Contemplating what they experienced will set them up for a more trenchant understanding of the poems. With the warmth coming from the intensity of our climb gradually finding its way out our muscles, as we look at the coming of evening, we are reminded that there is more to do tomorrow. We must go, and so we do.

Edinburgh

> *O Caledonia! stern and wild,*
> *Meet nurse for a poetic child!*

(Sir Walter Scott, *Lay of the Last Minstral Rokeby,* Canto V)

To catch the train from Northallerton to Edinburgh, we have to be on our way to the train station by 6:15AM. With the fatigue of yesterday's climb lingering in our bones there is both excitement at the prospect of a "day off," and some frantic, last minute assembling of jackets, hats, and lunches among the students. Questions abound, "Do we need our passports?" "Is the currency different?" "Where will we eat?" Since there is so much commotion and answers to the questions are unheard by some, the questions are repeated. And so, it goes. Shivering in the early morning damp on the railroad platform unites us, a choreography of eyes flicking to the station clock in the hope of hurrying the train's arrival. Once on the train, I settle into reading their journals while most of the students fade into the sleep they did not get enough of last night. Students are required to write a series of journal entries in three categories. The entries can be on cultural similarities and differences that they have experienced, or entries that describe a landscape we have hiked through with special emphasis on making the entry come alive by describing what senses are most involved in responding to the landscape, and communicating that sensual response in their description, and another choice is to respond to a poem the student finds interesting and thought provoking, or to explain why the poem does not work.

With the students' composition books leaping and shifting at each lurch of the train—more or less embodying the students' normal energy levels—I find myself in a tug of war with gravity. In time I adjust to the vicissitudes of the train's movements, and I lose myself to what the students have written. On the whole, they follow instructions fairly well, but there are notable differences in the range of detail and nuance in their writing, at this point in the program most students seem reluctant to write about poetry critically, though some do. I suspect that the students who shy away from writing about poetry do so from uncomfortable past engagements where they were uncertain about how their reactions might be judged. Over the next two weeks I will collect and read their entries and comment on their work. For the most part the students focus on what they have been experiencing. Their entries recount the ways they have found a resonance between what they have been reading and what they have learned physically. The tactile quality of the examples they cite reassures me that the somewhat elusive goal I have for them, about discovering within themselves their own way of understanding their interaction with the natural world and the meaning it has for them, is being realized. One entry in particular, from Sofia Colvin, stands out and needs to be included here, "I signed up for The Kiplin Hall Program because I wanted to explore the Lake District and Kerry in Ireland, but I had never even considered climbing an actual mountain before. The first day of hiking was the hardest of them all. I barely knew the people I was with, my legs were shaking all the way up the mountain, and I was the first casualty of nettles. I had been warned to stay away from them only moments before I felt my legs stinging. I learned two important things that day about climbing mountains. One was that Mrs. Gillin would get me up that mountain regardless of the amount of complaining I did. When I began to fall back in the group, she handed me chocolate and started an unrelated conversation to get me going again. In later hikes I knew that there was little point in attempting to stop because Mrs. Gillin would not accept that sort of defeat." Sofia's candor was widespread. The other students' openness and forthrightness in writing about their personal struggles during the mountain climbs also raises my concern about whether I have been pushing them too hard, but then continuing on as they express the value, they have discovered in extending themselves assuages my conscience. Many go on to note their surprise at how British English is so different from American English. Reading my handwriting is a challenge in the best of circumstances, but with the gyrations of the train, I work consciously to write slowly in the hope that my observations about their writing might be useful in opening their confidence, and also readable.

Edinburgh seems to be just waking as we arrive. Air heavy with a mixture of the preceding evening's mist punctuated by surges of fresh air battling into the stagnant musk within the station greets us with the promise of a different kind of day. Bagpipes roar an accompaniment to blustery winds seeming to come from all directions amid the guttural chug of taxies and weighted down, lumbering busses. The big city vibe takes hold of the students as we all step-out quickly, eyes riveted forward with a purpose. The cacophony of sounds, the steady flow of people moving in several directions, tips up our steps as we go to a central meeting point. The floral clock is a working clock with flowers embedded on the hands and the background of the clock's face. It is a longstanding feature of Edinburgh, and its location on Princess Street, in my mind, makes it an easy find for the students. I instruct the students that we will meet here at five PM sharp and then proceed to dinner at a nearby pub. I ask them to stay with at least one other person since some of the students are less comfortable in a city and intimidated about getting around. With a check to make sure that they all have my cell phone number, we escort the group to Edinburgh Castle. The walk-up Castle Hill is steep with flights of steps taking us through a rapid tour in stone of Scottish history and governmental buildings. There are also seemingly innumerable souvenir shops selling a good range of vulgar items, street performers, and at least one opportunity to have a photo taken, for a price, with a blue-faced William Wallace impersonator. The castle is imposing in its massiveness; two of the men take pictures of each other under the statue of William Wallace. Perhaps the William Wallace impersonator inspired their Scottish heritage, or maybe just the movie.

Over the years we have purchased tickets to the castle for each of the students, only to find that many of them went in and came out in a short period of time. Since the cost of each ticket is high this year we asked if there were individuals who would prefer not to go through the castle. Surprisingly only one person said he would prefer to go off on his own. I expressed my concern for his decision to go it alone, but I respected his desire for time by himself. He told me that he had no plans to spend the day in a pub or doing something that could lead to trouble; he just wanted to test his skills at chess with people in Scotland. Knowing his deep love of the game I told him, "good luck, and see you at five." I told him that it was very early in the day and in Scotland, particularly on Saturdays, things warmed up slowly. Off he went. The rest of the students entered the castle and began their "day out." Barbara and I sat for a while near the castle's entrance and speculated about the students' interests. On our first visit here when we were just a little bit older than the students in our group, we were fascinated by the visible history embedded in the Royal Mile. Every building seemed rife with age and stories. The very cobblestones that made walking awkward brought to each of us a literal feel of history. Learning more about that history and the literature by the Scots was more than an urge, it felt basic to our shared fund of knowledge. I hope the students find that sort of connection in their own way. For now, we have the new day before us, and as we look for a place to have tea; I cannot refrain from remembering events from past visits to Edinburgh.

The floral clock has claim as being the site of a deeply upsetting event many years ago during one of our earliest visits. Feeling confident that students listened to everything I said and remembered it perfectly since they were college students, not children, I gave the students instructions to meet at the floral clock at five PM so we could have something to eat before boarding the train back to England. My wife, who was an elementary teacher, signaled me several times and said repeat your instructions so they will remember. In a gust of reprimand, I stated that they were not elementary children; college students did not need additional reminders. Barbara looked at me in dismay as the students went off for the day. Once they were gone, I said that she should get out of the mindset of an elementary teacher and realize that we were dealing with adults.

At five o'clock, all the students except one showed up. I suggested we wait though my insides were churning like a motorcycle slipping slowly into a ditch. After an hour of waiting our time frame for catching the train back to England was closing in like a matador moving in for the kill. This was a time before ubiquitous cell phone use, but one of the students had met a former soccer coach from his high school and he had a cell phone. He called the police to see if there were any incidents involving a young woman, as well as the local hospital. Very calm day for both venues and no report of problems. I sent Barbara along with the students to find someplace to eat while I waited. An hour later I was still waiting by the clock when the group, minus one, returned. There was a later train to England and Barbara, and I decided to call the college to report what was going on and seek direct police help.

When I talked with the Dean, he said that I would need to call the parents to tell them about their daughter's disappearance. I have two daughters and the very thought of the phone call made me almost ill, but I knew it had to be done. I told the Dean of my plan to seek police help and he confirmed that it was the best plan. Since there existed a five-hour time difference between Edinburgh and Maryland I felt that I had some time to try to locate the missing woman before making the call. At the police station the officers were very relaxed and kind-hearted. When I related the story in hurried gasps the two officers looked a knowing look at each other. "She has probably found a young man and is sitting in a pub with him, "they chuckled. I explained that the missing girl did not drink and was not likely to take up with a stranger. She was always the person who was ever ready. If someone needed a band-aid, she had it. If something in the Study Centre needed to be done, she was first to volunteer. She was utterly reliable up to this point. The policemen shrugged and after a few deep breaths and long exhales they looked at each other seeming to acknowledge what the other was thinking. I surmised that they realized I was out of possibilities and truly needed something helpful at this point. The one policeman asked where anyone in the group last saw her. I said that I saw her near the Scott Monument about three o'clock and asked why that was important. A knowing stare between the policemen followed, and I had the sense that I was the stupid American who was clueless. "If we know where she was last seen we can pick her up on camera and follow her throughout the city centre. "What was she wearing?" "An orange fleece," I replied. Indeed, I was the clueless American, I had no idea that cctv (Closed Circuit television) cameras were located all around the city, and by knowing where she was at a particular point in time, they could focus on her and track her movements. I was astonished; grateful for what the police officers described seemed a wonderfully workable way of finding our missing student, but shocked at the intrusiveness of cameras capturing every passerby. How naïve I was. The world has taken up surveillance with little push back since that time.

The police suggested that we wait outside as they would begin the process of scanning the tapes. Putting my hand on the doorknob to leave, the mobile phone belonging to the former coach rang and it was for me. Given the Alice In Wonderland texture of the day it never crossed my mind how the call could be for me. The caller was the Warden at Kiplin Hall Study Centre. She said that one of the American students was with her. My throat contracted and I could not talk. Barbara took the phone and the Warden related how the student arrived in a taxicab after taking the train from Edinburgh. "Put her on please," replied Barbara in a tone of barely controlled urgency mixed with anxiety. The sobbing woman said she went to the train station at five PM and waited for the group. After a prolonged amount of time waiting, she saw a man with a backpack in a red jacket, just like mine, walk quickly to the early train to England and get on. She followed and it was not until the doors closed and the train was in motion that she realized that the man was not me.

She stayed on the train to Darlington, where we had embarked in the morning and got off. She was frightened by being in a strange place that looked suspicious in her eyes and made her uncomfortable. When she saw a taxi, she asked if the driver would take her to Kiplin Hall, and he did. Fortunately, our earlier call to the Warden at Kiplin Hall provided her with the mobile number, hence the student's ability to call us at the police station. I took the phone and asked her why she went to the train station and not to the floral clock where we had agreed to meet. She said that she was not paying attention to the directions since she was very excited about being in Scotland, the land of her ancestors. Not sure what to do as five o'clock approached she said that going to the train station seemed most logical to her. The man with the red jacket had to be me she reasoned and just followed him.

Her tears were genuine and profuse, and, if I were not in a police station, I might well have given way as well. I felt choked up with gratitude that she was safe and bewilderment. How could she get things so wrong? Barbara read my expression and with a single gesture of her forehead I understood what she meant earlier in the morning about giving instructions to college students. They were not much different in certain ways after all from her elementary students. Needless to say, since that day instructions are repeated to the point of rebellion. I called the Dean, and both of us felt that a staggering weight had been removed from our shoulders. I did not have to make the call to the girl's parents, though I did tell them the story when we returned to the USA. On the train ride home, the students joked with each other and me, asking me in light-hearted tones what I would have done if it were one of them who got lost. I told them I did not even want to consider the question; my resilience was depleted.

Different nationalities play out stereotypes: Germans, aloof and strong-voiced, French breaking the queue, Spaniards wearing funny hats, Japanese following the umbrella-equipped leader, Chinese in beige, Americans loud and laughing in thick soled shoes, and so on. Any temptation to sarcasm halts with my awareness of my status as a visitor, with a group. It is what drives us all, the desire to know and learn by travelling and visiting historically significant sites. Who am I to get sarcastic about these large— and probably in their own way—efficient groups? In a very broad sense, our overall motives in coming to the city are similar. This leads me to consider further dimensions of those motives. I am here today with a group as well, though now dispersed on their own, with the intention of providing time for them to feel Edinburgh and link those feelings to specific places they encounter. My hope is that clear memories of today's encounters will serve as a base for their growth as individuals.

Poking on through the sidewalk crowded increasingly with young university-aged people, the tourist shops yield to bars, small restaurants, and coffee shops. Even in the hours before noon young people in good, Saturday spirits talk in loud, throaty voices, leading me to think that perhaps they were still enjoying Friday night. No matter, they are enjoying themselves in that first enfranchisement of youthful freedom; their volatility gives a charge to the street the way the return of electricity after a black out brightens everything with a new sense of value. Many of the food shops carry the logos of American fast food restaurants; it has been a steady growing phenomenon for many years. The tidy tea shops abundant in the past are long gone, along with a particular element of Scottish culture.

Cities develop their own character by the intersection of geography, history, and the inhabitants. "Old Reekie" was the name given to Edinburgh since air pollution on a grand scale was characteristic throughout the industrial period. The stone buildings still have years of mold, mildew and pollution embedded in their roofs and walls, and enhances a dour mood like a prolonged rain storm in thirty-five degree weather in February. Yet families out for Saturday, teenagers, and old-age pensioners often flash smiles and seem to be very pleased in walking about the city, darting into shops, taking a food break, or just gossiping. The sidewalks on Princes Street in particular are wall to curb with a large cross current of inhabitants. Street performers, some in their rendition of Celtic Bards sing, bang drums, play guitars, accompanied by a base layer of bagpipes echoing down streets and alleys. The grayness of the buildings is upended by a vibrant spirit of people going about their ordinary business with verve and low-level excitement.

Time is evaporating, and since everyone meets at the arranged time we walk to a pub, The Abbotsford, for an early dinner. Walking to dinner provides us with some time to tell of the day's happenings. Several women talk about shopping, they stop us all in the street to show us their finds, their voices high with excitement, and a good-humored challenge to see if anyone can top what they did. Three men talk about the pubs they visited in the interest of cultural diversity, while two women and a man recount their enriching and satisfying time in the National Museum of Art. Once again, the students' enthusiasm and good-natured silliness is satisfying to me, and I share their pleasure. On the walk I feel especially fortunate that while Barbara and I are three times their age they feel comfortable enough with us to show themselves as they are and trust us to understand them. Perhaps the most important unreported joy in continuing the Kiplin Hall Program is being with really good yet widely diverse individuals whose energy and perspective on the world makes me think through how I can teach them about literature. Coming to know students as we do during the program reinforces the way we see them in the traditional classroom on campus. The very unsettledness that can prove wayward with deadlines and academic structures are clearly important but knowing the students as young and energetic individuals helps to provide room for mistakes and blunders. It is one thing to know that eighteen to twenty-two-year olds are still maturing but sharing their take on things as we do makes us much more understanding. I have learned that this is a valuable aspect of teaching.

The Abbotsford seems to be the real thing in traditional pubs. It is located on an ally behind the line of department stores on Princes Street. The swinging doors lead into a scene out of a history book. The mahogany bar is wrapped at the base with a brass rail and topped with frosted glass partitions behind which hang a multitude of glasses. The beer taps are as large as baseball bats. The prevalence of brass fixtures, the black and white tiled floor, and ancient-looking bar stools and tables battered by decade upon decade of stout conversations, wise cracks, and arguments create an air of gracious anarchy. We fit right in. At dinner across several tables I remind the students about what faces us tomorrow: Helveyllan. I tell the students that they must be prepared for anything in regard to weather conditions. Barbara and I have climbed in very warm, sunny weather, as well as very cold, wet, and windy weather. The climb will be long, probably between six and seven hours; therefore, extra water and food should be carried. Facial expressions drain their animation, and the voices of the people in the bar below are clearly audible in the silence that has fallen on our portion of the Abbotsford. I am certain that the students are thinking of recent climbs and the way they handled themselves. Reminding them that they have already ascended three mountains and that the major difference between them and Helveyllan is height and the time it will take to reach the summit. Bolstered by a level of self-confidence the mood brightens, chairs shift, coats and newly purchased treasures are gathered, and we set off for the train station and Kiplin Hall. Recollecting his experiences in Edinburgh Jack Despeaux wrote to me the following, On the day that we went to Edinburgh Castle, I went about an interesting social experiment that has kept me thinking to this day. I explored the castle with a small band of friends that day, all from different backgrounds. I knew I was a country bumpkin, my friend Devin was from a city, and he seemed to protest normalcy, there was Shannon, who was from Baltimore and wealthy, and Casey, who was a quiet but adorable friend of mine, who might live in Delaware? I'm not entirely sure. Regardless, when we reached the top of the castle and could view the city and the countryside, I had a surging sensation inside of me.

"Casey," I said, "When you are on top of this castle, do you feel humbled or powerful?"

"I would say that I feel humbled," she responded. Shannon felt powerful, like a queen, Devin stated that he felt neither, but was rather entertained. I was like Shannon, in that the grand view I had with the city and castle below me, made me feel like I had acquired some kind of ambition. I had a similar experience atop Helvellyn, and it made me crave the heights that I was formerly afraid of.

We could watch clumps of rumbling clouds, practically at eye-level, cross the sky in front of us, and make out the border between the incoming storm and the clear weather. The North Sea and the curvature of the Earth were awe-inspiring, and on the other side of the castle there was a great expanse of Scottish hills and land. It was beautiful, and inspiring." It was a day well spent.

Helvellyn: "Seeing into the life of things"

What a vast abyss is there!
Lo! The clouds, the solemn shadows
And the glistenings—heavenly fair

(Wordsworth, *On Her First Ascent to the Summit of Helvellyn,* 10 – 12)

Figure 21: Ascending Helvellyn

Source: Barbara Gillin

It is the mountain that Wordsworth almost reverenced; it was his favorite mountain. He and Coleridge met on Helvellyn often, each climbed from opposite directions. Sir Walter Scott climbed with Wordsworth and was deeply moved by the effort, not to mention the scenery. The story of Bobby the Cairn Terrier who stayed near the body of his master after he had fallen to his death and somehow survived several months in a particularly inhospitable section of the mountain captured the sentiments of Scott. He commemorated the story in a poem. It is the second highest mountain in England, and it will take us about seven hours to complete the climb. Striding Edge and Swirl Edge are two features of the mountain that are well known in climbing circles. Sir Edmund Hillary in preparation for his historic ascent of Mount Everest in 1953 practiced on the edges. Though the height is substantially lower than Everest, the terrain is similar and provided a useful place to negotiate challenging mountain features.

We will ascend from the Wythburn approach. The small car park is almost hidden from view, but very convenient for our purposes. Using the trail from Wythburn will allow everyone to reach the summit without serious risks. In the early days of the program we followed the Glenridding approach. That route led to the base of what is known as Striding Edge, literally a breathtaking portion of the mountain. After a long, winding ascent the summit with a mostly vertical face can be seen dominating the view to the west. The trail upward leads to a small path about two feet wide which traverses the several peaks. Following the trail means stepping out on the trail atop the peaks with a severe drop off on either side. Wind is a menace since it is not only strong in this place, but also highly variable. The very first program set out some of the problems in taking the Glenridding route. There were twelve students in the group, including my younger daughter. By the time we reached the start of Striding Edge the weather had deteriorated, and I emphasized to the students that we would abandon trying to make the summit if things turned wet; bursts of turbulent air already countered my hopes for the day. Stepping out on the narrow trail over the peaks seemed to me to be the signal that brought on heavy mists and a scattering of wind-driven, pelting rain. Immediately I knew that we had to turn back, the increase in danger was not worth a second thought.

Huddling with the students out of the wind I pointed out the trail we would follow down. My directions were greeted with some sighs of disappointment and petitioning to continue on; a few though were glad with the prospect of going down. I told the group that people do get blown off the edges every year, and that I had a very large responsibility for their safety, and I was not going to act foolishly. As they started moving, I noted to them that they needed to stay on the trail since there were bogs and bog holes all over what is essentially the floor of an ancient caldera. By the time they started walking the mist had intensified substantially and visibility was reduced to a few feet. I shouted that they must keep in eye contact with the person next to them until we reached the caldera floor below.

Our progress was deliberate and slow; I stayed in the rear to ensure that no one was left behind. On the trail below the mist blew off almost as quickly as it arose. I was relieved that we descended this far at a critical point in the climb without incident. My joy was short-lived. My daughter decided to take a short cut across the bog instead of staying on the trail as I directed. In no time it seemed that she was calling out to me. When I reached her, her face was red and her eyes somewhere between searching and embarrassment. She stepped into a bog hole, her legs were anchored in the muck, she could not get out, and she was steadily sinking downward toward her knees. Always the professor, I asked everyone to gather around as best they could without slipping into the bog hole and told them that this is indeed a bog hole. They are especially dangerous since once you sink to a certain level it is very hard, perhaps impossible in some cases, to get out without help. "Did anyone remember that I warned about staying on the trail in order to avoid the problem Courtney discovered?" I asked. Sniggers all around except from Courtney. She was very angry with me and now wet and cold. In a concerted effort we pulled her out, a sucking vacuum pulling off her boots in the process. Clearly, she was embarrassed and angry with me for making her the object lesson. She stomped off into the reappearing mist and as I gestured to follow her down, one of the students pulled on my arm and said that we were missing three men. My chest clenched and my throat constricted; for a few seconds I could not speak. The worst imagined horror seemed to have come true. All the self-congratulatory feelings connected to what I thought was a safe descent to this point vaporized. I looked around, counted the students, realized that three were indeed missing, and shouted into the mist for them.

We had stopped for several minutes and in that time most everyone was shivering. The misty wetness in the air by this time soaked into our clothing making the cold all that more discomforting. I told Barbara to take the students down to the base of the mountain, there was a pub there where they could get warm. My plan was to retrace our steps from the start of Striding Edge in the hope of finding the missing men. Racing through my mind were visions of them slipping on the rocks and getting injured. In my best moments I hoped that they were simply disorientated by the mist, had wandered off the trail, and that I would meet them on my return. My body was shaking I think as much from the cold as from fear and concern for the missing. After two hours of searching I found no trace of them and knew that I would have to get help from Mountain Rescue. Shaking continuously did not warm my body, I knew I was approaching a dangerous threshold if I did not get warm very soon. So, I began to descend morose in the darkest of thoughts. Tripping and stumbling I drifted downwards; my balance largely lost by the endless shaking and twitching. The days of cell phones lay in the future; we had whistles that we planned to use in case of emergencies. About a quarter of the way from the bottom I heard a whistle, momentarily raising hope that the missing men were found. Straining with as much energy as I could command, my legs stuttering more quickly in the downward direction toward the sound of the whistle.

A very fit young man from the group caught up to me, and breathlessly announced that the missing men were safe and waiting for me at the pub. The weather conditions were abominable, but I felt a glow of happiness immediately brightening my interior weather and taking a dreadful weight from my mind. I was deeply thankful that they were fine. While walking together, I asked the student what happened to the missing students. He was slow in his reply, and sheepishly told me that they had planned to do a keg stand on the summit. To that end they had carried a mini keg of beer with them. When I told everyone that we were not going to the summit, they stayed in place as the mist hid them from view. On they went to the summit and had their beer. In their descent they lost the trail in the mist, met a woman who said she would guide them down, and arrived at the pub.

Now I was conflicted with genuine, heart-felt relief, yet deeply angry that they disobeyed and put themselves in serious danger. Besides, I was near frozen, my fingers and toes numb from exposure, and my body saturated in cold rain. The student reacted to my grim silence as we walked by trying very hard to make light conversation. I wanted to reassure him that I appreciated his kind intentions, but I was too miserable to even crack a smile. When I sent the group down the mountain to the pub, I envisioned everyone having hot chocolate, coffee, or soup. When I entered the pub, the students were doing shots. Barbara read my face and she said to me to calm down; the missing students were here, and everyone was safe. What she said made perfect sense of course, but my emotional and physical discomfort led to me barking out to them to get into the vans, we were leaving.

The missing men apologized, but I was blind in the moment with disappointment and cold, soggy clothes, so I ignored them. Laughter and high spirits flowed through the van but stopped with me. I could not let go of my sense of failure. Once on the road I remembered that Ullswater, which was on our right was the lake where William and Dorothy caught sight of the daffodils immortalized in the poem of the same title. The road was very narrow, but I pulled onto the side as best as I could and signaled to Barbara to do the same. My intention was to tell them the story related to the poem and then read the poem to them here. Before I opened the door, several girls called from the back of the van to let them out immediately. I asked if they were going to get sick, since they had been drinking. "No," came the response, "We have to pee!" Before what they said registered with me, they were out the door and doing what they had to right there on the road. Quickly they were joined by others. Giving up on "the teaching moment" I sat in the driver's seat and began laughing at the entire situation. Disaster had been averted, and I had myself to blame in thinking that sending college students to wait in a pub on a cold nasty day to have coffee or hot chocolate was ludicrous. What the missing men did was something I would discuss with them later, and the yellow flow on the roadway would forever color my associations with the golden daffodils of Wordsworth's poem. My sense of order was not theirs, and while I had an obligation to help them mature in understanding the need for doing things in a certain way, I knew that my way was not the only way. Coming to understand how they thought and perceived what we were doing was the eye-opening lesson in the day for me. My treatment of my daughter was smug on my part, so sure I was in my position of authority, and shatteringly insensitive to her.

So it is that we no longer take the Glenridding route to the summit. The Wythburn approach carries a large number of obstacles to make it memorable in a different way. The trail through the base ascends steeply through a magnificent stand of pine trees. Cascades of water pummeling from the mountain provide something akin to nature's mood music, the thick canopy of pine boughs make the sound of the water flourish and diminish. The air is moist and fragrant from fallen pine needles; everything seems fresh and promising. The very steep angle of ascent through the forest takes a toll on everyone very quickly. Cool as the atmosphere is, everyone takes off outer layers of clothing. Perspiration drips from noses, chins, and lips. A stile in the trail makes for a good reason to stop and catch our roaring breaths. Some students are struggling already after only a few hundred yards. With the rest at an end, Barbara suggests that I take the lead group while she will stay with the students who are likely to need help and support. We agree to regroup frequently through the next section. Facing us is a series of switchbacks deceptive in the way they seem to promise an easier climb. The process through the switchbacks seems endless; each turn brings a view of yet another switchback. Much of the effort to reach the summit requires a resolute will, and hiking up through the switchbacks does much, I believe, to enhance each person's determination.

With the switchbacks behind us, we pause so everyone has time to collect themselves and get ready for the long arching trail that will take us to a series of stone steps in front of us. Footing becomes more uncertain as we negotiate fallen rocks, boulders, and mountain run off. Several stops are needed in this section as some students push against their limits of experience. Barbara is especially good at talking to the students and encouraging them to pace themselves, and to focus on what is directly in front of them and not worry about what comes next. The stops make it possible to take time to take in the vistas that surround us, particularly in the north-west. Lake Thirlmere bordered by forest-land leans northward catching sunlight in a dazzling array of blue and silver. Jackets and fleeces have been shed, though the air is getting cooler as we ascend. Looking upward students ask if what we see is the top. "No," I answer, the top is far to the left, and from this vantage point, out of sight. Their response is the definition of plangent. The stone steps immediately break our whole group into a series of small ones. Like bouldering on Langdale Pike the steps require concentration, balance, and strength. Moving quickly to the right or left with a backpack on accentuates the move, and consequently balance. The spastic gyrations make some students laugh, while others become frustrated.

Food is always a focal point for our combined attention, so just above the steps I suggest we take a long break for lunch and a class. Sweaty as we all are the chill in the wind causes everyone to bundle up. Earning this much of Helvellyn makes our humble sandwiches deeply pleasurable. Bars of chocolate, sleeves of biscuits, and bags of potato chips, give indulgence a new dimension. Reading from a selection from Coleridge's Notebooks where he portrays his hikes through the Lake District, scholars have noted that he was the first to write about climbs in the Lake District, I ask them to look around. Part of the scene he describes takes place where we are seated. Coleridge goes on to relate how he relied on moonlight to guide him down to Grasmere. The students are surprised that he survived. They have climbed enough to know at this point in the program that going up a mountain requires a certain set of strengths but coming down another more difficult set. The fact that we are in a place described creates a special resonance. We read further into Wordsworth's Prelude, and his time in the Alps where he had expected to experience a spiritual awakening in the Vale of Chamouni, but it did not happen at that time. Years later in recollecting the event in Switzerland he had an enlightened insight and came to understand that nature is the embodiment of the creative process in the mind of God, man, and in nature itself. According to Wordsworth reflection on the elements of nature can lead us to a deep self-awareness, and our connection to all of creation. In spite of their weariness and too many potato chips they understand the way that Wordsworth's depiction of process and creativity manifest themselves here where we are. We can see woods decaying never to be decayed, and streams seemingly stationary, with winds buffeting winds just the way Wordsworth describes. The passage is a very important one in Wordsworth's work as a poet, and the students as they talk with me show that they have a tangible grasp of what the lines mean. As one student added, "The physicality of the place, crossing the Alps, is only the starting point, but fundamental. The meaning of the passage has to do with the power of the imagination that stems from physical awareness, and where that leads us." Our immediate presence on a slope on Helvellyn, and the physical and mental effort to reach the site, play more than a mere accompanying role. Experience informs meaning.

With a considerable section of the mountain ahead of us before we reach the summit, we need to push on. After a climb among boulders, the trail oscillates in broad arch-like curves as far as we can see from here. The steepness in each of the arcs is deceptive; once again we find our group stretched out. The summit is the main hiking objective for today, but for some there are other options. Two trails descend from the summit; one is called Swirl Edge the other Striding Edge. Before we began the climb, I told the students that I was willing to take some members of the group out on Swirl Edge and then back up Striding Edge. I told them that the edges were especially difficult and would involve hand over hand climbing. A very good sense of balance was necessary since we would be hiking across a series of peaks on a trail about two feet in width. The drop offs on each side are considerable, and wind can always be unpredictable. The going down Swirl Edge and then up on Striding Edge would add at least another hour onto the climb, and that if anyone had reservations, they should not go. My aim is to discourage anyone who is not in very good shape but who, not wanting to be the only one staying back, might feel pressured into going. Typically, about two thirds of the group decides not to go. To make sure that everyone who goes can actually complete the circuit I offer them a challenge, if they can keep up with me to the summit following lunch they can go. If not, I will not wait for them. This challenge worked well for many years, though in recent years my stamina is not what it used to be. The groups remain made up of eighteen to twenty-two-year olds, and Barbara and I just keep going in a straight line, adding years. I have had to push hard to create enough distance between us and the main group of students; ironically the challenge is now on me.

Another rule regarding the edges is that if the weather is wet and windy, we will not go. About one third of the time we have walked away from the edges because of bad or deteriorating conditions. Wind is the primary concern, but rain and mist have played havoc with our plans as well.

We descend by going down Swirl Edge. The first step is the most daunting. The edge cannot be seen easily from the summit, to see it means going to the very edge of the summit and looking down where rocks jut out in fearsome angles. The rock formations came about when Helvellyn was an active volcano. What was the caldera is now known as Red Tarn containing water just above the freezing mark, so it seems to me. Rocks splintered by the force of eruptions and locked into place during the cooling afterwards give the immediate landscape a surreal character, like so many dragon teeth pointing upward and outward, menacing in their sharp points. Looking downward is like looking into fearsome and dark fairytale landscapes, with jutting rocks and a steeply twisted vertical view to the base. Our progress down is measured and careful, conversation is reduced to noting footholds and handholds for each other. From above we can hear the calls from the rest of the group, which has arrived at the summit, apparently in very good cheer. Once through the rock face the trail opens up considerably leading to the shore of Red Tarn. Two of the men and a woman want me to join them in a swim in the tarn. I decline. At their age I did go in, but the shocking cold of the water, which I clearly remember, is embedded in my body memory. In they go amid shrieks and laughter, their joy is infectious, but not enough for me to join them. I have grown wimpy.

Looking up to the beginning of Striding Edge looks unremarkable, but of all the climbs in the Lakes this one section about four hundred yards in duration is the most physically exhausting for me. The grassy slope deceives the eye. It appears gentle and relatively short in comparison to the massive face leading back up to the summit. It is the angle of ascent and the way the slope curves that have our legs burning as we begin, and a new round of profuse sweat disgorging from everywhere on our bodies. Among the six of us we sound like steam engines as we huff and puff out way up. Stops become more frequent as we move on, and everyone keeps looking longingly at the ridge where the path over Striding Edge is located. My method of climbing here is to just keep going in small steps without stopping. Legs and lungs seem to be on fire, and my knees are perilously close to buckling, but I know from experience that I need to get up in one go. With my shirt and shorts soaked through, I wait for the others, downing a bottle of water in the process. While catching our breaths the rest of our group on the summit is busy waving at us as they begin their descent down to the base. When the students with me see what lay ahead, a single narrow path at the top of the peaks leading to the very face of the summit, the rise to the summit like a gigantic wall pitched at a frightful angle, "Cool" is the universal response. Stepping out onto the path still takes my breath away after all the years. Even the slightest wind makes me want to drop to my knees and crawl to feel safer. After a slight hesitation the students move on comfortably and excitedly, animated by the exhilaration of being where we were. I caution them about keeping their focus. Capturing the moment on film, now in digital form, is inevitable. Pictures of each of them standing on the highest point I feel will harness their personal pride well into the future, giving them bragging rights among their friends.

Before the final section up the mountain's face to the summit, there is a choice of two ways to descend from the last peak in Striding Edge to the base of the final climb. Each way demands a shimmy down a narrow, tunnel-like formation with few apparent foot-holds or hand grips, and a notable drop-off straight ahead. Since I have come each way in the past, I have a reasonable sense of how to maneuver the descent. Once down I guide the next person, and she in turn helps the next student down. The wall looming up next before us means that we will have to climb hand over hand in a careful fashion. The first time I climbed here with Barbara when we were graduate students we inadvertently drifted to the right and ended up directly on the sheer face of the mountain, and then it began to rain. Retracing our way back seemed more dangerous than going straight up, so we did. The climb was frightful, and never forgotten. So, I tell the students, who are very eager at this point to launch into the final section, to stay very close to me to make sure that we, as individuals, do not get dangerously distracted. Between the large blocks of rocks are loose rocks that seem to shear off at each step. The tumbling of these loose rocks is a hazard that the students comprehend quickly. Knots of grass between the rocks provide useful hand-grips as long as the grass does not come loose. There seem to be many deceptive elements in this landscape. What looks simple is usually not. We have been exposed to the elements for a long time at this point and on the move steadily, now cramping becomes another concern for us. "Drink water, it will help," I tell them. The rocks give way to grass and I know we are almost at the top. A few steps on and the monument to Bobby, the Cairn Terrier who guarded his dead master, emerges ahead. Even though we still have to descend the entire mountain the students are delighted with themselves and overjoyed at the experience of a lifetime. Physically depleted as they seemed a short time ago, they are now overflowing with new energy and they are eager to go down. Since the main group is down or near being down by now, I tell them to go ahead and I will meet them in the car park.

The time I have alone in the descent permits me to reflect on the day and the program. The day has gone well; we all have come to respect each other in ways impossible to understand earlier before coming here. The physical and emotional challenges were unique in their experience, and they maintained balance and a new level of respect for each other. The overall experience is parallel to what I aim for in my classroom on campus. By introducing students to difficult poems challenging because of the language used and the cultural, historical setting, I hope they come to levels of understanding arrived at by the process. My awareness of this connection warms me. The aches and pains in my body remind me of my advancing age and lead me to wonder how much longer can we keep the program going. I want to continue but I know that there is an end out there.

Memories of other groups flood me at certain points on the mountain associated with groups or individuals. Limpid images come on me in wonderful excess. The first ascent with Richard Wordsworth, the great, great grandson of William, talking casually up and down the mountain, as if it were nothing but an afternoon stroll remains clear in my memory. Dressed in a trench coat he seemed ghostly at times as the mists came and went about his gaunt appearance. On another occasion the windiest climb with gusts of fifty miles an hour I was knocked to my knees by the wind, while a very thin, light woman near me, Sarah, had fears of being blown off the mountain. She was not, but afterwards she wrote the following, "Then one June day, we decided to tackle Helvellyn, one of the Lake District's and England's highest points. It was raining, which was not unusual during our hikes, but it was the type of rain that chills you to your bones. As we hiked, I could not stop shivering, my teeth chattering involuntarily. I was scared. I did not want to climb any higher, but we progressed.

At the summit of the mountain, Dr. Gillin could see how cold I was. He, and a few of us, sprinted down the hill so quickly that I do not remember how we got down. All I remember is getting into the running car with full heat blasting from the vents and feeling thankful. It's one of the days I remember most vividly from our trip because it embodies a valuable Romantic teaching. Not all days are perfect, but there is a certain beauty in that."

On another climb the weather was uncharacteristically hot, truly hot as in eighty-degree heat hot. In contrast, at the summit is a stone-wall in the shape of a cross. Since the wind is normally the major source of discomfort, it is possible to sit out of the wind for a while within one arm of the cross. I have often huddled with groups trying to keep as much heat within as possible. In the heat the opposite was true. We sought shade from the blistering sun. Now as I descend by myself, there is time to take in the particularities around me. I can clearly hear the birds twitter and see them hover in the calming breeze, and I hear the relentless sound of water flowing in a low roar muffled by the shape of the mountain-side as I descend. I think of Matthew Arnold's line about the "eternal note of sadness" he heard on Dover Beach, and I am reminded of all the awfulness in world events. Amid all the natural beauty that surrounds me I know that I am privileged to be here, and to be in the position of a faculty member enabled to do what I do. The special poignancy of dark thoughts in a scene that opens on the uncluttered landscape in the clear process of being shaped by wind, water, and sunlight reminds me of Wordsworth's depiction of his descent in the Alps that I discussed with the students earlier in the day, and feel heartened somewhat by the fact that Wordsworth kept faith with the power of what he discovered there in that natural setting amid the depredations of the counter revolution in France. The air warms in gradations as I continue in a low-level shuffle downward until I reach the pine forest where its freshness and deep green color at this time of the day makes my step lighter.

When we were all together at the base of Helvellyn members of the group that took on the edges were discrete enough not to make much of their accomplishments in front of the others who did not go. Their maturity and consideration said much to me about their characters. "Elation" best describes the mood of the entire group. We had climbed the second highest mountain in England together, our muscle aches earned and oddly enough pleasurable because our own efforts and further possibilities seemed limitless in this moment. Spirits were high all the way back to Kiplin Hall. Megan Viviano wrote in retrospect, "There were steep hikes uphill, and it was the first time I'd encountered hand-over-hand scrambling. Some of the peaks we traveled across were very narrow, with dizzying drops on both sides. Helvellyn stands out the most. That climb brought me out of my comfort zone and made the accomplishment feel very satisfying. I left the trip leaner, stronger, and more confident than when I arrived." Because fatigue would win out over high spirits the next day was scheduled as a less active one; we would visit the city of Durham. I told them they could sleep in later; we would depart at 10. Amanda then added, "The hiking was the reading, the internalizing, the feeling. The exploration of this new world—-that was the purpose of connecting art to life. We were not just reading the Romantics but discovering why they were given such a title. Why they woke up every morning, and decided to create within the surroundings they inhabited." Her comment was greeted with weary good spirits. They acted as though they won the lottery, joy and more high spirits prevailed.

Helvellyn can be approached by a variety of ways. The one we took most often started at Wythburn Chapel which is located on the A591 north from Grasmere. The advantage of the Wythburn route is that everyone can make the summit without having to ascend the very challenging Striding Edge or Swirls Edge. By car there is a Pay and Display Car Park just off the A591, just behind the chapel. The trail is clearly marked all the way to the summit. There is a bus stop at the Car Park as well. Swirles is another alternative. From Grasmere the Swirls Car Park and trailhead are about a mile from the Wythburn Car Park on the A591 and on the right. The trail is marked clearly.

Figure 22: Kiplin Hall

Source: Dawn Webster

Kiplin Hall

The history of Kiplin Hall and its families is in many ways the story of England written from the point of view of the local gentry and community rather than the rich and powerful, royalty and aristocracy, with whom 'history' is too often associated.

(Dr. Constance B. Schulz, *Kiplin Hall and Its Families: A History*)

When Barbara and I began the Kiplin Hall Program years ago, Kiplin Hall itself was in tenuous shape. University of Maryland students under the direction of David Fogle initiated a process of restoration that would take years to move forward. David's relentless work to get funding for the restoration project was remarkable for the intensity of his efforts, and his devotion to the goal. What is now the Kiplin Hall Study Centre evolved from paddocks and the coachman's house. It includes en suite bedrooms, a well-equipped kitchen, a dining room, a classroom, and a common room. The conditions in the Study Centre deteriorated after its establishment since there were very limited funds to make repairs. At one point the upstairs shower water was running into a lighting fixture below, and with twelve people using only two showers the bathrooms became bogs.

Since those early days the Study Centre has been renovated with room for additional students, and amenities many levels above what things were like in the past. With a budget for repairs in place now, the future looks very good for a comfortable level of accommodation. Students over the years have liked the quirkiness of the way the rooms are laid out and enjoyed the relaxed atmosphere in the Study Centre. The easeful quality of the Study Centre during our stay each year is enlarged considerably by a visit from Jay Griswold, who has supported the program from the beginning. Jay makes a point of traveling to Kiplin Hall from business in London to meet and talk with students. When he arrives, he is always invited to meet with the English Trustees and is asked to join them for dinner at what I assume is a notable restaurant. He does meet with the Trustees but always declines dinner in favor of having dinner with the students. Amid the commotion and noise of the kitchen, and upwards of eighteen students chatting, Jay stands in the buffet line with us all. Students are somewhat awkward at first, not knowing what to make of a man of stature from Washington College's Board of Visitors and Governors joining them, and for the academic year 2014-2015 the Interim President. Jay's engaging manner relaxes them quickly, and they respond to the honesty of his questions about what they study at Washington College, and what they think about the Kiplin Hall Program, candidly. From my point of view, it is wonderful to see him take the time and effort to find out what actually happens on a ground-level basis. In the 90s and 00s there were relatively few visitors to Kiplin Hall, and the forward motion of restoration on Kiplin Hall itself seemed glacial and uncertain.

The concerted effort of Trustees on both sides of the Atlantic saved the hall from catastrophic destruction; their dedication supplemented by a corps of volunteers from the local community who take great pride in preserving their historic heritage. The Hall itself is large, but not a great house on the scale of Castle Howard for example. Its history is woven into the time of its construction with all the political complexity of the seventeenth century. Suffice it to say here that it was the Calvert family who established the Free State, Maryland. Every year to commemorate the signing of the charter for the development of a colony in what would become Maryland there is a ceremony alternating between Kiplin Hall and selected historical sites in Maryland. Local leaders, trustees, political figures and a rich assortment of guests take part in the commemoration. Since we are always at Kiplin Hall each June when the event takes place, we have only joined the celebration in England. On several occasions the Ark and Dove Society of Maryland members have attended in noteworthy numbers along with political leaders from Annapolis. Coming to the "birthplace" of Maryland reminds us all of our newness as a nation and enhances our respect for the ideals of our fore bearers. At a time when America is held in poor repute in so many places in the world, it is warming to know that at Kiplin Hall America is honored and Americans are welcome.

The Hall and its grounds have been sensibly and very carefully renovated over the last eight years in particular. Gardens were almost obliterated in places, eighteen years ago, and in great need of work. I always found that sitting in the formal garden to the left of the front entrance to Kiplin Hall haunting. The hedges were unruly, and the topiary bushes had lost their precision, but it was possible to see the liniments of what was there at some point in the past. On warm sunny days I wondered who spent time where I was on a lovely June day, and speculated about how what I could feel in the sun's warmth in the protection from the wind outside the enclosed garden was probably similar to what those people unknown to me felt in the same summer circumstances. The bond between my feelings in this place and the past brought to light how we must derive our own meaning of our time in the time we are alive. The garden has remained essentially the same though in much better trim than our early visits, but how I experience it is significantly different culturally from the way they did. From the garden, on good days, I can call anyone on the planet with a cell phone; that was unthinkable in the past. The flood of information and the speed at which communication and transactions take place runs directly against the grain of a world-view they had with England at its center. Such speculations lead me nostalgically to hope that the students absorb the layers of history in this place, and that they will form connections of their own.

It has been speculated that Kiplin Hall, originally built in a cruciform configuration was meant to be a symbol of resistance to the monarchy. At a time when religious differences set English people against each other, great landholders in the North maintained their allegiance to the Catholic faith against the wishes of the king. Construction of Kiplin Hall can be seen symbolically as a form of Northern defiance to the king. There was a price to pay for that of course, which led to the king's offer of land in America to Lord Calvert. Shipping recalcitrant land-owners thousands of miles away from the king, with an ocean separating them, was a reasonable alternative tactic to blood-letting. While the interior of the hall has been restored with careful attention to decorative details, the room I find most interesting is the library with its almost grand spaciousness, tempered by the collection of books rising high up in the room and around its border with the ceiling. In the nineteenth century this library was added to the original building, much to the chagrin of architectural purists. Forces demanding that the library be torn off were ranged against others who reasoned that the library was crucial in the development of the hall over time and needed to be saved. In the end the library remains and in itself is a delightful relic of nineteenth-century gothic. It is a period piece within the bounds of the building, just as rooms used by officers during World War II have been preserved in all their spartan dinginess on the second floor. The second floor hallway was a place where ladies in the eighteenth and nineteenth centuries could exercise while the men were out hunting. Exercise for women was not considered good form, so ladies were consigned to walking moderately. In foul weather they were relegated to sauntering back and forth in a space about fifty feet in length and twenty feet in width. The hallway brings home to me the pressure on women to conform to stringent social standards alien to our world today and make me wonder how social and cultural restrictiveness shapes the experience of life itself.

Protecting women from the harsh realities of life was a major motivating factor in having women restricted to walking indoors. Jane Austen in her fiction depicts that sort of crushing world in vivid detail, as do a number of 19th Century English women novelists such as the Bronte sisters, Elizabeth Gaskill, and George Eliot. Adoration of the angel of the household put women in the position of staying within narrow social bounds and very limited experience. The implications of experience are numerous and complex, and the changing nature of experience available opens the world to us differently and in unique ways. Since the nineteenth century in particular women have been striving to free themselves from cultural curtailments with impressive success, though the task is not complete yet. As the women from our group go from room to room through the house, I think about how the way they are dressed today would have been unthinkable in the not-too-distant past. Flip flops, shorts, brightly colored tee shirts ordinary in our day would have received hard stares even a few decades ago. The grounds of Kiplin Hall, in which delightful flower gardens have been resurrected, particularly the rose garden, have also been transformed by the woodland walks. Attention to the grounds has been created so that visitors linger in this northern landscape. Walking in the woods brings me to several students and we talk about our impressions of the hall and the grounds. One girl said that she could see herself descending the grand staircase dressed in a stylish gown, much like some of the female characters from Downton Abbey. Another cites the amount of work needed to keep the house clean and in good repair. I tell them of my thoughts about the young women relegated to walking around the second-floor hallway. "Dorothy Wordsworth" did not conform to conventions, says another. "But she was seen as being odd," came in reply from another. This off-the-cuff conversation went on through dinner and some time at the pub in the evening, and it is indicative of the kind of communication that was well established at this point in the program. The students were comfortable with me and Barbara as well as with their classmates, and the combination of reading and experiencing things well out of their conventional comfort zone made honest conversations frequent.

Scafell Pike

I ascended Sca'Fell—by the side of a torrent, and climbed, and rested, rested and climbed till I gained the very summit of Sca'Fell—believed by the Sheperds here to be higher than either Helvellyn or Skiddaw tho' the wind is strong, and the Clouds are hasting hither from the Sea—and the whole air Seaward has a lurid Look—and we shall certainly have Thunder—yet here (but I am hunger'd and provisionless) here I could lie warm and wait for tomorrow's Sun, and on a nice Stone Table am I now at this moment writing to you—between 2 and 3 o'Clock as I guess—surly the first Letter ever written from the Top of Sca'Fell! But O! what a look down just under my feet! The frightfullest Cove that might ever be seen, hugh perpendicular Precipices

(Coleridge, *Notebooks: The Natural World Science*)

Figure 23: From Scafell to Scafell Pike

Source: Barbara Gillin

After our initial visit to the Lake District in 1970, Barbara and I talked about climbing Scafell Pike, the highest mountain in England. While we were in the Lake District, we often heard people talk about Scafell Pike in tones ranging from reverential to lurid. Scafell is located in a remote area of the lakes, and it is a mountain that needs time and good luck. For many years, I did not include it in the schedule for the program; since Barbara and I had not climbed it I did not think it a safe thing to do with students of

136

markedly different physical capabilities. When my Son-in-law, Frank Fitzgibbon, volunteered to help out in the program I knew we should climb Scafell. Frank is a very experienced hiker and climber and having him in our group assured me that an ascent was feasible. The journey to Keswick was similar to others we had taken to other mountains in the Lakes. But from Keswick to Seatoller the road narrows, the trees look solemn as they stand in very dark shadows created by the nestling of several peaks, and the mountains themselves seem to be crowding in on the road as if to repel the world beyond Borrowdale. After parking on the side of a farm road, the group was giddy as we disembarked from the vans, a frisson of expectation made us move in a jangled bump fest as excited nerves played out some pent-up energy from each of us. Knowing that we were about to take on a very major climb loomed in the atmosphere among us. Once we began walking, nerves settled. During our approach into the base of the mountains, the day seemed to promise fine weather. Mists were rising and clearing from the wet low lands, checkering the sunlight straining to insert itself into the day.

My map seemed useful as I planned the day, but as we began climbing the landmarks, we should have found easily were not evident. The trail was clearly marked so it seemed reasonable to follow it and forget the map. The climbing was strenuous and prolonged at first, but then it mellowed to a long gradual ascent toward the base of Scafell Pike. Jokingly one student shouted out, "Are we there yet?" He meant the completion of the hike, but I answered that we were still on the long approach into the beginning of the real climb. The giddiness and energy evident when we parked evaporated into a group response, "Really!" "Push on, we have a long way to go," I responded. We stopped for a lunch break and a class by the Head of the Sty a place bordered on one side by the Sty, a stream vigorously splashing its way to the valley below, scouring the rocks in a single-minded purpose, and pine trees with their rich and refreshing scent raising our spirits. I read passages from Coleridge's prose account of his ascent of Scafell in 1802, and how his method of descent was to jump from one ledge to another. In a short amount of time he found himself on a ledge without any clear way of going down or up, and how at the moment of his consternation a thunder and lightning storm arose. The dramatic rendering of his fear and exhilaration seemed to bring a sharper focus to the eyes of the students since being where we were, we felt the power of the natural world, and were very vulnerable. We seemed to be like a miniature species in comparison to the implacable fells around us, our own strength puny.

When we arose from our rest and regained the trail, the sky darkened, and a wind roared its way to us. For several minutes we were wrestling with our flapping clothes and striving to maintain balance in the blasting wind. A burst of rain erupted and quickly subsided. What appeared to be a glorious gem of an English day in the brightness of June when we arrived turned into a slice of November. The air temperature dropped significantly. We hiked on determined to get to the summit in spite of the weather: the students in particular were resolute on reaching our goal. Clouds descended and shrouded much of the anticipated view from the upper reaches of the mountain. The more we advanced the more natural impediments rose up to challenge us. A group of other hikers, English by their accents, overtook our group and marched ahead with a fast, determined pace. I noticed that they were not carrying backpacks and were dressed in tee shirts and shorts. They moved as I would like to, quickly and steadily, but I was surprised by what they did not carry. My experience in the Lakes taught me that being ready for weather surprises is basic. Our packs hampered our movements, but we had extra clothing and food.

I calculated that we must be near the summit by the number of hours we walked. Clouds descended on us, reducing our vision to a few feet. The hope for the summit sharpened as the wind came back with greater force and rain joined in as an accompaniment. Looking up, I saw what seemed like an endless boulder field. Balancing on the shifting boulders in the wind, fears of slipping interlaced our wrestling with the wind, making our movements slow and tedious. Coleridge's words came back to haunt me in my growing sense that things were becoming very complicated. By the end of the boulder field, I was ready to turn back when I caught a glimpse of the cairn at the summit. The wind now ripped at us with hail lashing our clothes like the sound of miniature machine guns. The boys who passed us lower down were at the summit shivering and looking not at all well. They were huddled against the base of the very large summit cairn. Members of our group were intensely cold, but they had layers of clothing protecting them and keeping in body heat. The English boys were dangerously exposed, and I urged them to descend with us, movement being the only way they were going to get any kind of warmth. They laughed about my concern as they gleefully said that they were Englishmen and could handle the weather. I gave them candy and cookies left over from lunch in the hope that sugar would supply them with energy, and for that they were delighted. We began to go down without any delay at the summit. Movement back over the boulder field was frustrating and painfully slow, my hands and face were numb from the wind, and the students showed their firm bonding with each other as each person encouraged the person next to them to stay strong and keep going. I was glad to see their mutual support for each other and wanted to take away the discomfort they were experiencing. Their movements showed that they were essentially fine although cold and wet, but not in any very serious danger from exposure, at least at this point hours later we were reaching the upper thrust of the valley. The sun that had greeted us in the morning was gone, replaced by a landscape soaked in every way possible. Running water trickled in a deceptively benign way. At first it seemed gentle the trickling sound was outsized as we descended; everywhere there was running water growing more aggressive in its sound as time wore on. Once more the wind reasserted itself, catching me off guard and knocking me knee first into a rock. In less than a nano-second pain flooded my sensibilities, and the pain in my knee, not the cold wetness, became my main focus. The injury would prove to be complicated later, but for now I wanted to catch up to Frank and the lead group.

Without a watch, I did not know the time of day, but the sun was just about down; it had to be very late, and I guessed that we had been out hiking for over nine hours. Alas in time, we were all the way down. Relief rather than excitement reigned among us this time. Wry smiles wrinkling from tired and weathered faces, powerful in understatement, said it all. No additional words were necessary. Given the conditions we had pushed ourselves to new levels of endurance and will power, but success was not a central concern at the moment, finding a place for dinner was. On our drive in, we passed several country pubs that looked cozy and inviting. I had visions then of settling in with a hot meal near a fireplace with a crackling fire. Entering the vans, mud splattered, with cold rainwater still soaking its way to shivering skin, we endured it all with resolve and fellow feeling. No one was spared from the difficulties of the day, and the mutual concern that the students showed to each other high up on the mountain as they encouraged each other flowed unreservedly now that we were in the vans. The good-natured bragging after completing other climbs as, without saying anything specific, the students understood that they had achieved something remarkable in their lives, and that the discomfort was worth it. The shared experience established a bond among them that no one else outside the group would understand. Truly, "You had to be there," and they knew it.

The quaint pubs I fantasized about were past the time when they served food. From pub to pub we traveled unsuccessful in finding the availability of food. It was approaching ten o'clock and hungry and tired as we all were, I suspected that we would have to travel all the way to the Study Center to have dinner. The almost two hours that that would take was a crushing thought. As we entered Keswick, I decided that it would be best if everyone fanned out through the town to see if a meal could be had somewhere; it would save time that way. No cars were in the car park, not a good sign I thought, but I parked anyway. When I got out of the van a magenta neon sign announcing an Indian restaurant appeared before me. Like a moth to a flame I moved irresistibly to the front door and was greeted by a hospitable man who when I asked him if he could serve our group of eighteen people, looked at me in puzzlement, and said, "Of course." I think he thought it a silly question; he was open for business and we were welcome. Fine with me. On the way into the restaurant some students said that they had never had Indian food, the man who greeted me in a loud voice said that cultural diversity happens best through food. I could not have put it better myself, besides we were so hungry preferences seemed not to matter. Our day brought us together well and provided much to talk about for a long time.

Barbara and I talked about the climb up Scafell Pike the next day in a state of physical recovery and agreed that it was at the edge of everyone's capabilities, and that we ought not include it in the future. With my knee throbbing from yesterday's fall the decision felt right, but there was a lingering sense for me that the benefits of pushing to the limit were invaluable. Taking on a substantial challenge and succeeding in meeting it cannot be packaged, and that element was central in many ways to what we were aiming at in the program.

Two years later, with the promise of clear, dry weather, we set out again to climb Scafell Pike even though we had some reservations. On our arrival at the farm road the air was indeed warm and dry. On our last visit the entire landscape seemed more a waterscape with darkness adding to the gloom. As we walked small puffs of dust surrounded our feet, and there was no need for a jacket or fleece. In talking with students about a number of events in Wordsworth's and Coleridge's lives I missed the trail I intended to take and instead we were well off course from the plan for the day. Using my map, I figured out where we were and where we needed to connect to the main trail, my inadvertent diversion adding about forty minutes to the climb. The landscape in the Scafell region looks like pictures from the moon. There is little vegetation, except for our movements and talk there is remarkable silence, and no shade. The clear sky urged the sun to dry what was muddy and soupy on our last visit. Heat steadily intensified became uncomfortably noticeable as we made our way to the summit. Several of the students were panting and we were all soaked in profuse tie-dye patterns of sweat and caking dust. On big hikes I tell the students that they need to take extra water even though it adds weight to their back-packs. On the earlier hikes there was no need for extra water, but today was notably different. At the summit a woman asked me if I had anything spare to drink in my pack. I told her I did and asked if she had used her extra water. She said that she did not pack extra water and had drunk the water she brought with her earlier on the way up. I gave her my extra water and was then asked by two other students for water. Their flushed faces indicated that they had to have water right away. I gave them what I had left in my pack as well as a container of apple juice I did not drink during our lunch break.

Other students said that they had the same problem, either they drank all the water they had, or they did not bring extra. Though it was later in the afternoon there was still several hours of sunlight left in the day. The way down was long, and I was not sure how well several of the students would bear up in the heat. I was not sure about myself either. From the summit I could see the valley a long way off where our vans were parked. I took a compass bearing and told the group that we would aim to descend in a more or less straight line toward Derwent Water, which was clearly visible in the far distance. The sooner we could get down the better; we were all of the same mind on that count. For about forty minutes we covered a fair amount of ground fairly quickly, though much of the terrain we could see from the summit was obscured by the convoluted pitch of the trail. Ahead a rolling descent down a grassy decline leading to a small ridge looked inviting and easy in comparison to the rocks and boulders we had been picking our way through up to this point. At the ridge I immediately thought of Coleridge's description of his descent from Scafell Pike where he found himself on a ledge with what appeared to be no exit. I really did not want the duplicate Coleridge's situation. Below the ridge I could see what I was sure was the trail leading to Sty Head, but to get there was another significant issue.

Sizing up a way to move on made me deeply uneasy. I could not see an obvious way of descending; every possibility seemed to arrive at a dead end on the side of a cliff. With the heat and thirst as incentives I looked with greater precision and followed a very small ledge angling downward with my eyes. A section of the ledge was very narrow, but it was near the end of the downward line. I talked with the students about our options. We could go back up and look for the trail we had ascended, although that would take time and a lot of energy, or we could take the unconventional, teasing way before us. Great care and discipline were essential; our movements would be measured and slow.

One fellow, head down and red-faced, said that he had a fear of heights. My instinct was to sit down, talk to him, and reassure him that he could sift his way along the ledge; we would all be with him. But I did not do that. We had a long way to go; he was strong and athletic, and the group needed to go ahead. I told him I would guide him by staying next to him and talking him through. Barbara set out in the lead and I stayed at the back of the group with the fellow who was in some distress. Each step was calculated and as the group moved onto the ledge and advanced, I could feel in the movements of the student I was guiding a rising confidence. I told him to look just at the rock face before him and shuffle slowly to his left toward me. His movements were deliberate and light footed. Stopping at one point he breathed deeply, looked up with a pained expression, and then continued to move steadily. We were two thirds along the ledge; I could see that the rest of the group was safely down and watching the student with me intently.

Time seemed to have disappeared, I felt there to be no movement forward in time; we were in an apparent unending present. My shaking legs and hands seemed to be radiating electric static in the center of immobility. The ledge wrapped around a jutting rock from the cliff face, and next to the rock a small spring of water created a break in the otherwise smooth rock face of the cliff. The spring was only a few feet above my head and some grass peeked over the cliff. The student with me was much taller than I and he said that he could see a way out. Instantly, shocking me, he hiked himself up on the broken rocks in the spring, and he kept going. The suddenness of his movements unbalanced me briefly before I followed him. Internally my emotions were scrambling to sort out what to do. I believed that going up as we were doing was going to make things worse, and I had doubts about how I could get him and myself down again.

Rising onto the cliff top I could see immediately that the grass stretched out for hundreds of yards, and the land sloped downward. The young man was sitting calmly, and apologized for bolting, but more so for being afraid. I assured him that he showed courage in dealing with his deep-seated fears, and he had come through with a far better solution than I had. Standing up and looking down we could see the rest of the group below and loudly cheering. The ground we were on connected to where the group was. Where we were could not be seen from above, the protruding rock from the face where the student and I had come up blocked the connection. No matter, at this point we were safe again.

Rejoining the group brought sincere expressions of cheer for the student and praise for his fortitude. Smiling broadly, he accepted backslaps and chest bumps. We were on our way again. Gaining the lower ground brought some relief from the heat as parts of other mountain peaks in the range cast welcomed shadows. Near the base a small tarn with its ice-cold water proved to be a temptation not to be resisted. Three of the men stripped off their clothing and plunged in the blessed relief of the tarn. Some women with greater discretion, after the men left the water and were dressed, simply jumped into the water, clothes and all, a few emulated the men. Barbara and I were invited to join them, but we declined. Thoughts of riding back the two hours to Kiplin Hall in wet clothing had no appeal for us. Besides I felt too drained to make the effort. Perhaps the womens' impulsive behavior was foolish, but they were young and in spite of some later discomfort owing to saturated clothing, they would have the distinct pleasure in this moment of bringing immediate relief from the parching heat we had endured today. Kelly Topita captured her impressions in a journal entry this way, "We climbed to the summit of Scafell Pike, the highest mountain in England; we also hit two other peaks on the way, hiking 16 miles in 8 1/2 hours to about 4,000 feet high. I never thought I could do something like this; I feel incredible. On the mountain we discussed Coleridge. I only remember "Kubla Khan." It wasn't hard to see how Scafell could have inspired him. I felt as though we might be trapped in a crazy man's "pleasure dome," in fact I've felt that way most of the time here. It's like living in a fairytale: everything is more vivid, felt more acutely. Plus, they have potato chips, I mean crisps, in every flavor imaginable. At the bottom of the mountain we jumped in a pond. It was the most satisfying victory dip ever, then we had to hurry up and change into dry clothes before a shepherd saw us naked. And we couldn't understand a thing he said." Reflecting further she later added this observation to her journal," I still consider climbing Scafell Pike one of my proudest accomplishments and I still think back to one of the best lessons I learned in the mountains which is that if you're going to get anywhere—if you're going to travel the world or climb a mountain or write poetry—sometimes your entire world has to be the three feet in front of you, because the present is the only place when you can accomplish anything new."

Yet again, Barbara and I decided not to include Scafell Pike into future itineraries. The hike is difficult enough, but so much depended on weather conditions. Our first ascent was bone chilling and the second was roasting. Two years later, however, prompted by the urging of Frank, my son-in-law, we talked about the possibility of taking on Scafell Pike. The students were looking for challenges and they were a spirited group. We put off making a decision until, in the second week of the program, a crystal clear, cool day with a weather forecast without a mention of rain or excessive heat, led to another journey to Seatoller and Scafell Pike. Often the air in the Lakes has a unique quality where an underlying chill gets covered with a layer of rapid warmth from the direct sunshine. The effect is bracing, pushing emotions high. The hike up to the summit was what we had come to know, and everyone was moving at a sustained, lively pace. The boulder field preceding the cairn at the summit was the only section that slowed us down. Recollections of conditions and feelings at this point in the past came to me with vigor, and I felt very confident that we had finally reached a secure feeling in connection with this mountain. Students were singing "The Wind Beneath My Wings" loudly as I approached them.

Indeed, it was a day for soaring spirits. They were overjoyed at reaching our goal for the day in a time well ahead of what we anticipated. We all sat facing north with the stones of the cairn at our backs, protecting us from the chilly wind. Just looking out at the tops of the mountains, illuminated vibrantly by the midday sun, and seeing the vast number of valleys way below allowed us to think our own thoughts peacefully. The joy that comes from earning the view from hours of climbing was not spoken of but felt by all and evident in the eager and smiling expressions on the faces surrounding us. Normally we do not spend much time at the summit of mountains we have climbed, largely because the weather can change rapidly, and typically the summits are generally windy and cold. Today was the remarkable exception and we were luxuriating in the unique tranquility enveloping us and absorbing the gigantic view from the top of the tallest Mountain in England.

But we did need to begin the descent since it would take several hours to complete. As I rose to put my backpack on, I heard Barbara cry out that she was hurt. Several of us converged where she was lying in the boulder field with her left leg caught among several rocks. Barbara has a remarkably high tolerance for pain, when I knelt down next to her, she was quivering, her eyes watering, and I knew this was a serious injury. As she stood up to begin the descent, the stone she was standing on wobbled, her foot slipped into a crevasse among the boulders, and her body weight shifted as she fell, while her right ankle was locked between the rocks, causing a "pop." Frank immediately tightened her boot to keep imminent swelling down, and in a short period of time Barbara had composed herself. Here we were literally at the top of the highest mountain in England facing a major descent.

Figure 24: Approaching the Summit of Scafell Pike

Source: Barbara Gillin

Barbara and I talked over the options. I could call Mountain Rescue and it was likely that they could fly since the weather was so favorable. The associated problem with a rescue was that we needed someone to drive her van and no one in the group was old enough to drive a rented vehicle, not to mention the fact that they would need insurance. She rejected the rescue option, a good thing because our cell phones did not work from where we were. Scafell is in the most remote area of the Lakes, and in England for that matter. Carrying her was the next option, but the boulder field was treacherous for one-person walking let alone two people carrying someone. In the midst of going through possibilities Frank picked Barbara up, put her on his back and proceeded to pick his way among the boulders. I knew I could not match his strength and dexterity, but worried about how long he could keep going. He moved with deliberate, steady, and measured steps for more time than I thought possible. At the end of the boulder field he placed Barbara down, took a little time, suggested that we worry about the vans after we got Barbara down, and made a suggestion about the next section of the descent.

From the edge of the boulder field the trail was clear, but it plummeted at a gut-tightening angle. Carrying Barbara down was not a good idea since a misstep could mean a dangerous fall. Barbara was very appreciative of Frank's help, but insistent on climbing down on her own. I pointed out the foolishness of her desire; her ankle was already injured; it would not take much to make it worse, and given the sheer drop off from where we were, dangerous because it was weak. She was not to be deterred. With the boot tightened she could stand lightly. She took a couple of tentative steps, and I told her to stop for a moment, I had an idea. Along with us for a short time was a faculty member from another school; he was considering how to organize a program of his own/ and asked if we could show him what we do, which we agreed to. He was tall and my idea was to have him go in front of Barbara with Frank and myself behind her so we could more or less envelop her should she stumble or need a sure grip. His height put his shoulders at Barbara's waist so she could balance herself by gripping his shoulders. Advancing was foot by foot with many rests. The initial steepness was a constant threat, and the rocks, slippery with running spring water, did not provide any sense of security. The wonderful trek up to the summit turned into a fight with the mountain, yet again. With our collective attention riveted on each movement we all bonded in the single-minded focus on Barbara, but in a way that none of us would have preferred.

Hours passed and fortunately the weather was kind to us, it remained sunny, cool, and dry. The increase in the sound of trickling water signaled that we were getting close to the tree line, and we could see the trail broadening. Students volunteered to take a position with Barbara and continued chatting encouragingly about the progress she was making. Throughout the climb down, Barbara never complained and continued to encourage students to keep up with her. Her enthusiasm and concern for the students was undiminished by her injury. Arriving at the farm road where the vans were parked brought no change to Barbara's face. She looked ahead steadfastly and said that she would be ready to drive when the students had changed out of their boots. One student said that he could operate the accelerator and Barbara could steer and work the clutch. She merely looked at him and thanked him for his consideration, but, no, she would drive without help. The drive back to Kiplin Hall seemed easy in comparison to the events of the day. On the way I kept thinking about why it was that something always seemed to go wrong for us on Scafell Pike. I concluded that climbing was something like baseball, success as a batter means one hit in three at bats, in climbing there are multiple contingencies and overcoming a third of them makes for success. As opposed to Wordsworth I did not believe that nature always has our best interests at heart, but I do feel that we can learn much about ourselves in our connection to nature and the natural rhythms of nature.

Our experiences at Scafell were dramatic, exhausting, and frightening. In the process we learned that experience and perseverance allowed us to find our waythrough significant difficulties. The parallels with studying literature and the way literature means were clearly evident to me. Barbara's heroic descent was an object lesson in courage in spite of pain, and an example of what we as humans are capable of in critical circumstances. Frank's willingness to ease Barbara's pain at a considerable cost to himself as she faced the boulder field, and the willingness of students to give of themselves in helping throughout illustrated fundamental human kindness. My understanding of the natural world and our relationship to it as a way to find who we are by reflecting on our plans and expectations and how those plans and expectations collide with unforeseen and uncontrollable circumstances deepened on Scafell Pike. It is not that we define ourselves, but that we can discover what is in us, and what we can rise to do.

Were the Scafell climbs worth the discomfort and fright? Yes. None of them was easy by any means but the demands put on us by circumstances made us get out of our conventional perception of limits and led us to the realization that there are ways through the most trying of challenges. Hope is a driving force in life especially in our collective desire for a more congenial and civilized world and hope experienced in the harshness of painful circumstances cannot be easily discarded. Every generation has to face a world that seems destined to destruction by one force or another. The causes and reasons for dreadful circumstances like the proliferation of barbaric terrorist attacks, a political system that seems at a breaking point, and cynicism about the value of higher education can drain hope from the most optimistic individual. Living in the first world gives us a legion of privileges, but also limits us. Most of us are insulated from the daily and ordinary privations suffered by millions of people in the world. I believe that we cannot know and experience that world fully because of who we are and what we know. I am not suggesting that slum tourism is a useful choice; that is merely a manifestation of our societal limits. I do believe that the experiences the students have had in the Scafell climbs as well as all the other climbs in England where we had to extend ourselves physically and emotionally, provide a means by which the essential elements of our respective characters are shaped and confronted in creative ways. The climbs and what was gained from them captures what Humanities teachers aim for in the scope of readings they assign students. Former students have written to me and told me how much their lives were changed by their participation in the Kiplin Hall Program. I attribute that change to a discovery of hope; hope learned in the confrontation with nature where the unexpected and how we respond to change is the norm.

Scafell Pike is in a particularly beautiful and remote area of the Lakes. From Keswick take the B5289 toward Seatoller. The drive is remarkably beautiful. Turn left just before Seatoller at the Thorneythwaite Farm. Park along the farm road. The trail is straight ahead through a residence and farm buildings.

Ireland

I who have stood dumb
When your betraying sisters,
Cauled in tar,
Wept by the railings,

Who would connive?
In civilized outrage
Yet understand the exact
And tribal, intimate revenge
(Seamus Heaney, *Punishment,* from *North)*

Figure 25: Shamrocks: West Cork Ireland

Source: Kelley Holocker

In Ireland, our days are somewhat different from our time in England, though the essential aim of connecting literature with the various landscapes remained the same. Students by this time in the program have learned to expect the unexpected, and Ireland never fails us on that point. Meals are served at the Perrine Inn; we only need to prepare our own lunches, so we begin our walks at ten in the morning instead of eight. The change in the day's start also underscores the way that time moves differently in Ireland. We all learn to absorb the moment and diminish the urge to get things done immediately. The ordinary seems to be more purposeful without a preconceived sense of order. Being in Glengarriff we are located in the heart of the West Cork and Kerry mountains; consequently, we do not need to drive very far to launch into the landscape. As in England the aim of each day is to hike through various landscapes and connect poetry by Irish poets to what we encounter. Unlike England there are no trails in general, so we make our way in good spirits and faulty directions. The well-worn trails of the Lake District provide a notable contrast to the adventure of setting off on wet ground that devolves into bogs in West Cork. Staying dry is not an option even for the most fastidious individual as the students learn in the first ten steps. Sliding and slipping quickly become the norm; bolstered by a good sense of humor.

Gouganbarra for years was our first hike from Glengarriff. The location is picture perfect on a clear day, with the secluded pine forest at the base of the horseshoe shaped mountain range, suggesting freshness and comfortable isolation. Even on a wet day the mists chasing each other up to the summits are enchanting. As is often the case appearances and reality can diverge markedly. During our first experience the richly tinted green moss growing profusely on the trees and everything else rising out of the ground should have been a clue that endemic wetness comes with consequences. Opening the doors of the vans had us sucking in clouds of midges, everyone twisting and waving to fend the flies off. Comical as we probably appeared to bystanders, no one was laughing in the vans. The offending midges could hardly be seen, but their descent on us was suffocating. Driving away from the pine forest was prime, and once away from the stately pine trees clad in velvet like moss, Barbara and I had to re-imagine how to start our climb.

With the luck of the Irish or the luck of being in Ireland, we both noticed a sign with a hiker on it, a sort of international indication of a trail. The sign was a revelation. We never encountered designated trails in the past, so our foray into the haunt of the midges ended in a most valuable discovery. We began with a good-natured laugh at ourselves for being so overwhelmed by the flies, and an optimistic attitude since the sky was deep, enchanting blue, and a gravelly trail was clearly marked. A series of steep switchbacks led us along a farm road to a stile. Over the stile we were on rough ground without a path but with trail markers. Large grass tufts seemed to get larger as we plodded our way upward. Suddenly as we approached the first in a series of grassy cliffs held in place by a substantial number of rocks, the ground became sodden with water and muck. The suck and wheeze of each step was tiresome and unpleasant. Muddy water splashed everywhere and irrigated our shoes in just a few minutes. Socks laden with mud draped over our boots. The prospect of slogging along was dispiriting.

The high ground before us raised our collective hope; once above the mud bath we believed that we would find footing that would be secure and light. So, we believed. Hand over hand climbing brought us up on top of a grand looking rock surrounded by boggy grasses. The longed for, dry portion of the hike, never materialized. Bogs were everywhere. Sliding and slipping and an ever-increasing amount of wetness in our boots made the climb something of an ordeal, until we reached the summit of a ridgeline running north and south. Rising over the summit brought a view of Bantry Bay opening itself to the Atlantic Ocean with an easy nonchalance. With the view came ruffling wind chilling our bodies soaked in mud and water, and also buckets of sweat. It was a place to linger, the beauty of the view taking our breaths as much as the climb. But the rapidity of the chill made everyone want to move to keep warm. Hunger dictated that we needed to stop to have lunch, so cold as we were growing, we found a huddle of rocks where we could find shelter from the wind. At that point I noticed that one of the students was missing, and Frank and I set out to find him. About a half hour later we found him, and he was profusely apologetic for his action. He just wanted to be alone and so he raced far ahead of the group and lost contact. Frank and I nodded to each other in gratitude that Doug was unhurt, and we moved very quickly to meet up with the group, lunch and a discussion. Doug sent me what he wrote about that incident after his return to the United States, and it revealed to me how much there is in any event that is greater than our initial impressions. It is like the way poetry often works where meaning keeps unveiling itself over a period of time. Doug wrote, "There was little to be viewed, as there often is on the Irish countryside, through torrents of fog, mist, and rain.

I forged on, running alone in air made of floating water. I don't remember much about the path. I could barely see a large rock licked with slime over here, a puddle there, a few gnarly trunks without their complement of leaves, the metal signs importunately welcoming travelers to a ruined castle a few kilometers away. For a minute I stopped running and realized how out of place I felt, more out of place than those metal signs. My pace slowed and my heartbeat eased its swell. Suddenly remembering there was a whole group of hikers and, I guessed correctly, two agitated professors searching for me, I plopped myself and my pack down on a large round stone jutting upwards from the ground. The wind calmed. The mist thinned out. I looked around me in every direction and noticed I was sitting on the edge of a small mountain meadow.

Lichens and moss crept over everything. Gale forces on the crisp air dazzled with motes of dew that flickered as they swirled. Tarns marked the deep places where rain gathered. I peered into one of those little ponds beneath the rock where I sat. Past my rippling reflection, scarlet and purple vines jeweled the undersurface. My hand permeated the moving mirror, and I inspected the fronds and leaves without bringing them above the water. After splashing my face and sipping enough from my palm to taste it, I looked up and continued gazing, counting more than fifteen shades of green among a host of other colors I had never seen in the real. My nose learned a different sweetness every way the wind breathed. Everything I touched was pleasantly damp, cool, refreshing. And there was the music—the cacophony of birds and insects whose patterned calls were entirely unfamiliar to me. You are dreaming or dead, I thought, you slipped on a stone that gave way and sent you toppling head-first into a nasty, skull-splitting end. Upon reasoning that I was neither dreaming, nor deceased, I experienced a sensation I didn't know.

I was terribly afraid of silence and loneliness, in the short- and long-term senses of those words. I used to do whatever I could to populate quiet with manufactured noise, empty space with company. But there, lost in the surreal dampness of that place that felt like a dream (Or a dream of a dream, I heard a book from my childhood whisper to me), I recognized how I had never felt so comfortably and happily alone. Those few minutes of solitude owned no concrete sense of time. I could have been there for hours, years, centuries. I imagined the crew finding me like Rip Van Winkle, my hiking fatigues tattered, my snowy beard long and wiry. There in the Irish wilderness, I found myself capable of simultaneously engaging with everything around me, my thoughts, my memories, my education, my faults, my hopes and dreams, all at once, and clearly. I had to confront who I really was.

In that self-awareness, I immediately made a personal connection with Wordsworth's "Lines Composed a Few Miles above Tintern Abbey," which we'd read in England just some days before. I saw myself like the speaker, who "bounded o'er the mountains…more like a man / Flying from something that he dreads, than one / Who sought the thing he loved." What had I been dreading in myself? I was drinking too much. I was acting out and speaking thoughtlessly in my daily haze. I wasn't focusing on the things in life I held to be truly important to who I am. In that inescapable, piercing solitude, I understood what caused me to burst away from the group was a reflection of my own behavior. Just as I saw my physical reflection in the clear tarn, my experience on Gougane Barra forced me to hold the proverbial mirror to myself and view my own humanity with abrupt and shocking clarity. Few other moments in my life have felt so real and revealing, and I continue to feel fortunate for how they colored my perspective."

Doug's account of his climb and flight along with his reflection on what it meant to him captures the resonance between the physical exertion and inward sensing of both the environment and himself. Seeing himself from a new perspective in strained circumstances brought about a new and important level of understanding for him. The echo from Wordsworth provided the frame for his self- reflection, and also provided a new and greater meaning for the poem. Doug embodied what I aim for the Program

Given the chill in our bodies and our experience of bogs first hand, Seamus Heaney's bog poems were especially appropriate. "Punishment" details the imagined execution of a young adulteress, and the speaker's outrage until he confesses that he understands the social and cultural push to go ahead with the execution and acknowledges his silent complicity in the imagined past and the present time of turmoil. Heaney's directness and spare language makes the poem lean and powerful, haunting the reader's sensibilities in the poem's atmospherics and its relevance to contemporary troubles. Much about Irish history is unknown to the students, and North/South, Catholic/Protestant significance needs clarification.

I explain to them that the fight is not religious in the sense that each side is trying to convert or eliminate the other over religion alone; it is about civil rights. The longstanding legacy of deadly religious differences is the substructure of contemporary strife. No one cares where people go to church; they do care about having a future. From the Protestant side there is fear that Catholic rights will endanger employment, political power, and educational opportunities, from the Catholic side being able to secure a job, decent housing, and political justice. The habit of hating the other side is generations old and fertilized by ever new killings and maimings. Like all history Irish history is convoluted, complex, and sad in ways that defy logic. The lines:

> *I almost love you*
> *But would have cast, I know,*
> *The stones of silence*

are the cause of strong responses from the students. "The ghastly situation cannot be ignored," comes from one girl, complemented by another girl's outrage in support. I respond by asking, "Is Heaney being honest in the lines by showing how even under revolting, particular circumstances there is a bigger cultural picture?" By degrees the students come to feel the terrible pull of human compassion on one hand, and the pull of custom on the other. As the center of the diametrically opposed forces Heaney must contend with forging a self without a resolution beyond the honest exposition of how he feels and acts. Human nature is capacious and formulations about the reasons why things develop, what they mean, and what they might portend about the future demand a broad perspective and careful scrutiny.

Preconceptions about what being Irish means is freighted with distortions largely cooked up in popular culture. In a film where the sound of a penny whistle and a fiddle precede an actor's entrance there is a kind of shorthand leading the audience to expect an Irishman, who is probably going to be drunk, looking for a fight, a trickster, and slightly dim individual. The Irish stereotypes crop up in the nineteenth century, particularly in the popular Punch magazine in England where the Irish were represented as being brutish, dirty, and ape like. Sub-human imagery of the Irish continued into the twentieth century in England and America. On stage the "stage Irishman," thick brogue, a tendency to the irrational and other worldly and at odds with social sophistication became a mainstay of American entertainment. At mid-century, film absorbed the stereotype but softened the brittle edges from earlier depictions by infantilizing the Irish. In "The Quiet Man," for example, Ireland is portrayed as a natural fairyland pastorally perfect, with a beautiful, young and innocent girl, the natural partner the American, Sean, coming "home" to a place he has only heard about in glowing terms. To Sean as an outsider everything the native Irish do is perplexing, childish, comic, and frustratingly immobilizing by customs he does not understand. However, amid the cultural confusion that Sean encounters, paralleling the audience's experiences and assumed reactions, there is a good-natured subtext assuring the audience, and Sean, that all will be well in the end. Fierce issues connected to drinking, religious strife, poverty, and political control are glanced over, as is right in the kind of film the "Quiet Man" is. The general effect of the film is to strengthen a particular perception of Ireland and the Irish natives.

It is against those stereotypes that I discuss the way that Heaney uses history and his vibrant reactions to contemporary conditions in Northern Ireland. The stony, empty landscape scoured by winds rushing from the Atlantic Ocean where we sit supplement the directness of Heaney's poems and serves to undermine the conventional nod to the Irish stereotype. The grey, white mountain side streaked by strands of green moss and ragged grasses seductively embraced by feathery mists is the stuff of contemplation and the poetry of Patrick Kavanaugh. The Beara Peninsula is the subject and controlling metaphor of Leanne O'Sullivan's re-writing of the "Hag of Beara." These three poets serve as our connection to the landscapes of West Cork, Kerry and rural Ireland. Supplementing the reading assignments is Vince Fitzgibbon, my Son-in-Law Frank's father. A native of Cork living first in the country, and later in the city, Vince brings with him what seems like an unending series of stories both literary and historical, as well as the ability to recite from memory vast tracts of Irish poetry. He can recite literally for hours and sing even longer. His good humor and his willingness to sing a hefty variety of Irish songs from the past have made him a natural asset to our time in Ireland. In his mid-eighties he climbs mountains with us, often leading the way with his thorn stick in hand, and under his tweed hat. His tales about growing up in rural Ireland fascinates students because of the gap between their lives and his. Talking about self-reliance and finding joy in simple pleasures resonate with the students, and their questions about endurance and perseverance reflect their concerns as they look out to a world where fear, social and economic discord, and conformity seem to have the high ground.

Vince takes the students' concern seriously and as he tells them about his family history in the context of Irish history, they respond by peppering him with questions about what it was like to grow up on a farm isolated from the diversions of city life. With a chuckle he describes simplicities, and without rancor challenges them to try living without the intrusions of various forms of electronic media. Reading was the great staple in his life and has remained with him. One student adds, "That before the Kiplin Hall trip he would have scoffed at what he is saying, but now, having been away from his cell phone he likes the sense of freedom." Others note how they feel that they can absorb their environment now more forcefully and have a clear recollection of what they have felt on the trip." Vince suggests reading, especially poetry as a way to human wisdom. The students assent by nodding their heads.

To get to the Gougan Barra Forest Park from Bantry take the N71 toward Ballylickey. At Ballylickey turn right onto the R 584. Continue on to the entrance of the park on the left. In addition to several trails the park contains the remains of Finbar's Monastery and the beginning of the Lee River which runs through Cork City.

Molly Gavigan's

What was better then

Than to crush a leaf or a herb
Between your palms,

The wave it slowly, soothingly
Past your mouth and nose

And breathe?

(Seamus Heaney, *A Herbal*, from *Human Chain*)

Figure 26: Along the Way on the Old Cart Road, Kenmare

Source: Kelley Holocker

For years, we have traveled the road between Glengarriff and Kenmere; about midway we passed what looked like a tourist trap, woolens for sale, as well country hats, wax jackets, thorn sticks in a farm setting with farm implements and tools set out. Last year we stopped and found much to my surprise a wonderful place to hike from, and, yes, to buy an array of Irish goods. Molly Gavigan lived on the farm, enduring a very hard life, typical in many ways for country people. Farms are even now far flung, but there is a communal sense of belonging in the landscape by the inhabitants whose families have lived in the area for many, many generations. As a way to keep the land as it has been, and to protect it, a man named Stephen explained that the local people have agreed to develop a kind of tourist trade so that they can keep living where they are. Part of their vision is to open the land for people just like us, hikers. To that end they have marked trails over a diverse landscape of rolling fields, rocky cliffs rising to the top of the Healy Pass, and grassy valleys.

Our walk took us initially through displays of the traditional farm and then on to wide-open spaces undulating among working farms toward a mountain summit. Since our time driving to the beginning of our hike was only a half hour, everyone was rich with energy. Without bogs to contend with in the early stages of the hike, and the pulse of energy in the fast pace of the group, we ascended well up toward the summit in relatively quick order. For lunch I found a grassy perch out of the wind presenting us with a panorama of the far-reaching valley below.

During lunch, I read some poems by Patrick Kavanaugh to the students. One of them was "Spraying the Potatoes" where Kavanaugh depicts the yearly act of doing an important but routine duty. Since we had just walked through fields with potatoes the connection with the poem was direct. The ordinariness of Kavanaugh's setting in the poem leans into his recognition that the old man he meets and their talk "was the theme of kings, a theme for strings." The ordinary in his view is never ordinary, great value can be discovered in any moment. And so Kavanaugh describes himself as a "poet lost to potato fields." Remembering the sensual specifics in the scene brings unity to his life and sensibilities as he acknowledges. Having shared a good range of experiences together, and studied a fair array of poetry in the program most of the students have developed a keener sense of how to look at the natural world surrounding them, and the apparent simplicity of Kavanaugh's poem strikes an elemental cord for many of them. "Inniskeen Road: July Evening" celebrates wonder and imagination stemming from the conventional aspects of an obscure village life and leads the speaker to embrace his world as, "A road, a mile of kingdom, I am king/Of banks and stones and every blooming thing." Joy in the act of living provides a sub-text for what we are doing in connecting with the landscape, its physical features and the sense impressions made on us.

Particularities of where we are in Ireland, the physical elements such as the wind, rocks, grasses, and streams have counterparts with what we felt and saw in England, but they are not identical. The light is different here in its relentless glare through roiling clouds, making the landscape hard and secretive. Farms below, rich in the prospect of a fine harvest, jar against history, the potato blight bringing starvation, emigration on a staggering scale, and general misery for those who stayed and barely survived. Now where there is abundance once there was nothing. We are travelling through a landscape for pleasure and instruction where people in the past suffered greatly. It is hard to put the two realms of experience together; they seem and feel so diametrically opposed. Imagining the earlier time requires cunning to try to get around our way of life and the consequent view we develop of the world. Total success is impossible, we cannot shed who we are and all that shapes us but willing ourselves into a sort of Keatsian Negative Capability and taking in the hard landscape enveloping us, our imaginations can make an authentic connection. Students talk about their perceptions and feelings linking Kavanaugh's gratitude and joy for living in his physically constricting and limited world, to the severity of our environment high up as we are. The students have been living largely without technical assistance. That is, they have disconnected from cell phones and the internet because of where we are and have been in areas not served consistently by technical services. Leaving the technically connected world and finding other resources to take their attention was not easily nor entirely desired by them. But freedom from the continual bombardment of messages and the expectation of immediate response, not to mention the amount of time spent on Facebook and the like, has altered the way they construct the tempo of their days and led to a recognition of a different perception of time to think and contemplate about what they are doing. Ireland and literature are beguiling.

After lunch, we continue ascending and our bus driver, Martin, who has asked to join us on the hike, tells us about a Bronze Age quarry just before the summit. Looking at the quarry, I would not have known what it is but for the information from our driver; it serves as a reminder of how much we miss when we think we have taken the scene in. It is a reminder of how our perception of the world around us filters what we think we are seeing. We miss much, though we feel we know what we see. I mention this thought to the students and one replies, "Isn't that why poetry is so important; our sensibilities get altered?" She has made my day! Yes, literature makes a difference in intensely valuable ways. The side of the mountain looks carved to a height of about twelve feet and about fifteen feet deep. It does not exactly blend into the mountain scape, but it could easily be passed by with no notion of it. The layering of the rock seems parallel to how we live in one layer of time and place and can come to a conception of what we perceive as real. Understanding our relationship to other layers of time and place provides a richer insight of our vantage point in existence; poetry in conjunction with experience can give us that altered perception.

A short time later, we achieve the summit of the Healy Pass and can look out at what seems to be the whole world. Audible gasps come from the students, as they respond to the dramatic interplay of light, sky, earth, and in the distance Bantry Bay with its deep blue color in sharp contrast to the gray, green and sepia hues leading up to it. Wind is no less dramatic, its staccato pulses alternately pushing us back and then releasing its force. Breathing deeply in the crisp, moving air purifies our lungs and revives our desire to absorb what we see and sense here. There is little talking going on. Each person seems to be concentrating on his or her own thoughts, and it is my hope that they are storing up impressions that will give them insights into what their experience in gaining this summit means to them. A student breaks the silence with the observation that next week at this time she will be back in the USA where it will be very hot, and that she wishes she could stay here longer. The process of reflection and perception is beginning for her I think to myself.

Picking our way down is always more difficult for me than going up a mountain. Given the precariousness of the trail with very steep descents at each stage, every step must be calculated, at least for me. Several students bound down with deer-like surety, while my legs shimmy and shake to the edge of seemingly endless bog land. Almost on cue someone ahead of me has stepped directly into a bog up to her waist.

Flailing vigorously and shouting she seems to be a comic performer, and laughter surrounds her. Her wide-eyed and clenched facial expression, with her emphatic shrieks to, "Get me out!" make it clear that nothing is comic for her. Yanking her out brought immediate relief to her, and after a few shaky moments she bloomed into a broad smile and laughed at herself. Soaking in slimy, wet mud made her want to get moving again before she became cold, so on we went, becoming wet and muddy ourselves as we tramped through bog after bog.

Our arrival at Molly Gavigan's brightened our flagging spirits and sore bodies. Tea was available so most of us squeezed into a small stone walled room with a roughly hewn table and benches worn down with age and use, while others looked for the perfect Irish sweater or hat. After a day outdoors and especially after a demanding hike up a mountain and back, the snug warmth of a small room with the shared sense of having used our bodies well, anticipating tea and freshly made scones with butter, whipped cream, and jam, is a delight to me above all others. The palpable conviviality in the smiling faces along with the banter recounting the challenges in the climb, and personal successes in reaching the summit magnify the warming pleasure of freshly brewed tea. The warm glow following the taking of tea is enhanced by the guilty pleasure of eating scones laden with whipped cream. The best in the world seems to be in this humble cave of a room. As everyone talks in successively louder tones, there is a sub-tone of understanding going on as well, heard underneath the chatter, and made visible in everyone's eyes. No one is interested in leaving the room; it is a time to hold onto and embrace. Without saying anything we all recognize the rich pleasure in each other's company that has been contoured by our hike and the food we have consumed together. Reluctant to break the spell as the glow diminishes, we must get back to Glengarriff, so one by one we sort our way out. The afterglow continues as the whole group reassembles, then off we go. I hope they cherish the afterglow as much as I do.

The N71 leads from Glengarriff to Kenmare. About mid-way, in the heart of the Bonane Valley, Molly Gavigan's tea and gift shop and farm museum is the beginning of a trail which traverses a variety of landscape elements, and eventually leading to remarkable views of Bantry Bay and its surroundings.

The Perrine Inn

In fact, the whole truth about Ireland is as elusive a commodity as Irish coal.

(Terry Eagleton, *The Truth about the Irish*)

With the sun lowering the evening beckons with the promise of music in the pub as well as singing and dancing. While in England the pub closest to Kiplin Hall, the White Heifer, is a convivial place, and we have enjoyed our time there. The patrons and the owners are very welcoming to us, and there is a generally friendly atmosphere. One memorable occasion was when the World Cup was in progress and England had a big game with Portugal. Ordinarily there was no television in the pub, but because England was in a big game a wide screen television was set up, and the pub was out the door with people. When England scored a goal there was a roar from the patrons. When Portugal scored my Irish son in law, Frank, cheered loudly all by himself. I looked to him perplexed and a little afraid. We were in England among English football fans. It was like making fun of Nascar in Alabama I thought. The people in the pub knew us and remained gracious, and we left after a pint. I asked him why he had rooted for Portugal, and he said that as an Irishman he could not root for England. As much fun as our experiences at the White Heifer have been, in mostly subtle ways, we are clearly outsiders, tolerated and enjoyed, but outsiders. In Ireland, though, pub life is markedly different. Patrons are expected to contribute to the evening's entertainment either by singing a song, telling a story, playing a musical instrument, or some other form of entertainment.

The owner of the Perrine Inn, Pat Sommers, has consistently gone out of his way to make us feel welcome in his pub and in Glengarriff. He arranges for musical entertainment for each of the evenings we are there and embodies a generous informality. After living four and eight to a room at Kiplin Hall, the two to a room accommodation in Ireland are a welcome change for the students. The pub is a three-story building, the bar and dining room downstairs, and the upper two floors the Sommers' residence. Surrounding the pub on two sides is a series of cottages with four rooms to a cottage. Seeing it brings to mind the sort of motel with cabins built in the late 1940s across America as highways opened access to a nation on the go. Students since our first arrival at the pub many years ago have enjoyed its rustic simplicity and friendly atmosphere. Several students over the years have stated that they feel as though they have come home because of the natural and unforced way conversations arise. Local people seem interested in them and their views on world issues. As opposed to home though they also remark on how time does not seem to be important to local people. I explain that "Irish time" is time out. Only two years ago, Wi-fi access became available, though cell phone service is erratic. Interestingly with Internet communication now available, most of the students do not rush to check their email. Being without email contact for the preceding two weeks seems to have tempered their urge to connect electronically. As wonderful as electronic communications are and all the related benefits of technology, which are undeniable, I think that many students understand a new level of joy possible in their lives as a result of what we have been through in the program. Seemingly simple things such as breathing the clear crisp air at the top of a mountain, or seeing a difficult day in wind and rain through to its planned conclusion leading to a reward of hot tea with friends in a warm dry room has made students' unique experience of their emotions in conjunction with the natural world richer and more trenchant.

From Bantry follow the N71 to get to Glengarriff. The Perrine Inn is on the right in town.

Glengarriff

A light that might be mystic or a fraud
Played on the far hills beyond all common sight,
And some men said that it was Adam's God
As Adam saw before the Apple-bite.

(Patrick Kavanaugh, *After May*)

Associating with local people in the pub makes us feel that we belong and are openly welcomed. Conversations run from politics to literature, to popular culture and the arts without the hard edges of ideology or missionary work aimed at conversion. The physical layout of any place tells a story. In America, where strip malls serve as punctuation marks between highways, and the majority of buildings are assembled for utility and functionality, there is little patience for the past. Old buildings yield to new ones that often arise in a very short time, only to be replaced by even newer ones in relatively few years. In Glengarriff, seemingly adrift along the coast-line of Bantry Bay, the buildings seem to grow from the rocky terrain. Damp filters into the stonework camouflaging the buildings, and at continual odds with the perpetual work throughout the year of dressing up the businesses with new paint. The surrounding hills stretching out of the tree line give the town center a snug feeling, and the surfeit of pubs in the four-hundred-yard line of businesses, brings assurance of a place to go out of the elements. The apparent simplicity of the one main street is counterbalanced by a wonderful bayside park filled with walking trails and a children's play area. Winston Churchill stayed in the village, as did George Bernard Shaw, and even Queen Victoria. Actress Maureen O'Hara has lived in Glengarriff as well. It is not hard to speculate about their reasons for staying here.

Early mornings are especially rich in texture. Watching the sunrise as the mists from the bay waft up in feather lightness, and then languidly dissipate before fully evaporating, makes me feel the scene as a reenactment of some timeless moment from the mythic past. Everything seems fresh and new in the morning dampness. The slap and splash of anchored boats in the harbor serves as background accompaniment to the squawk and chirps of birds alternating in the flow of air aloft. The local post office is also the only grocery store in the village. Opening time seems to be the signal for street activity in the village as regular customers arrive. On a daily basis we buy supplies for lunch, which means that we practically strip the shelves of baguettes, cheese, cold cuts and peanut butter. The O'Shea's who run the store have become used to our visit each year and they make a point of baking additional bread for us among other supplies we commonly use. The post office cubical at the rear of the store offers stamps, post cards, phone cards, the weather report (always the same it seems), and gossip. Other shops include Irish- made clothing and souvenirs; the proprietors are glad to see our students since they make purchases. The feel of the village is one of purposeful peacefulness. Tourism seems to be the life-blood, and in order to keep people coming much work goes into support services, and a proud aesthetic. In Glengarriff, the streets are clean, flowers adorn light poles, and hanging baskets rich with colorful blooms accentuate the tidiness of public spaces. Though our time in the village is relatively short we feel comfortable and connected to the village rhythms.

A Day at the Beach Irish Style and Three Castles

As between clear blue and
cloud, Between haystack
and sunset sky Between
oak tree and slated roof

I had my existence. I was
there Me in place and
the place in me

(Seamus Heaney, *A Herbal*)

Figure 27: Three Castles, East Cork

Source: Courtney Fitzgibbon

Discovery is among the delights in Ireland and discovering connections with the Irish is the best. While discussing a visit to Barley Cove Beach with Martin, our bus driver and all-about guide, he mentioned a place very much off the tourist grid by design, and one which he believed strongly that would appeal to the students. And it was located fairly close to the beach. There was a peculiar complication though. We would have to cross privately owned land, and the man that owns it has an aversion to groups. There was a degree of perversity in the situation since the man does not want groups to traverse his property, but he also has a café with signs welcoming visitors, according to Martin. He said he had a plan; he would have us all get off the bus out of sight of the land-owner. It was the bus more than anything that raised the land-owner's ire, so by hiding the bus things should be fine. The mischief involved convinced me to follow the plan, so off we went to visit the Three Castles, as they are known, as well as the beach. Hiking and swimming seemed like a natural to me.

As we began our trek across a sharply sloping hillside, I could see a man coming to us. His agitated way of walking made him appear nervous, at close range he seemed to want to smile but could not quite get there. With a degree of bluntness, he asked me who we were and why we were hiking in the direction of his land. I explained to him the purpose of the program and why we hoped to see the three castles. His face brightened and his shoulders relaxed as he explained his rudeness. He told me, lectured me more precisely, that he was at war with much of the twenty-first century, and the Irish tourist industry, in particular. In short, he did not want tourists gawking about the environs without knowing anything about where they were and having little sense of Irish Culture. The fact that we were reading Irish poetry and making connections to the landscape made us very welcome. I felt somewhat guilty about our bus deception, and I did understand his genuine concern about the commodification of Irishness. What seemed to me at first as quaint, odd, and Irish behavior forced me to think about the way our contemporary culture treats value primarily in monetary form. My sense of his tilting at windmills at first gave way to the realization that he was putting into action the essence of what we were doing in the program. My aim to get beyond the distractions of the tech culture that envelopes us by expanding the feelings and knowledge that experience and careful reading of poetry brings as a way to find our center, was like the man's wish to cut off his part of the world and to reject the superficiality of tourism.

In dazzling sunlight, we skirted the cliffs bordering the surging Atlantic Ocean below us, in air that seemed to be purified just for us, so lovely was the isolation. At the castle thoughts prompted by my discussion with the land-owner entered into the class discussion of Seamus Heaney's The Singer's House. The section of the poem:

> *What do we say any more?*
> *To conjure the salt of the earth.*
> *So much comes and is gone*
> *That should be crystal and kept*
>
> *And amicable weathers*
> *That bring up the grain of things*

Their tang of season and store,
Are all the packing we will get.
(5 – 12)

led to students speculating on what people would be saying about our time on earth in a hundred years from now. "Being here in Ireland makes me wonder about what is going on back home, and little things connected with home seem much more important because I can't be there right now," added a young man. Another student responded, "There is a lot about the ordinary that gets lost or ignored, and isn't that Heaney's point? Valuable, seemingly little things easily drift away and are forgotten. We need to think about the particular context of our lives, and not get lost to a commercial version of what life is." In a journal entry by Jack Despeaux for this day he wrote, "There is a series of hills, plains, and cliffs to explore that must have come from a storybook or one's imagination. We hiked to the remains of a castle to have lunch, but just before we reached the castle, we passed through a rock wall, and on the other side might have been the most beautiful place I have ever seen. Hundreds of feet below me, and on the other side of a wired fence, was the Atlantic Ocean. The surrounding cliffs were behemoths of rock towering over another, a single rock, jutting from the ocean. The waves crashed against the single rock that was between the cliffs, and I couldn't stop watching the water play with the earth. I was pulled away for lunch by the castle but rushed back to the view as soon as Dr. Gillin had finished his post-lunch lecture. I told my friend Amanda that I wished I could stay standing there forever." I trust that his memory and the feelings he discovered will stay with him and prove to be a source of stability like a rudder as he moves into life beyond college.

By the time we rejoined our bus the sky clouded over, but everyone was determined to go for a swim. Barley Cove Beach is dramatically stretched in about a quarter mile sandy arc between cliffs. Much to our surprise Martin started stripping down to a bathing suit and dared everyone to race to the ocean. Like children just let loose from school we dashed across the beach and splashed into the water. The air temperature was about fifty degrees and the water temperature was about the same. I dove into an oncoming wave and immediately took on a choking mouthful of water. My gag reflex had me inhaling ice water as I drove through the surface. Spluttering and instantly cold I was the focal point of glee and laughter. Iron shards of cold seemed to be piercing me all over. What a wimp I thought to myself as I scurried out of the water and into an off shore wind, as if I was not cold enough. Most of the students frolicked and teased me to come back in. I was astonished at their resistance to the cold. Mindful of our discussion at lunch at the castle Carly pointed out how as cold as it was this was an experience not to be had at home in the summer, and therefore it needs to be embraced. Well observed and said.

From Bantry take the N71 south to the R591. Turn right on the R591 through Duras to Barley Cove. Parking at the Beach is clearly marked. Mizen Head and the Three Castles are very nearby.

Hungry Hill

Like shadows courted
Between the rushes,
They climb one by one,

In the night-ebb
Over the borders
Of the rain waxed fields,

Dropping their lichen loads,
Their fossil-loads,
Their darkly pitched breaths

(Leanne O'Sullivan, *The Stones Turning into Mountains Cailleach: The*
Hag of Beara, 1 – 9)

Figure 28: Black Valley Path

Source: Kelley Holocker

Just beyond Ardrigole, a tiny village on the coast line, the mountains rise up into what always seems like perpetual mist, especially in the morning. The UCC (University College Cork) Mountaineering Club regularly climbs in the area and the challenge of making the summit became irresistible to me. Things are getting better in regard to mapping trails and access points, and as a group leader the pressure is on me to make sure we do not trespass, but there is much that remains in a gray area. Gathering information from local hikers and using a tourist map I pieced together a route that seemed straightforward and careful. On our first visit we turned off the main road onto a farm lane a little wider than the width of the vans. A bouncing mile later the road ended at a farmhouse and I developed a sinking feeling that the day's plans were about to be scrambled. Taking a few minutes to size up the immediate surroundings led me to see a stile, a new one clearly. The stile was a trail marker, as good as it gets in this remote area of Ireland, and a lift to my otherwise diminishing spirits. We parked precariously along the verge, made a quick inventory of our supplies, and set off. The first step to the stile should have been seen as a forewarning. The rain sodden grassy bank leading to the stile became a slip and slide venue, everyone quickly drenched in sepia colored water and thick mud. The way up seemed mild, the rise toward the summit lost in the clouds at this time of day looked unthreatening. Two hundred yards into the climb, however, brought the reality of boggy ground well into our awareness of just where we were. Squelching and squishing our way forward, slipping backwards and side-wards, tripping on tufts of grass and the occasional rock, slowed our progress.

We sounded like old-fashioned steam engines as we rasped and huffed for air. At each resting point we could look back at our hard-won progress, only to be admonished by what lay ahead. Vince in his early eighties urged the students on. With his hounds-tooth cap, street shoes, thorn stick, and sports coat topped off with a wool scarf, he stood in contrast to us in our fleeces, brightly colored goretex jackets, boots made out of materials never found in nature and impervious to all manner of elements, it was hard not to feel well below the mark. Being who he is was a non-verbal message to go beyond the lassitude growing among us as the way became difficult.

Then, almost on cue, the sky darkened quickly, winds blew sharply down the slope at us, and the air filled itself with moisture. My hope for a lovely rest in the sun radiated summit looking out at the glazed Atlantic fragmented almost in unison with the deterioration of the weather. Through the rifling raindrops I could see a notch in the ridge ahead and told the students that we would stop there for lunch and a class. "A class?" was the unified reaction from the students. "Well I will try," was my reply. At the ridge the rain dropped with heavy enthusiasm and dampened our own. Urging everyone to get close to the rock outcropping at the ridge, I added that we would eat our lunches here. Water seeped into every seam in my clothing, chilling every movement I made as the wind blew at about forty miles per hour. Uncomfortable as the students were, they never complained. Stoically they ate lunches in the downpour, many of them making light of the situation in a good-natured way. "This will be something to tell our friends at home, or perhaps our children or grandchildren. It's the stuff of legends." As I unwrapped my sandwich the wind, blasting at gale force now, took it, perhaps all the way to Boston, the next landfall.

Vince was the image of resignation and defiance of the weather. He recited poems as we all put our backs to the rock wall in the hopeless desire for relief from the scouring elements. The absurdity of the situation instigated a few chortles among the students, then some giggles, and before long, general laughter in the wind. Talking was useless; nothing could be heard above the roaring wind. One of those moments similar to ones in our earlier treks, arose without expectation. In circumstances well beyond our control, and painfully unpleasant we shared a single focus; we felt a common bond, albeit a shared misery, and knew that we were being changed by our joint bond. We were on our own and at the mercy of harsh natural elements; we had to take responsibility for ourselves as individuals and as a group, and there was will to do that.

As quickly as the rain and wind started, they ceased, and the air warmed enough to be noticed. Glee replaced the somberness of our sodden lunch, and the students wanted to push on to our goal, the summit. Our initial joy at the absence of rain and wind gradually sifted into another level of resignation as we navigated among bogs that had recently been cut for fuel. The sponginess underfoot lapsed into muck and almost every step had to be calculated to find the least likely soft, wet spot. Frustratingly slow, considered movements eventually landed us on a series of rock faces in the rising cliff, raising spirits with the change. The top of the mountain now visible I could feel the energy of the group surge, only to be tempered by a very large bog, followed by an ascending order of ridges, about seventy feet each before our goal. No one was dry, nor unmarked by freely flowing mud, now crusting over on our upper bodies. Picking our way for solid footing became a sort of game. One good foot placement followed by a knee-high sink into the murky ooze. Like some mythic creature the bog kept trying to suck us in, but the deep fellow feeling among group members now pushed back against the bog as each person simply took responsibility to help out anyone who was sinking or stuck. One woman in utter frustration with the slow pace decided to run across what looked like a field of grass. Five yards into her run she sank with a slick slip, high up to the top of her thighs. Finding herself immobilized she began to panic with the sensation that she was sinking and cried out for help. Immediately, the students formed a human chain, themselves sinking as they moved. Gathering her under her shoulders they extracted her from the mud with a whooshing sound, heartening to her ears. Her terror melted into laughter, abetted by her classmates in a wash of emotional support. Back to slow, steady, and safer progress resumed, the climbs over the remaining ridges taking us to our hands and knees. In that moment I saw another confirmation that important changes had taken place for the students. They understood almost instinctively what had to be done, and they moved without regard for their own comfort.

By the time we reached the summit clouds cleared away, the sun smiled on us, and the vista opened so we could see the land caressing the boundary of Bantry Bay, and the Atlantic stretched to the utter end of the horizon. Compensation for all of our efforts to reach this point seemed to inform the moment. Pictures were taken, laughter was in the air, fist pumps in triumph, and bragging rights noted, and something more. The differences among us and the petty irritations inevitable in group efforts were forgotten. Having persisted to our goal, in spite of severe conditions, linked us on an emotional level of self-revelation, we encountered and found substance in the wonder of it all.

I had the students read Leanne O'Sullivan's Cailleach: The Hag of Beara, and as we look at the vista before us a few of the poems make us feel we are in them. We are on the Beara peninsula and the Hag of Beara is a poem dating back to the 9th century, Leanne O'Sullivan, a native of Beara, reinterprets the ancient poem creating a mythic rendering of place and character. As we consider the lines from Meeting Place:

> *The mist rolls from the hills like an airy*
> *moss, mottled with heather, and my*
> *weather-eye*
> *is cast to the clouds hanging wildly above us.*
>
> (Leanne O'Sullivan, 1 – 3)

We can literally see and feel what she describes. A frisson of recognition laces its way among us. The mist, hills, and wild clouds are our immediate reality. The fusion of emotion in gaining our vantage point, I feel, brings us closer together and sets up a receptive awareness; the way each of us experiences the lines of poetry opens space for our individual, unique understanding of what they mean. In this moment the discovery of poetry's power to reach the recesses of our being is on us. Links between words and landscape like the very rocks we sit on are visual and tactile. We can see what we feel and feel what we see. Reiterating the cosmic duration of time and weathering lines from Birth Dream:

> *Once I made mountains, carried stones*
> *and earth in my apron and set them in*
> *piles along the coast, raised them up like*
> *the skin of a healing wound.*
> *They are old now, and I am still here, wading*
> *the river's clay bed to the lush meadow on the east.*
>
> (Leanne O'Sullivan, 1 - 5)

capture the mythic recollection of creation and render our surroundings with sensual precision and evolving order. With an emphasis on natural and human process in the poem, what might appear to be a desolation in the random scatter of rocks, bogs, and grassy patches before us, becomes alive and reassuring. The Hag looks forward to the way love will carry her onward, the excitement of discovery lingering ahead like a promise in the movement of time. The success in our overcoming the physical hardship of hiking up to this point serves as a parallel to the poem.

The descent became a kind of frolic. I decided that we would take a direct route down to the clearly visible valley below. Using a stream as my guide, all water moves downward after all, I assumed that the bright green grass before us would cushion our weary bodies kindly. What I could not see was the way grass mounded up on top of considerably large rock formations creating a number of very steep drop offs. If I had been looking up I would have seen the rocks jutting out of the mountain face, but as it was, looking downward, the rocks were hidden from view. Trying to follow the stream we ran into many cul-de-sacs and had to traverse the fast running water frequently. Just as we were more or less drying out from the rain storm earlier we were soaked again as we stumbled and shifted off and onto the stream banks. The more individuals tried to stay dry the more they became awkward in their attempts to do so, losing their balance against the fear of falling. We were all scarred by various mud patterns all over our clothes and backpacks, but the prospect of more mud made everyone tentative in their movements. Then it all came undone. Once one person fell into a bog, more followed. Amid the laughter and mock terror, everyone was gleefully sliding down the grassy parts of the mountain. Ideas about the best way to descend from a cliff or whether it was better to go around a small bog hole or through it, flew through the air. One woman who was a sort of fashion plate and described by another student as someone who never shopped anywhere else but Nordstroms, was the queen of these mountain bogs. From her hair to her boots she was soaked and mud-smeared, and she laughed in full body shakes throughout the descent. After another hour of skidding, falling, and general low-level acrobatics we arrived at the base physically drained, but emotionally high, the elevated good will very much alive among us.

Well, into the third week of the program, bonds among us were firm, and the kind of experiences we were involved with now could not have been done well at the beginning of the program. Trust and consideration for others has evolved among us, and everyone has a clearer understanding that what looked like limits in ability and will power can be overcome by determination. As in academic learning small things need to be accomplished first so that more complex elements can be situated on a strong, firm base. I am reminded about the way our society seems to be very willing to short change the steps into the complexities of life confronted in the study of the humanities. Too often I believe the rush to get to the useful means homogenizing significant differences and the individually unique and missing a way of seeing in favor of the conventional. The dismissal of the arts and humanities in general as being "frills" can lead to a blunting of our sensibilities, a diminishment of our capacity for compassion, and a divorce from the natural world. Becoming fully human requires a good deal of effort; it is the antithesis of barbarity. The tensions between these two states come home to us everyday as we learn about new horrors in the world. There is beauty and joy in the world, poetry and the physical engagement with natural forces reaffirms a way of rising above our fears and reflexive reactions.

Follow the R572 from Glengarriff toward Adrigole. Just past Adrigole Village follow the road south to a green metal style on the right. Turn and go to the the end of the road. Park along the road.

Epilogue

As much as we wanted to develop the Kiplin Hall Program, neither Barbara nor I really thought that the program would continue on for as long as it has. Setting up the twenty first year of the program has the comfortable wear of familiarity, and with new students excited about participating in the program our own energy takes on new voltage. Yet we know that mortality is a fact of existence and there is an end point out there for us. Our hope is that another faculty member will take the opportunity to develop their own version of a Kiplin Hall Program., fostering the values incorporated in the liberal arts, and that has happened. Professor Katherine Charles has agreed to develop her own version of the program, and we are delighted. What has worked very well for us is not necessarily the best or only way to proceed. Just as I believe that the study of the Liberal Arts is not a matter of specific courses; a Kiplin Hall Program can take on a myriad of possibilities from a wide number of academic disciplines. The key to what I have outlined above, and future successful programs, has to do with students' experiences that will excite their fascination and wonder. Wonder humanizes us and sets the beginning of the ever possible, while our fascination brings infinity to a personal level. Giving students responsibility for their welfare and for control of their actions not only enhances their growing maturity but it also can lead to a life- long quest for meaning.

In the last several years, voices have been raised about the value of higher education, and in particular, Liberal Arts education. While the students today are under significant financial pressure to be able to stay at a liberal arts college, and are potentially distracted by the myriad of technological devices, each with its own lure, they are still captured by the power of literature and the meaning it has for their lives. Gaining mastery over how the study of literature, for example, opens a realm of understanding others, providing the basis for taking leadership roles and avenues of cooperation is fundamental for our age. The elements of this sort of knowledge are tied to individual works and not easily, if at all, deducible to a metric. Understanding comes from immersion in the subject. My bedrock belief is that the shaping of intellect and fostering the power of the imagination are the most useful things we can do in our age. Because Washington College is small, students and former students tend to keep in touch. Letters, emails, and cards from participants in the Kiplin Hall Program truly make the effort to lead the program worthwhile and fulfilling, among the best aspects of teaching. Megan Viviano notes, "On the personal growth side, I think I grew in two ways:

1) Pushing my own physical boundaries gave me confidence and joy.

2) Leaving most modern technology behind for three weeks gave me the opportunity to be quiet and think. It also forced a group of us college

students, all of whom used TV, cell phones and the Internet regularly (though it was before social media and smart phones), to find imaginative ways to entertain ourselves. We sang songs while climbing mountains. We played cards or walked to a pub to pass the time. We took turns making dinner. Mrs. Gillin taught me how to make real whipped cream. We had to be present. I think that, above all, is what made Kiplin Hall such a cherished memory to this day! Amanda, from a group years later confesses, "To this day, it has been one of many experiences in my life (and I, personally, have had too many) that has shaped me into the woman and artist I am today. I will forever be grateful to Richard Gillin for providing such an eye-opening experience, on so many levels. This program, however, was tough for me. More than I could have ever expected. A lot of reflection, both about art, life, or (mostly) myself happened after I left England and Ireland. Learning through the various experiences in the program could not have happened any other way for me."

Doug Carter, ready to embark on his chosen career, added this, "Recalling how fulfilled I felt helping Connie and Michael find new emotional perspectives as they climbed the mountain with me, I discovered a career path where the great outdoors serve as a backdrop for helping others make positive changes in their lives. Without the Kiplin Hall trip, I would probably not be preparing to enter the Wilderness Therapy field, where I'll guide backpacking expeditions with young people facing problems with drugs, alcohol, and depression. My time abroad with the Gillins and my classmates significantly affected my understanding of who I am. Were it not for the trip, I may never have discovered a sense of purpose in my life."

Amanda, a recent student is heart-warming in her comments, "What I received from the trip is a debt that I can never pay back, I owe so much to the Gillins, Kiplin Hall, and Washington College. The Kiplin Hall experience is something that is truly magical."

And Sarah from years ago, "Kiplin Hall was without a doubt my most rewarding college experience because it shifted my perspective of myself. I am athletic. I am outdoorsy. I will have good days, and bad days, and successes, and failures."

Sofia claims from her experiences in 2011, "My involvement in the Kiplin Hall Program was one that I reminisce on most days. I think about the friends I made and became roommates with, and the poetry I read. But the largest impact that the Kiplin Hall Program had on my life revolves around the changes I experienced physically and mentally. It is difficult to explain all of these lessons and memories to people who have not experienced the Kiplin Hall Program. So, when I have a moment when I am lost in my nostalgia of my experiences, I reach out to the friends I made on the trip and they knowingly laugh and tell another story and another and another."

Chelsea, who was new to climbing and hiking, reflected, "It is hard to put the Kiplin Hall experience into words. I have always gotten enjoyment out of being away from busy life and enjoying the beauties of nature. Kiplin Hall students take those experiences to the next level by creating their own connections with nature and the authors who came before us. You come to realize how much we depend on our surroundings and the impact they have on our life. It is easy for one to read literature whether it be works from Bronte or Wordsworth, but it is another thing to actually live it. Whether it was sitting in the mountains, reading poems in the Moors, or meeting the local people, we got to immerse ourselves into what we were reading and what was lived. I will share a bond with my fellow classmates that is indescribable. How many people can say they got to walk a wide expanse of territory where some of the world's best and most creative writers drew their inspiration from."

I really could go on with testimonials, but what threads former students' comments and observations together is that what they experienced in the Kiplin Hall Program had degrees of life changing dimensions; the essence of a Liberal Arts education. Barbara and I are forever grateful for Washington College for giving us the opportunity to develop and run the Program and have faith that the ideals of the liberal arts will continue into the future.

Figure 29: Barbara and Rich near Hadrian's Wall

Source: Joy Irvin

BIBLIOGRAPHY

Bronte, Emily. *Bronte, Poems.* New York: Alfred A. Knoph, 1996

Coleridge, Samuel Taylor, ed. Ernest Hartley Coleridge. *Poetical Works.* New York: Oxford University Press, 1969.

———. *The Table Talk and Omnia of Samuel Taylor Coleridge.* Oxford: Oxford University Press, 1917.

Eagleton, Terry. *The Truth About the Irish.* New York: St Martin's Griffin, 1999.

Heaney, Seamus. *District and Circle.* London: Faber and Faber, 2006.

———. *Human Chain.* New York: Farrar, Straus, and Giroux, 2010.

———. *North.* London: Faber and Faber, 1975.

Holmes, Richard. *Coleridge Early Visions, 1772-1804* New York: Pantheon Books, 1999.

Kavanagh, Patrick. *Collected Poems: Patrick Kavanagh.* New York: Allan Lane, 2004.

Keats, John, ed. Elizabeth Cook. *John Keats.* New York: Oxford University Press, 1990.

Scott, Sir Walter. *Lay of the Last Minstre*l, 11th Edition. Edinburgh: Landon, Longman, Hurst, Rees, and Orme, 1810.

———. *Rokeby: The Lord of the Isles.* Boston and New York: Houghton Mifflin, 1913.

Stoker, Bram. *Dracula.* Hertfordshire England: Wordsworth Editions, 1993.

Webster, Dawn. *Kiplin Hall: North Yorkshire.* Scarborough: Adverset Printer, 2016.

Wordsworth, Dorothy, ed. Pamela Woof. *The Grasmere Journals.* New York: Oxford University Press, 1993.

Wordsworth, William. *Poetical Works.* New York: Oxford University Press, 1965

Webster, Dawn. *Kiplin Hall: North Yorkshire.* Scarborough: Adverset, 2016.

Lightning Source UK Ltd.
Milton Keynes UK
UKHW022330191220
375501UK00001BA/13